FROM RESTORATION TO REFORM

Jonathan Clark is currently Hall Distinguished Professor of British History at the University of Kansas; he was previously a Fellow of Peterhouse, Cambridge, and of All Souls College, Oxford, and was a Visiting Professor at the Committee on Social Thought of the University of Chicago. His best-known book is *English Society 1660–1832*.

JONATHAN CLARK

From Restoration to Reform

The British Isles 1660–1832

VINTAGE BOOKS
London

Published by Vintage 2014

2 4 6 8 10 9 7 5 3 1

First published in Great Britain in 2014 by
Vintage
Random House, 20 Vauxhall Bridge Road,
London SW1V 2SA

www.vintage-books.co.uk

Addresses for companies within The Random House Group Limited
can be found at: www.randomhouse.co.uk/offices.htm

The Random House Group Limited Reg. No. 954009

A CIP catalogue record for this book
is available from the British Library

ISBN 9780099563235

The Random House Group Limited supports the Forest Stewardship
Council® (FSC®), the leading international forest-certification
organisation. Our books carrying the FSC label are printed on FSC®-
certified paper. FSC is the only forest-certification scheme supported by
the leading environmental organisations, including Greenpeace.
Our paper procurement policy can be found at:
www.randomhouse.co.uk/environment

Printed and bound by Clays Ltd, St Ives plc

Contents

Preface

History is always young, its youth preserved by fresh enquiry; and whatever the validity of its arguments, this book is at least the result of much enquiry and self-criticism. It is addressed especially to the young in spirit, of whatever age, who are willing to rise to the challenge of rethinking what they thought they knew. It is perhaps distinctive in its aim of showing its readers that they do not have to agree with their teachers. Nevertheless, its author has his intellectual debts. To acknowledge them in full would demand an autobiography, not a preface; here I prefer to address the action, not the author. Rather, I wish to express a general thanks to all those who have provoked me to develop my ideas. Patrick O'Brien kindly read a draft, and my understanding of economic history, especially the themes of taxation and national finance, owes much to his extensive expertise.

One's view depends on one's vantage point. A position outside the high windows of British universities has often allowed me to range beyond present-day preoccupations, to hunt across a broad landscape not enclosed by current fashions.

There are, in my world, no methodological fences that cannot be jumped. Never having been a modernist, I find it easier to manage postmodernism: I can grant leases to each, without adopting their strangely similar agendas. In this book and elsewhere I seek to revert to discourses and concepts closer to those of the long eighteenth century. But this is no 'linguistic turn', since I have always cultivated my fields in just that way. Here, seed time merely gives way to harvest.

Reviewing the state of the subject has reminded me of the remarkable degree to which conventional interpretations remain entrenched for present-day reasons. Yet if I have often reacted to the conclusions presented to me by ordinary historiography with doubt, and sometimes with scepticism, I extend the same privilege to others: readers are invited to take this work as a starting point for their own explorations, not as a set of definitive pronouncements. Only dead subjects can be understood through textbooks, as the most famous textbook of all, Henry Gray's *Anatomy*, continues to prove. Rather, as R. G. Collingwood rightly argued, history is a dialogue of question and answer, and this living and youthful dialogue must have a future. Like Collingwood, too, I regard history as the master discipline; as an intellectual creditor, not a debtor. These are my rationales for what follows.

Callaly Castle
Northumberland
June 2014

List of Illustrations

Introduction

The long eighteenth century, the central third of British history since the Reformation, has a special significance in historical debates, for here, more than anywhere, old orthodoxies once had their rise and have now been overset. Two in particular demand attention. In the first older interpretation, these years had a special significance. Somewhere during this era was conventionally located a Great Divide: on the far side of it lay the fascinating (or comic) but irrelevant early modern or premodern 'world we have lost'; on this side lay the utilitarian but relevant world we now have: modernity. That divide was identified in various ways: constitutionally, with the Whig rejection of 'absolutism'; intellectually, with the Enlightenment's repudiation of 'superstition'; economically, with the escape from a Malthusian population regime and the launch of an emancipating 'Industrial Revolution'; socially, with the defeat of patriarchy and a move towards the emancipation of women. There were several models; but they all shared the premise of a liberating Great Divide, and used ideal types like these to characterise it.

This book argues a different case. It contends that the idea of a great discontinuity is at best a rhetorical exaggeration, at worst deeply misleading, and that the evidence reveals both long continuities in many areas of life, and complex but often unrelated changes in others. Change was important, but it was generally evolutionary, not revolutionary; it obeyed no 'laws'; it exemplified no 'processes'; it responded to no 'underlying' determinants; it was highly contingent, and could never be taken for granted; even within the narrow geographical bounds of these islands, it often took different forms in Scotland, Ireland, Wales and England, and in their regions.[1] That these four societies constituting the polity assembled in 1801 survived the challenges of these years, prospered, adopted political union and extended their power around the world was remarkable. Yet no single concept, no single model of development explains it; a general history should reveal events as the results of the complex interplay of every cause, not as the simple unfolding of any single overriding theme or totalising category, whatever the passing appeal of those on offer from 'progress' to 'identity', least of all 'modernisation' or 'the modern state'.

Other scholars, uncomfortable with the disturbingly dynamic and theoretical notion of a Great Divide, fell back on a model of this era as safely unchallenging: prosperous, progressive, conventional, secular, middle class, polite, achieving 'modernity' by consuming 'luxuries' rather than by heroic revolution. Such notions, for them, identified the age's changes, which sometimes indeed disclosed assumptions close to a scaled-down but essentially similar version of the Great Divide, transposed to other areas. This second old convention, operating within the time frame of a short eighteenth century of 1714–83 (or even, shortest of all, 1727–83), helped those who subliminally preferred to contemplate 'the quintessence of the eighteenth century' as 'a rather dull interlude' in which politics was only 'a game'.[2] Extending our time frame to 1660 and 1832 at least helps us better to integrate change and continuity. The long eighteenth century, from the restoration of the monarchy to the era of reform, emphasises a different story: a long defence of the hegemony of certain social forms in the face of continual challenges, domestic and international, political and economic, ideological and religious. It is a story of change, not of stasis; of conflict, not of consensus; but of continuity and change largely held together (except in 1688–9, and in the American colonies) in an era of threatened instability.

These two broad emphases or orthodoxies have come under criticism in recent years, but despite their adherents' minor concessions it is remarkable how far they survive. This book seeks to redress the balance by showing that alternative views are not merely criticisms of secure orthodoxies that call for only minor modifications; the alternatives can, on the contrary, be set out on a broad canvas.

That canvas is indeed full of action. Enthusiasts for expansion and success find here all that they seek, as England, Wales and Scotland metamorphosed into Great Britain and then into the United Kingdom of Great Britain and Ireland; but explanatory certainties are undermined by the demonstration that even the largest developments were dominated by contingency. The Restoration of 1660, the Revolution of 1688, the American Revolution and the French Revolution were game-changing reversals, episodes in which the obvious failed to happen and different and unanticipated social forms were born. An era that contains such significant developments in population, power and political theory poses the most urgent historical questions. It is no coincidence that more and more historians have returned to this continuum, and their preoccupation with its interpretive challenges shows no signs of diminishing.

Some disavowals may be in order. Others rely explicitly or implicitly on the notion of consensus; I employ that of hegemony. Historians tend to project backwards the phenomena of which they approve (whether political change, like the arrival of democracy; social change, like class formation; intellectual change, like pluralism or radicalism; economic change, like urbanisation or industrialisation) into earlier and earlier years; this book resists that temptation, and dates many such phenomena to later time frames. It begins (but only begins) that hardest of historical tasks, the comparative analysis of England, Wales, Ireland and Scotland, taking the view that none of these societies was normative for the others and that patterns of change could be very different in each. Some historians treat English party politics and political discourse as seventeenth-century conflicts that became institutionalised and safely contained in the eighteenth; this book points to the revolution of 1776, a British episode, as a refutation of that idea. Most books leave out most themes, and this book is no exception. Reasons of space alone compel the omission of many areas that deserve attention (including taxation and finance, the slave trade, the West Indies, India, and many areas of social history, from crime and consumerism to art and literature); but this volume makes no claims to complete coverage. Indeed, that notion itself can only be a dictatorial one.

Finally, there are no historical 'periods', no time frames more privileged than others, but there are influential events nevertheless. This work is open to the idea that many social forms persisted in some strength until the full flowering of mass industrial society by the 1880s,[3] but it balances this thesis against, first, the origin of many hegemonic ideas and practices in the Restoration rather than after the Revolution of 1688, and, second, attention to the significance of the major changes of 1828–35. It does not reify a long eighteenth century, or the state form that prevailed during its course in these islands; but it is open to the consequences of abandoning the idea of a single Great Divide, of lengthening the short eighteenth century, of dispensing with anachronisms, and so of extending our intellectual estate.

Part I
Material Cultures

The long term

It is hard to write the history of the British Isles in these years as anything other than a success story. Earlier decades had been scenes of catastrophe. In material terms, the British Isles in the mid seventeenth century were as marginal to Europe as they had been for centuries. Thinly populated, with few significant towns compared to the most prosperous areas of the continent, they were largely tangential to the wider European economy. The archipelago also counted for less than the sum of its parts. In 1660 its population was divided among three polities (England and Wales; Ireland; Scotland) that had long been in armed conflict. Yet by 1832 this weak position had been transformed into one of strength. The British Isles now counted for considerably more than the sum of their parts; they were politically united as never before; their population had grown by a factor of three where the populations of many rival states on the European continent had grown slowly or were sometimes stagnant; Britain's wealth and military power had increased by even more than her population. Even if this success story was primarily dependent on navies, armies, politicians, diplomats and popular patriotism,[1] it had an economic dimension too. Victory in war was a necessary but not a sufficient condition of national success.

A longer time span emphasises these changes. In 1550 the populations of the largest polities of western Europe (in Germany, Italy, France and Spain) averaged 12.25 million, against England's 3 million (24 per cent of the average of the others); by 1820 the continental four averaged 20.25 million, but England had grown to 11.5 million (57 per cent of the average of the others). Output and real incomes per head also rose by more in England than in her rivals, much of this growth occurring before the 'Industrial Revolution'. Put more starkly: between 1550 and 1820 the populations of present-day Germany, Spain, Italy and France rose by 51, 56, 67 and 79 per cent, but of England by over 280 per cent.[2]

Even these figures understate how much had changed. By the 1820s, the actor on the European stage was no longer 'England' but that cumbersome yet effective composite monarchy formally termed 'the United Kingdom of Great Britain and Ireland'. In 1660, England's population of about 5.28 million was hardly strengthened by Wales's 0.2 million, and was offset by the problems represented by about 2 million in Ireland and 1 million in Scotland. By 1830, England's 13.25 million was supplemented by Wales's 0.8 million; the union also now included 7.76 million in Ireland and 2.36 million in Scotland, a total of 24.17 million. This union was achieved even while the balance was tilting away from England: in 1660 her neighbours within the archipelago amounted to 60 per cent of England's total population, in 1830 to 82 per cent, much of it in Ireland. In 1660, Wales, Scotland and Ireland were agricultural areas of low productivity; in 1832 the first two were beginning to contain dynamic centres of heavy industry.

To explain this transformation we must reject the assumption that such changes had to happen as they did. They took place because incremental economic developments in agriculture, commerce and manufacture just managed to outrun major population growth; because social change, although continuous, was evolutionary rather than revolutionary; and because (with the key exception of the American Revolution) political action succeeded in building up rather than breaking down the state. These themes of continuity and evolution will be prominent ones; but, as we shall see, human agency was decisive: neither revolution nor evolution was inevitable.

Gender: population and the role of marriage

Why did the population grow in such a dynamic way? Economic historians have long celebrated Britain's industrial performance, and have more recently been joined by other historians who have tried to link statistics on economic growth with the political and military track record first of England, then of the archipelago as a whole. Such success stories depended in turn on sustainable expansion in population. We begin with population, and population increase or decrease was determined not least by gender relations. Gender relations are currently a growth area of scholarship. Yet research has often been based on evidence from ecclesiastical or civil courts: evidence of what happened when marriages went disastrously wrong. Using such material as evidence of male domination and female oppression is difficult, however, since we do not know how representative these breakdowns were. The statistical evidence for gender relations that left no record of litigation relates mainly to population.

Ideas of gender roles set marriage patterns, and the family was the main determinant of long-term population change.[3] In these years the chief object of marriage was widely regarded as procreation; and in a society initially on the edge of numerical decline, sustaining the nation's population was also a public policy goal. At the time, there was no reliable information on population trends, and anxiety about decline could easily spread; even the journalist William Cobbett (1763–1835) could cite the social problems of his day as evidence that England's population had fallen since the 1200s. A little earlier, this was nearly true: England's population in c.1300, just before the Black Death, is variously estimated at between 4 million and 6.5 million; it was probably not exceeded until the mid 1700s. Eighteenth-century farm labourers' wages were significantly below those of c.1400–1550.[4] Prosperity grew, but initially the prosperity was mainly that of the elite and middling orders.

For England at least, the overall pattern is now clear. Initially, the story was one of failure. England's population boom of c.1550–1650 slowed down and stopped during the Commonwealth; the population actually declined from the 1650s to c.1700, and rose little before the 1750s. This century-long hiatus was partly the result of crises of mortality, but may also have been a response to the civil wars of the 1640s and 50s. Demographic historians have recently solved an old problem for England: which was the stronger influence on population trends, fertility or mortality, births or deaths? In the sixteenth and seventeenth centuries, the two seem equally balanced, and at a low level compared to other European societies, but from the mid eighteenth century it was more a rise in fertility than a fall in mortality that boosted the total.[5] But why did birth rates increase without triggering a rise in mortality? In the face of insecurity and disruption, marriage strategies changed: the average age at marriage increased, and a larger proportion of people never married at all. Ireland and Scotland, often closer to the margin of subsistence, were perhaps harder hit by mortality crises. Subsequently, growth recovered, and from the 1780s it boomed.

England's 'low pressure' demographic regime, of relatively low fertility and mortality, seems in the long term to have kept population within available resources without triggering the crises of mortality still seen in Europe. This relative absence of deterrent crises may have encouraged a rise in fertility caused by a fall in the age of marriage, and a larger percentage marrying, as changing economic circumstances encouraged family formation. England's population growth was explained by Wrigley and Schofield as a rise in real wages producing a rise in the birth rate, but after a thirty-year time lag. At some times and in some areas England saw rises in both; yet the increases in real wages seldom seem enough, and the time lag too long, to be a complete explanation. Many other causes were probably involved. Population might also threaten to overshoot resources. From the mid eighteenth century much of the rise in gross national product went to support a rapidly growing population, so that GNP per head scarcely rose in the short term. Economic historians long debated the 'standard of living' question: did workers lose or gain from the 'Industrial Revolution'? This is still contentious, but the larger issue, irrespective of the merits of capitalism, was the relation of national wealth to the population total. Such rapid population growth almost meant that national wealth per head actually fell; why then did population still grow?

Why, too, did population not grow even further? A rise in fertility indeed posed major risks. England's greatest demographer, the Anglican clergyman Thomas Malthus (1766–1834), explained the problem in 1798: population naturally tended to increase in a geometric ratio (1, 2, 4, 8 . . .), but the output of food could rise only in an arithmetic ratio (1, 2, 3, 4 . . .). Population would therefore overshoot subsistence until it was reduced by the 'positive checks' of war, famine (after high food prices) and disease, reducing population until wages returned to the 'subsistence level': these crises in mortality were normally the chief agents restraining population. Savage setbacks could only be avoided, urged Malthus, by a form of social control he called the 'preventive check' on personal conduct to restrain population within available resources, involving chastity before marriage and late age at marriage (within wedlock, it was assumed, children followed inevitably). In pre-industrial societies, living standards depended to a large degree on the control of fertility – the social conventions and practices that limited family size and the number of families, so increasing the wealth of each. If so, it could seem that England, Wales and Scotland, with effective mechanisms of social control, narrowly remained within these constraints until the 1810s, but that Ireland increasingly did not, with catastrophic results seen in the population boom and collapse at the time of the Irish famine of the 1840s.[6]

Was Malthus's analysis correct? Economic historians often write of a Malthusian 'demographic regime' which had kept real wealth per head within strict limits for centuries or even millennia, and which England sensationally escaped at the 'moment' of the Industrial Revolution. The problem with this argument is that what counted as the 'subsistence level' varied widely between societies in the pre-industrial era: England was far wealthier than China per capita in the eighteenth century, and England's story was of a more successful commercial economy. Secondly, the real escape from a Malthusian regime came with birth control from the 1870s, after which the standard of living of the majority began significantly to improve. Nor was this at once a decisive improvement. Judged by real income per head in England, the major gains came long *after* the era normally labelled the 'Industrial Revolution', and even after 1945.[7]

We now know that even by 1700 England had moved beyond a pattern in which mortality fluctuated closely with food prices: this correlation steadily weakened after the 1640s, a problem largely cured by the market and by a rise in real wages. English poor relief based on local taxation was effective by the 1630s; by *c*.1700, a national market in England for wheat had developed to the point where it ironed out local harvest failures.[8] Even so, there was no sudden and decisive escape from old perils. There were many setbacks. Crises of mortality meant absolute falls of about 200,000 in England's population between 1678 and 1686, and again between 1727 and 1730.[9] Substantial emigration during *c*.1650–1750 also helped stabilise England's population.[10] Birth rates did not begin consistently to pull ahead of death rates until the 1740s. Even so, it was not clear at the time that such a change had occurred, and the interaction of these wider demographic pressures was not fully understood. Anxiety, and argument, continued. If England had escaped from a 'Malthusian regime', it did not realise it: 'preventive checks' were still seen as crucial in keeping population growth sustainable, defending a standard of living much higher than the subsistence level. Gender relations remained the key. By contrast, a seventeenth-century 'agricultural revolution' meant that England became a net exporter of grain by the 1670s; but this prosperity did not produce a population boom.

In seventeenth-century England, the average age at marriage was relatively high and did not fall markedly until the eighteenth century. With stalling population growth after *c.*1650 went a trend to more and more people remaining unmarried, a trend only gradually reversed in the early eighteenth century.[11] The high percentage of those never marrying influenced population totals in the seventeenth century even more than the late age at marriage: this may have reflected a deliberate rejection of participation in a world shattered by civil war and revolution. For a minority, otherworldly renunciation was succeeded after 1660 by worldly, even libertine, engagement; but this (as measured by illegitimacy and pregnancy before marriage) did not become widespread. 'Preventive checks' still worked; marriage survived.

If population growth in the south of England was triggered by rising real wages before *c.*1780, as Malthus's analysis might suggest, that growth continued afterwards when real wages stabilised (or, especially for agricultural labourers, were often eroded) for other reasons including the impact of enclosures, the demise of living-in farm labour, and the decline of apprenticeship and of opportunities for female employment.[12] Malthus's model was no sooner formulated than it failed to apply. As urban economic opportunity widened in the late eighteenth century, the 'preventive check' was not wholly discarded; but what was seen as a prudent response to limited rural economic opportunity was increasingly offset by wider horizons as communications improved. If elite culture became ever more preoccupied with 'respectability', an ethic of control and renunciation, urban life often widened economic opportunities for the non-elite, made anonymity possible, reduced the scope for Malthus's 'preventive check', and did so for that growing part of the population living in towns: economic opportunity now depended less and less on access to land.[13] So England's population growth accelerated. In the late seventeenth century its rate was zero; by the early nineteenth it was about 1.75 per cent per annum, the highest England ever experienced.[14] But it was a growth rate that still did not revolutionise family structure.

A minor statistic is an indication of the weakening but still substantial survival of social control. In 1650–74 illegitimacy rates were about 1.35 per cent of births; from there they increased slowly to 2.31 per cent in 1700–24, then more strongly in the second half of the century to reach 6.18 per cent in 1800–24. Similarly the percentage of children conceived before marriage declined from sixteenth-century levels, reached a low point of 16.4 per cent in 1675–99, and rose steadily to 37.6 per cent in 1800–37.[15] Marriage and 'social control' survived, although challenged; pregnancy meant subsequent marriage much more often than bastardy.

These demographic trends are evidence that productivity gains in the British economy in the century after 1760 were essentially unrelated to population growth in those decades: without the productivity gains, England, Wales and Scotland would have shared in Ireland's demographic disaster of the 1840s. Fertility levels were transformed by steadily reducing age at marriage, and by a halving in the percentage of women never marrying; and these changes occurred everywhere in England, not just in areas of growing manufacturing industry.

English population history has been brilliantly reconstructed on the basis of evidence from parish registers kept by the established church, but in Ireland, Scotland and Wales the fragmentary nature or lack of such sources obscures understanding before the early nineteenth century. In Ireland, Scotland and to a lesser extent Wales, it seems that war, famine and disease continued to produce the crises of mortality that England increasingly escaped: if so, Malthus's 'positive check' continued to operate in different ways across the British Isles.[16]

Where England is said to have had a 'low pressure' demographic regime of fertility and mortality rates low by European standards, Ireland and Scotland in 1660 showed 'high pressure' regimes with the opposite characteristics. How they coped with the differences determined their demographic outcomes. Ireland was probably hard hit by war and its attendants, famine and disease, in the 1640s and 50s, and again in 1689–91; but recent figures for the early eighteenth century suggest that rapid population growth of 2 per cent per annum followed in c.1706–12 (faster than anything England ever saw) until total population was actually reduced by the famines of 1727–9, 1740–1 and 1744–6.[17] Women's ages at marriage were lower than in England, and so, probably, was the proportion never marrying, although both were within northern European norms: denominational differences were not significant.[18] Illegitimacy rates, and prenuptial pregnancy, were lower in Ireland than in England: perhaps earlier marriage explains this.[19] With such characteristics, Ireland's rate of growth accelerated again after c.1750, reaching three times Scotland's rate of increase in 1755–1801.[20]

Scotland's, too, has been called a 'high pressure' regime,[21] but with more uncertain growth than England's. Initially, Malthus's 'positive check' may have dominated; later, his 'preventive check' took over. Scotland, like Ireland, continued to experience major crises of subsistence, disease and mortality in 1623, 1644–9, and 1695–9, the last reducing Scotland's population by up to 15 per cent, in addition to lesser crises in the early 1630s, 1649–51 and 1674–6; it may be that mortality rather than fertility was still the key determinant (the opposite pattern to England's), although historians of Scotland debate this.[22] From the eighteenth century the position improved, partly as a result of the absence of bubonic plague in Scotland after 1649 (as it disappeared in England after 1665). Harvest failures, like those of 1739–41 and 1782, tended to become more localised, and were belatedly alleviated by the movement of grain in a more commercialised economy. Scottish death rates, however, still fluctuated widely. By contrast, what little is known of fertility indicates figures declining in the second half of the eighteenth century to be close to England's;[23] the slow growth of Scotland's population between 1780 and 1800 suggests little change in marriage patterns. By the nineteenth century, Scotland's population characteristics came (unlike Ireland's) to mirror England's almost exactly.[24]

This convergence was slow. Where in England during the later eighteenth century the age of women at marriage and the percentage never marrying fell, in Scotland they remained constant.[25] Only from c.1800 did Scotland's growth accelerate, partly because of a remarkable initiative to vaccinate against smallpox. Yet major growth was still not a forgone conclusion. The rate of Scotland's population increase fell back after the first three decades of the nineteenth century, constrained by the return of mortality crises in the growing industrial towns brought by diseases like tuberculosis, cholera and typhus: there was no necessary upward trend, and by the early nineteenth century there were already complaints that the introduction of the potato in the Highlands was producing local populations for which there was no employment. Emigration was always a feature of Scottish life; in the early 1770s it reached epidemic proportions. After 1815 a Malthusian crisis threatened in parts of the Highlands; it struck in 1836–7, and again in 1846, as the result of potato blight. But massive relief operations averted massive mortality: Scotland was not Ireland.[26]

So Scotland's population growth came later than England's, and was less rapid. By contrast, the Catholic Irish hardly emigrated before the famine of the 1840s, and Ireland's growth exceeded England's: between 1781 and 1831, the population of Wales grew by about 48 per cent, of Scotland by 65 per cent, of England by 84 per cent, of Ireland by 92 per cent. What caused such divergent demographic outcomes? We still hardly know, although the different operation of 'social control' must have contributed. The alienation of the Irish elite from the masses for religious reasons may have weakened the force of elite doctrine and the 'preventive check'. Probably the easy availability of farm tenancies in Ireland kept the age at marriage low, and a fall in mortality (especially infant mortality) in the late eighteenth century with the disappearance of famine in Ireland also boosted growth. For whatever reasons, Ireland followed a pattern that was only narrowly avoided in England and Scotland: in Ireland the strong growth of population from the mid eighteenth century outstripped the growth of the economy, which prospered in Ulster but stagnated elsewhere.[27]

In demographic terms, it may be that society in the British Isles only narrowly escaped a general crisis. England's 'low pressure' regime allowed a substantial population increase that ran just ahead of agricultural output. Overall economic growth was on the most optimistic estimates just enough to sustain a much larger population without an average reduction in real wages, but in some areas precisely this reduction occurred: by 1820 the countryside in the south and Midlands of England too often saw a local world polarised between the mean, grasping farmer and the resentful, welfare-dependent labourer for whom there was too little work. Even in manufacturing areas, threats of revolution produced by economic distress were taken seriously by the government. Outside England, things were worse. Scotland's demographic regime now threatened to revert to its previous state: the second decade of the nineteenth century saw the return of crises of mortality caused by the diseases rampant in the new industrial slums. Although there is evidence of improving conditions of life for the Irish agricultural labourer to 1815,[28] Ireland's 'high pressure' regime was heading for disaster: the stage was being set by population boom and dependency on the potato for the massive mortality of the 1840s.

Did Malthus's 'preventive check' depend on gender roles? Older histories treated the forces of capitalism and democracy as the locomotives of history; today, demography seems one more plausible driving force, and demography describes marriage. Female 'virtue' was central to Malthus's 'preventive check': eighteenth-century English female authors today labelled feminists generally sought to establish the dignity of their sex, or personal independence, by ostentatious chastity rather than to advance their careers by exploiting their sexuality. The second strategy was open to only a small number of courtesans, and not at every court: William III and Anne looked coldly on sexual licence. For the majority of women, stable marriage was their aim. For them, it is not clear that any fundamental qualitative change in gender relations came about in these decades.[29] Images of gender relations (the power of husbands, the disobedience of children) were prominent in the political thought of the late seventeenth century, but are not evidence for a crisis in actual gender relations.[30] What changed was the average age at marriage, and the percentage of the population marrying.

Nevertheless, two models asserting profound change currently contest this thesis. One, derived from Engels, urges that the decline of production in family units, the growth of the factory and the rise of wage labour increasingly divided the sexes during the working day, diminishing women's power and wealth: patriarchy strengthened. This thesis is contradicted by another which claims that the Industrial Revolution eroded patriarchy and transformed relations between the sexes by expanding opportunities for female employment. Although these explanations cannot simultaneously be true, both might be false: both might fail to do justice to a complex picture in which overall shifts towards or away from 'patriarchy' were absent. Most obviously, a population boom meant that more women spent more of their lives bearing and raising children, a picture not greatly modified until the twentieth century. Many enterprises had never relied on family production; those that did, had hardly provided for the economic equality or independence of the sexes. For the great majority of women there was no transition from patriarchal subordination to radical-individualist emancipation, or from economic activity to leisured indolence, but merely incremental shifts from certain forms of work discipline and authority to other forms. In some regions women's employment was actually curtailed by economic change: population pressure in the countryside, and male monopolies in many industries, reduced opportunities; elsewhere, factories widened them. In many areas, especially towns, the pattern of female employment remained much the same over long time spans.[31] No single trend is apparent.

Because early research into gender relations was heavily

influenced by already-existing historical scenarios, grand narratives still flourish here. Some historians still identify the eighteenth century as the era in which Engels's division of spheres between men and women occurred, and this has newly been linked to the alleged creation of a middle-class identity;[32] both arguments are contested. Recently, the Marxist account of class formation has considerably weakened; and a yet more recent argument that class emerged as an idea in the ideological and religious polemics of the 1820s and 30s, rather than as a reflex of the emergence of ideas of domesticity and separate spheres, makes the claim about women's fundamentally changing role more problematic still. Alternatively, the 'separate spheres' model can be accepted as correctly describing an older patriarchal pattern, but this segregation can be argued to have broken down in c.1780–1830 as a result of women's patriotic involvement in an age of war and revolution; this argument, too, does not yet rest on quantified and systematically weighed evidence.[33]

Nor have these enquiries yet been conducted on a comparative basis: currently we do not know how Scotland, Ireland, Wales and England compared in respect of gender relations, or how each compared with continental Europe. The most accurate sorts of evidence are figures for the population; these show the continuing centrality of the institution of marriage and its increasing success over human mortality. Much did not change; but where women's opportunities narrowed, this sometimes derived from reforming zeal rather than from capitalist greed. Just as the Whigs attempted to exclude the mob in 1832, they formally excluded women from the parliamentary franchise in the same Act. Women were also excluded from the local franchise by the Whigs' Municipal Corporations Act (1835). Until this time, the legal status of women as electors was ambiguous: a few female burgage owners had voted in parliamentary elections, and a judgement in 1739 had allowed women to vote at local level in vestry elections; this was overset in 1835. What had mattered most was women's informal involvement in a widely conceived politics, but this is hard to measure. Gender roles changed over time, but in complex ways and seldom in attempts to arrive at present-day practices.

So the family remained the basic social unit, and household size (at least in England) was roughly constant between the sixteenth century and the early twentieth: recent demographic history shows that there was no transition from a patriarchal, 'extended' family to a 'nuclear' family under the impact of 'capitalism', as some sociologists used to claim. The fairly constant differences between ranks were greater than the changes over time: one sample of households in England from 1574 to 1721 gives the average size of gentlemen's households as 6.63, husbandmen's as 5.09 and labourers' as 4.51, with little variation over the decades.[34] The nuclear family seems also to have been the norm in Scotland and Wales as well as England. Only in Ireland did ancient assumptions about the primacy of the kin group give family life a more collective character, but this needs more research.

One marked change was a considerable increase in female literacy in the half-century after c.1670. Yet this new skill was initially put to old uses, to reinforce ideas of chastity and restraint. The Anglican clergyman Richard Allestree produced his classic work, *The Ladies Calling*, in 1673 (it was very often reprinted); it called on women to develop the religious virtues appropriate to domesticity. Few women writers stepped out-side this ideal: Lady Mary Wortley Montagu (1689–1762) and Catherine Macaulay (1731–91), who seemed openly to challenge men's roles in society, were rare exceptions.[35] The object of 'conduct books' was still to shape women's characters as wives and mothers. What the church taught as a route to morality, the political economists taught as a route to economic survival. Adam Smith (1723–90) distinguished between 'strict' and 'liberal' schemes of morality: the first meant breaking even, the second would be 'ruinous to the common people'; only the elite could afford it.[36] An emphasis on the moral dignity of family life increased in the decades in which England's population stagnated, and sometimes fell; as this doctrine took hold, population began to move upward again. How these things were linked, we do not yet know.

Contemporary debate on gender relations was limited in scale, small in practical impact, and often anonymous. 'Sophia' in 1739 set out an extensive case for the equality of the sexes, appealing to natural law from empirical observation of women's abilities. Only 'prejudice and custom' stood in the way of women's equal participation in almost every occupation, she urged, whether as politicians or professors, lawyers or doctors, admirals or generals. Men had no 'natural right of superiority over us'; indeed they were too often slaves to their passions, not to reason. Otherwise, they would be able to 'see that nature invincibly proves a perfect *equality* in our sex with their own'. As it was, men thought women only fit 'to breed and nurse children in their tender years' and manage household affairs; they excluded women from full participation by 'violence' and 'lawless oppression'. But as if realising that her teaching would imply social revolution, the anonymous author concluded: 'What I have hitherto said, has not been with an intention to stir up any of my own sex to revolt against the *Men*, or to invert the present order of things, with regard to *government* and *authority*. No, let them stand as they are.'[37]

Perhaps unsurprisingly, her male respondent seized on the main point: his 'Fair Adversary' was 'undoubtedly right' that men saw the chief calling of women as the bearing and nursing of children, but this role gave them no status higher than men. He supported the priority of men from Scripture, reason and tradition. Genesis, Micah, Ecclesiasticus and St Paul agreed on this point; of the Fathers, Augustine, Ambrose and Isidore confirmed the Scriptures. As to reason, 'the weakness of their intellects' set women below men; Protagoras, Democritus, Aristotle, Seneca and Plutarch wrote similarly. Tradition, too, was unanimous: 'From the beginning of the World till now, *our Sex* has enjoy'd an undisputed Sovereignty over the *other*, and their joint Consent in all Ages sufficiently proves our Possession not usurped'; this was true 'in every Country'. The 'universal Ease with which the *Women* of all Ages have supported this their Condition' proved it was 'a natural Duty'. Custom, in this respect, derived from 'right Reason and Prudence', not from prejudice. Sophia was inciting a 'Rebellion' like Lucifer's against woman's God-given 'Allegiance' to man.[38] Even such debates as there were took place in England, rather than Ireland or Scotland: speculation on a wholly new social order was the ultimate consumer luxury.

Demographic survival still dominated gender relations, but it did not specify their forms. Some things did indeed change. The growth of leisure among women of the middling ranks led to more and more books written for, and eventually by, women. Women's writings quietly shifted from religious prophecy in the mid seventeenth century to fiction in the late eighteenth. By 1800, women authors had devised a distinctive voice. Indeed they were a large fraction of the authors of novels, a genre non-existent in 1700, dominant in 1800. As a result, women played a prominent role in the development of the new style now called Romanticism, and gave a different spin to it than the male authors also identified as Romantics. These men were normally members of the social elite who had received the conventional classical education: they continued the focus of eighteenth-century male authors on the heroic, the epic, the elegy, satire and political action. Women's writing developed the themes of the 'sentimental' novel, especially the preservation of female virtue, domestic and personal friendships, moral reform, and, in general, 'feeling'. But many of these feelings and friendships were related to a common (and ancient) cause: marriage strategies.

Feelings were still expressed primarily within families, and in these years the family or household was the dominant social institution.[39] The main changes in 1660–1832 were in numbers of children rather than in gender roles, yet these changes were not large except in one respect. Fewer apprentices and servants 'lived in' with employers, but on this perhaps minor fact some historians build a major argument: that this meant a narrowing of 'the household' to create the nuclear family of husband, wife and children. This argument often claims that such a trend was driven primarily by economics (the extension of a monetised, market economy), but it is linked to an argument about sentiment (the alleged rise of 'affective individualism', which purportedly turned the family into a more egalitarian site of warm emotional relationships between kin). Yet demographers have now shown that the 'nuclear family' was by this time very old in much of Britain, and statistically changed little in the eighteenth century. The argument about a transition from 'patriarchy' to 'affective individualism' also looks problematic if we dispense with its major premise that the seventeenth century was dominated by 'patriarchy': much evidence exists not only for loving marriages in the seventeenth century, but also for male domination in the eighteenth and later. It seems likely that opposites were more compatible than was thought: male authority was consistent with loving relationships; the nuclear family was consistent with the wider and affective kin group.

The object of the family was not to fulfil present-day notions regarding gender relations, but to ensure demographic survival. For all except the rich, family formation and success depended on Adam Smith's 'strict code' of morality. Because women had most to lose, social order was defended more often by women than by men, and the rise of the female author is therefore revealing: many, like Mary Astell (1666–1731), Aphra Behn (1640?–89), and Delariviere Manley (1663–1724), sympathised with the Tory, and sometimes the Jacobite, cause as a route to asserting a larger social role for their sex. Only occasionally did the female voice take a libertine form, as with Behn; sometimes, as with Astell, it generated an opposite ambition of creating separate communities for women.

Mary Astell acknowledged that 'Custom' had an 'Arbitrary Sway . . . The only way then is to retire from the world.' She rejected fashion, calling on at least a minority of women 'to improve your Charms and heighten your Value, by suffering you no longer to be cheap and contemptible', instead transferring women's 'Beauty . . . from a corruptible Body to an immortal Mind'. Her scheme was 'to erect a *Monastry*, or if you will . . . a *Religious Retirement*', 'a Seminary to stock the Kingdom with pious and prudent Ladies', partly concerned 'to give the best Education to the Children of Persons of Quality'.[40] Astell, arguing from Scripture rather than natural law, advised women to seek 'Wisdom' and 'Goodness' in a husband, but conceded that the 'Husband must govern absolutely and intirely'; the wife 'must not attempt to divide his Authority, or so much as dispute it'. Women, in her view, 'have no business with the Pulpit, the Bar or St *Stephens* Chappel [the House of Commons]'; they should concentrate on their 'Necessary Affairs' in governing their families.[41] Much of Astell's writings merely acknowledged current practice; her ideal of female education had to wait for the foundation of Girton College, Cambridge, in 1869. Nor were mid eighteenth-century gender relations measurably affected by the development of the novel, especially those of Samuel Richardson, giving expression to a characteristically feminine perspective on gender roles and emotions. Life does not always mirror art. Perhaps it does so less than artists think.

If 'early feminists' looked to chastity to defend the independence of their sex, this ideal faded in the eighteenth century with significant falls in the percentage never marrying and in the average age at marriage. In this sense 'early feminism' failed: the key women authors of these years were Sarah Trimmer (1741–1810) and Hannah More (1745–1833), evangelicals, apologists for the family, propagandists for the education of children. Their adult lives, and the years of fastest population growth from the 1790s to the 1840s, were overshadowed by war and the threat of revolution. Women writers who saw the French Revolution as a helpful bandwagon suffered by identifying their cause with a revolution whose unfolding horrors polarised opinion against them; of these the most famous was Mary Wollstonecraft (1759–97). But just as the French Revolution diminished the role of women in France, its British supporters did the same in Britain: instead it was evangelicals, firm friends to the established order, who pioneered a growing role for women as agents of philanthropy, exporting the domestic virtues of the middling ranks to the poor.[42] Women's roles into the nineteenth century were dominated by demography, not democracy.

'Paternalism' partly overlaps with another ill-defined concept, 'patriarchalism'. There has been much debate on the ways in which 'patriarchalism' survived from the seventeenth century into the eighteenth. Yet if 'patriarchalism' is a synonym for 'collectivism' rather than for 'divine right', then however dominant the assumptions of individualism were in the early nineteenth century, the ideals of collectivism survived too, and found powerful expression after 1900. 'Patriarchalism' in the political sense of the doctrines peculiar to Sir Robert Filmer (1588–1653) was not prominent after 1688, but 'patriarchalism' in the social sense of the doctrines (more numerous and more important in practice) that Filmer and John Locke (1652–1704) shared was lastingly influential: the origins of the state in the family, the rootedness of the social hierarchy in natural law, and, as Locke put it, the ascendancy of gentlemen over plebeians, masters over servants, husbands over wives.[43]

Open society or ancien regime?

Whether Britain in this era can be termed an ancien regime society was not a question asked before 1789, since no such concept then existed. At the outbreak of the French Revolution both the prime minister, William Pitt, and his chief opponent, Charles James Fox, were hopeful and optimistic. But that revolution soon encouraged the French to conceptualise their own 'former regime'; France's declaration of war on Britain in 1793 defined the question for the British; and Britain's key role as the most consistent enemy of international Jacobinism carved this identity in stone. In daily politics, the post-war ministry of Lord Liverpool often pursued reform, but this did not prevent the profoundly disaffected from characterising their social order as 'Old Corruption', that mutually supporting system (as its critics claimed) of placemen, pensioners, contractors, sinecurists, and the unproductive elite in general, whether in church or state.

The question was made real by politics, not social analysis; but politics is overlooked when historians frame a false antithesis, asking whether Britain 'was' an open society 'or' an ancien regime. Those who supported the existing order supported what they saw as the most advanced, most rational option, a social form that had guaranteed security of property and encouraged commercial growth and the progress of knowledge. The French word *ancien* meant 'old' in the sense mainly of 'previous' rather than of 'outdated'. The issue is not whether society before 1832 was outdated (which would be a problematic argument) but whether the different world that followed 1832 represented a fundamental break with what went before (which is more plausible). This question is keenly debated.

The older orthodoxy was emphatic that England, then Britain, departed from a European absolutist model at an early date. Some historians pointed to the late seventeenth century as the moment of fundamental modernisation when patriarchy and hierarchy were rejected for the values and practices of an 'open society'. Such claims now seem to others to be historians' rhetoric, difficult to reconcile with observable data on population and poverty. The demographic restraints that Malthus later described remained in place: women remained unmarried, or bore children. The poor, as Samuel Johnson observed, had little choice but to work or starve. And as Bishop Horsley remarked in the Lords in 1795, 'he did not know what the mass of the people in any country had to do with the laws but to obey them'. Poverty created work discipline and family discipline; the 'open society' in the sense of a society offering serious choices to most people had to wait for mass affluence in the late twentieth century.

One determinant of openness was ownership. Primogeniture was later defined by revolutionaries as a practice supporting social hierarchy, preserving the unity of great estates. Yet it also promoted social mobility by forcing younger sons into other occupations, and minimising the number of landowning heirs for daughters to marry. From a demographic point of view, the basic fact about the 'old society' was *downward* social mobility, and the threat of it: richer families had more children than poorer ones, and more children in richer families survived. These children had to find work where they could, often less well rewarded work than their parents undertook. It has been argued that the downwardly mobile nevertheless carried with them at least some elite values: literacy, numeracy, industry, patience, imagination, investment, prudence, non-violence, ambition. At the top, this reinforced a patrician ethic in which recruits from the ranks of the poor into the elites could prosper only by displaying similar elite qualities. Downward mobility went with elite cultural hegemony (in the present, an opposite trend prevails). And whatever the stability of overall income distribution and of the ideology of hierarchy, these should not conceal 'the churning dynamism of the social fabric, with individuals headed up and down the social scale, sometimes to an extraordinary extent'.[44]

Effective 'openness' in society varied in different social strata and geographical locations. City wealth, not city air, made free; yet across Britain most wealth was still derived from land, which continued to be owned by the few. One recent estimate (Appendix, Table 4) suggests a strengthening of the great estates and of the gentry each by some 5 per cent between 1690 and 1790, at the expense of those owning less than 300 acres. The legal devices of primogeniture and the 'strict settlement' of estates acted gradually to consolidate ownership of English land; demographic disaster and the breaking of entails by private Acts of Parliament both occurred, but did not reverse this gradual trend.[45] In England the slight overall strengthening of the great estates and the decline of small proprietors went together, not necessarily in the interests of agricultural productivity but promoting the power of the great landowner.[46]

Scotland's landed society was even more polarised between great landowners and dependent tenants than England's, with a much smaller class of gentry. Scotland's landownership pattern changed more than its southern neighbour's, as the customary relations of clanship gave way to landlordism in the Highlands. Wales, meanwhile, largely lacked its own nobility. The strange failure of many gentry families in the early eighteenth century to produce a male heir led to a restructuring of landowning society: perhaps half of Wales's wealthiest families in the mid eighteenth century were English newcomers.[47] Wealth mattered everywhere; in Scotland, Ireland and Wales landed wealth mattered even more.

At the very top, therefore, society was largely 'closed', the position of the large landowner even strengthening from the late seventeenth century to the agricultural depression of the late nineteenth. As revealed by John Bateman's survey of 1870, the families of more than nine-tenths of the richest landowners had owned their lands since before 1700.[48] Few 'new men' bought great estates, although more of them bought small ones: the gentry was more 'open' than the nobility. The peerage as such remained more closed: of the 117 new peers created in the eighteenth century only seven came from outside the gentry. But the lower down the scale of landed wealth, the more movement into the ranks of the landed elite. Land was business, indeed the biggest business of all, and landowners had to be open to entrepreneurial opportunity if they were to prosper. Trade, therefore, did not automatically rule a line between 'open' and 'closed' sectors of society. And a richer top quarter of society meant more people employed as servants, a nexus only broken in 1914.

With the domination of landowning by the great estates went the domination of national politics by the great landlords, usually peers, a dominance which persisted into the late nineteenth century: the huge preponderance of peers in successive Cabinets is easily established. Although 'new men' increasingly bought their way into Parliament, the proportion of MPs who were sons or clients of peers also rose over the eighteenth century: the old society was strengthening, so that 'the old' and 'the new' were scarcely yet defined as antithetical. Here as elsewhere, it is not clear that we can speak of a 'new' society rising to challenge an 'old' one. The evidence suggests merger and co-operation more than division and conflict. Cross-group co-operation within parties was implicit while political conflict was being fought out between parties. Yet the political elite presented a less welcoming side to those outside it. The law commanded openness in electoral behaviour, but political practices expressed different values. The Treating Act of 1696 criminalised the giving of money, meat, drink or entertainment to influence votes in parliamentary elections, but it was widely ignored. The 'hospitality' offered by candidates to electors expressed a quite different set of social norms from those which later prevailed, ones in which mutual deference and service cemented powerful reciprocities. Only after these assumptions had slowly eroded could the secret ballot be introduced into parliamentary elections in 1872.

In Scotland, the smaller landowners had much less political power than their English counterparts: the tiny electorate, and the distance from Westminster, locked them out. In Scottish counties, even among the landowners only a small fraction possessed the parliamentary franchise. But their local role was much stronger than the English gentry's: these 'heritors' held large and growing power within the Kirk sessions, where civil and ecclesiastical jurisdiction coincided. In Ireland, the power of the landlords was magnified, and its significance embittered, by the alternating dominance of Catholic and Protestant communities. There the major shifts of landholding were the result of political vicissitude, as the Catholic interest backed the losing dynasty and was penalised by expropriation.

In some ways, British society had long been seen as 'open', and remained so; in others it was not so described and would not be until the social revolution of the 1960s. The 'open' aspects could be very old indeed. In England, representatives from the counties and the boroughs had sat in the same House of Parliament, the Commons, since the reign of Edward I; their children had intermarried; younger sons of landowners had pursued careers in the professions, or as merchants. The social distance at any moment between patrician and plebeian was real, but identities over time were not indelible. Nevertheless, not until the agricultural slump of the late nineteenth century did landed wealth weaken its grip on society and the political machinery. It was not clear that merchants or manufacturers made any breakthrough in status or political power before 1832, although their well-endowed daughters long found it possible to marry for status. The parliament of 1641 had included fifty-five merchants; that of 1754 included only five more.

The groups which did increase their representation among MPs were the professions, especially lawyers and army and navy officers. A shared characteristic of the major kingdoms of Europe at this time was the dominance of their national budgets by military and naval expenditure. During the eighteenth century this accounted for between 61 and 74 per cent of government spending (82 and 94 per cent, if debt charges are included), roughly twice the figures seen in the nineteenth century in peacetime.[49] Even in Britain, a growing military role on the world stage politicised the army and navy; although the armed forces no longer intervened to change regimes after 1688, a political role remained for them in Scotland and Ireland. Those kingdoms in turn produced disproportionate numbers of military officers, and later of colonial administrators. Yet although most MPs and peers were landowners, Parliament was responsive to trade: these were landowners for whom land was big business.

Some historians have celebrated the growth of English towns in the eighteenth century as a proof of increasing 'openness', hailed as a magic marker of modernity. Against that conclusion, most 'towns' remained very small by today's standards; there was only one major English city, London, which accounted for a large share of the urban sector of the population; and England had little to compare with the network of very substantial towns and cities that characterised long-developed areas of the continental economy, including France, northern Italy, the Low Countries and the Rhineland. Towns were not a prerequisite of political consciousness or political change: the American Revolution broke out in a society far less urbanised. Until after 1800, Scotland, Ireland and Wales were substantially lower in the league tables of urbanisation than England, yet Scotland and Ireland were major political destabilisers. Historians' older rhetoric about the effects of urbanisation assumes an English model that hardly fits England's nearest neighbours, let alone agricultural North America.

Towns had representative institutions, but they were not essentially democratic. They varied greatly in their structures of government: Manchester, the archetypal city of Victorian progress, was still administered in the eighteenth century by its court leet, a medieval survival. Yet such structures could be well or badly run: many towns in the eighteenth century pursued schemes of improvement while still being in the hands of oligarchies, while other towns did little. Many corporations were well conducted before the Municipal Corporations Act of 1835 regularised and opened up their governance; many were badly conducted after it. Corrupt enclaves persisted in some cities through subsequent centuries, merely serving new interest groups; it is not clear that an 'open society' argument can be sustained on such evidence.[50]

A preoccupation of the eighteenth century came to be the theme of 'improvement'. Daniel Defoe, in his *A Tour Thro' the Whole Island of Great Britain* (1724–6), celebrated 'the Improvements in the Soil, the Product of the Earth, the Labour of the Poor, the Improvement in Manufactures, in Merchandises, in Navigation'.[51] Remarkably, this awareness did not produce a generalised idea of 'progress': that term still meant geographical movement, not the general amelioration of the human condition. Defoe also described a society that was run by local elites (as was even more true in Scotland, Ireland and Wales) without major intervention from the central

government except for the collection of excise (a tax on commodities like beer and tobacco) and the periodic visits of assize
judges. Local elites, not subject to the spotlight of publicity,
could be more unaccountable than national elites: the idea of
the 'open society' is partly an invention of twentieth-century
cities.

Some historians have adopted the recent German notion
of a 'public sphere' to argue that government became
decisively more subject to popular participation and consent,
but this thesis must be doubted.[52] The coffee house, the
pamphlet and the newspaper, spreading rapidly after 1660, had
long been preceded by the tavern, the sermon and the news-
letter, and these older forms and forums of communication
continued: the new culture of the *Spectator* (1711–12, 1714)
supplemented this older culture but did not abolish it. Nor
were they necessarily antithetical: the same people could
attend both coffee house and tavern, and continue their old
disputes in both. An informed public outside Parliament grew
with the growing number of newspapers, and participated
even though they lacked the vote. Yet this was not new: the
Reformation, and the wars of the 1640s, showed informed
participation before the advent of newspapers, and eighteenth-
century newspapers were far from populist.

The concept of *communitas regni*, the community of the
realm, can be traced to the thirteenth century or earlier in
England, and the Reformation revealed similar group
solidarities in Scotland. In Ireland, sectarian communities
were aware of themselves as such long before the franchise
became an issue. People had long felt involved (or excluded
where they expected involvement); this assumption did not
wait for the invention of a concept of 'society' distinct from
the state. 'Society' in this sense was unknown to Locke and

was an idea only invented, for polemical reasons, by authors like Thomas Paine. Nor did the career or writings of Locke validate the notion of a 'public sphere'. Locke's political theory was underpinned chiefly by natural law, not by contract, and Locke did not appeal to any essentially contractual or voluntary character of social relations in his day. Contract was an ancient device, but not necessarily a revolutionary one; it did not automatically supersede status and custom.

Social mobility, too, is not a single and easily measurable thing. If the middle ranks increasingly aped the fashions and consumer goods of the elite, this has been read by some historians as evidence of the ascendancy of cash; others interpret it as showing the cultural hegemony of patricians.

Whether 'new men' were acceptable in elite landed society is a question that some historians seek to answer with an assertive 'yes', others with a robust 'no'. But the situation is likely to have varied greatly by region (London being almost a different world) and occupation (different occupations of equal wealth commanded different status). An acceptable 'character' mattered: the colonial Benjamin Franklin found many doors in London's elite society open to him; the native Thomas Paine found doors shut, and chose exile. Yet however 'closed' the landed elite and the political class, society in the middle was increasingly 'open' in the sense of mobile. In a diversified economy, growth meant thousands of new opportunities, seized by men of little or no fortune. This quickly became an easy boast. In 1728 Defoe claimed that:

It is the Trade that has made the common People rich, as Pride has made the Gentry poor . . . however the Gentlemen may value themselves upon their Birth and Blood, the Case begins to turn against them so evidently,

as to Fortune and Estate, that tho' they say, the Tradesmen cannot be made Gentlemen; yet the Tradesmen
are, at this Time, able to buy the Gentlemen almost in
every part of the Kingdom.[53]

Yet Defoe exaggerated. Statistics now available suggest that
although *income* did flow into 'new' hands, it flowed into 'old'
hands about as much, except in a few areas; meanwhile, the
balance of *wealth* was still heavily towards land. Nor did the
rise of manufacturing always have an egalitarian outcome.
Some enterprises fell into the pattern of the 'artisan republic',
the workshop coercively dominated by the customary
expectations of groups of skilled craftsmen; others were
organised on a top-down basis by the employer. Neither was
obviously 'open'. New manufacturers from the ironmaster
Ambrose Crowley to the social reformer Robert Owen
borrowed from the gentry a patriarchal model of labour
relations, theoretically idealised, practically coercive. If modest
wealth opened many opportunities in the middling ranks of
society, this pattern did not obtain at all points in the social
hierarchy: in many trades journeymen remained trapped as
wage-labourers. The measure of openness depended on one's
location and ambitions. The son of a farm labourer who rose
to be an innkeeper might consider himself well rewarded; a
struggling author who narrowly failed to be accepted as a
gentleman might become a Jacobin and an enemy of the
aristocratic ideal.

To the rural poor, society could seem even more 'closed',
especially when economic change undermined living standards
and eroded customary entitlements. Scotland saw a similar
transition to England as customary use-rights slowly gave way
to commercially disposable freehold. In Scotland, even before

the suppression of the Jacobite rising of 1745 ('the Forty-five'), the Gaelic idea of landowning (*duthchas*, or heritable trustee-ship, whereby the clan chiefs were obliged to provide security of possession to their kin) began to give way to an idea of heritable freehold title (*oighreachd*). This 'legalist concept of heritage' entailed a subordination of traditional ideas of entitlement to market opportunities, growing after 1745, in full flood by the 1820s. This legal shift in ideas of land tenure, it has been argued, was the most important cause of the demise of clanship; it was a change equally promoted by landowners who inclined to the House of Stuart and those who sided with the House of Hanover.[54] Eighteenth-century Britons competed without a sense of 'the new' transforming 'the old'. Even when changes in landownership had their effects, they were not necessarily what recent assumptions predict. In 1776 Thomas Bentley, reformer and partner of Josiah Wedgwood, on his way across northern France to Paris, noted: 'Another observation occurred to me in passing through this open country. *Enclosures* have an affinity with *free government* and open fields with *monarchies*. This is a political paradox, that requires and will admit of explanation.'[55]

The criminal code has been used as another measure of 'openness'. Supporters of a 'closed society' model have empha-sised the growing number of offences that incurred the death penalty, including ones that defended property in various forms. Capital crimes, about fifty in 1680, rose to over 200 by 1820. But few people convicted under these statutes were executed: the criminal law worked by show and by deterrence rather than by bureaucratic efficiency. There is evidence that homicide rates per 1,000 of the population had declined steeply since the lawlessness of the sixteenth century, and con-tinued at a low level.[56] Since most major crime was committed by the poor on the poor, and was punished only with their consent, expressed via the jury system, it can be questioned how far the criminal law was seen as an agency of class domination in a closed society.

Some social historians have interpreted parliamentary legislation in the eighteenth century as favouring private property, capitalist enterprise and elite authority (as in laws against poaching) over customary rights. The people's customary entitlements and sports, they urge, were implicitly legislated against. Economic historians by contrast have sometimes argued that the legal system was slow in promoting capitalism, being too often swayed by respect for custom, and not effective in providing a legal infrastructure for modern business. In the countryside, legal challenges to enclosures show that the law could still be used to defend customary relationships in the village community rather than being a simple instrument of capitalist domination.[57] The history of the law is a fertile but as yet insufficiently tilled field.

The laws against poaching have been used as one index of the old order, beginning with the Game Act of 1671. By this Act, the landed gentry (defined by a property qualification) enjoyed the sole right to kill certain sorts of game wherever found, not just on their own land. Further statutes were added to this code into the early nineteenth century, until the laws were repealed, and game turned into private property, by the Game Reform Act of 1831. As with the secret ballot, it can be debated whether repeal initiated changing relationships or was made possible by them. Certainly, the gentry defended the game laws as epitomes of a hierarchical, landed society. One historian has traced the 1671 Act to the desire of the gentry to distinguish themselves from the rising urban financial interest by the institution of a symbolic group privilege tied to landowning; it was not primarily intended to defend the gentry against any perceived challenge from the labourers. But by the 1820s, this was indeed the dominant theme, with a bitter 'poaching war' endemic in many areas. Landowners might restrict any form of hunting on their own land, defining it as poaching, and enclosure greatly extended private property rights over animals, far beyond the practice of 1671. What changed in 1831 was merely the abolition of the property qualification: now, all game was redefined as private property. The Game Reform Act of 1831 is therefore open to two interpretations: that it was intended to destroy a whole social order; or, alternatively, that it was intended to reformulate that order to permit its survival. As with the Reform Act of 1832, both interpretations have some plausibility.[58]

Poaching itself is sometimes analysed as class action, and as part of a repertoire of rural protest to defend customary rights that included (but especially from c.1815 to the 'Captain Swing' riots of 1830–1) arson, rick burning, the maiming of cattle, and the smashing of agricultural machinery. The old order in the countryside was not idyllic, any more than the later class society in the towns; assertions of old entitlements could be as ugly as the assertion of newly formulated class rights. But which was present in the Swing disturbances? Historians disagree. It is clear that the Whig government reacted harshly, with special commissions replacing the courts and sentencing at least 500 rioters to transportation. But these facts do not prove the existence of class; and it is difficult to present the game laws as class legislation in the 1670s if (as is argued below) class was a concept not framed until the early nineteenth century.

'Class' is conventionally taken to be a marker of a closed society, and the arrival of social class is sometimes postponed by a claim of the survival of paternalism despite the challenge of an unfettered free-market ideal; but this antithesis needs careful examination. Such an argument takes paternalism (an imprecise notion) to be in good repair in the early eighteenth century, but undermined by the decline of yearly hirings, the rise of wage labour, the progressive difficulty of obtaining a poor-law entitlement (a 'settlement') and a wave of enclosures that eroded economic independence. It has been argued that there was a watershed in the mid eighteenth century when practices in the labour market moved away from ones that respected paternal relationships towards ones that attended only to market forces. This scenario seems most persuasive as a general model, but the local variations were so great as to make it problematic as an account of England as a whole, let alone Wales, Ireland and Scotland.

What mattered most with any system was the degree of humanity with which it was run, and this varied unpredictably. Symbolically, compassion and coercion still alternated, the first reasserted in the Speenhamland poor-relief system of 1798 which indexed cash handouts to the price of grain. Yet there was no natural pendulum: the old statutes regulating prices and apprenticeship regulations weakened as the eighteenth century went on; the old assize of bread, allowing local JPs to set prices, disappeared after the 1790s. So did traditional rural entertainments, once provided by farmers for labourers: social distances were increasing in the countryside, as in manufacture. Even so, one study of Lincolnshire has postponed the essential shift in labourers' attitudes to the 1840s.[59]

Yet changes in paternal relationships were not necessarily all in the libertarian direction of individual autonomy. Indeed there was arguably a revival of paternalism in the late eighteenth and early nineteenth centuries, after years in which many complaints had been made of the self-interest of rural elites. From the middle of the eighteenth century, this argument runs, the rural gentry acquired a new interest in their local roles, a trend that found one expression in the much larger number of country clergy appointed as Justices of the Peace. This revival of paternalism, it is argued, mitigated the wave of violence, arson and strikes in the 1830s and 40s caused by the triumph of laissez-faire principles, not least in the new poor law of 1834.[60] Whether this 'revival' was sufficient to count as a new paternalism is a subject for debate.

Perhaps paternalism and free-market forces had co-existed all along, but as ideals. It may be that old assumptions about community and reciprocity, sometimes overstated by historians' use of the term 'paternalism', were undermined less by the rise of industry (for factories were highly organised, and their owners sometimes showed much involvement in workers' lives) than by unemployment in the countryside: total annual expenditure on poor relief in England and Wales rose from £2.004 million in 1783–5 to a peak of £7.87 million in 1818 before being pared away by Whig reforms to about £4 million in the later 1830s.[61] The rural population boom had produced a workforce often too large for the rural economy to sustain in full employment. Wages were eroded; poor relief had to take up the slack. Landowners blamed the labourers; the labourers blamed the landowners, but often also the clergy. Apart from a long-standing drain to London from neighbouring counties, not until after the arrival of the railway did unskilled rural labour become much more mobile, the rural population decline, and rural poverty shrink. The problem was never solved.

'Patriarchalism' is too fashionable a concept. Much recent

writing on gender relations assumes that a social-anthropological 'patriarchal model' of the family characterised the seventeenth century but was dismantled by social change in the eighteenth. This relies on an older model of the 'extended' peasant family, holding land in 'impartible inheritance' by collective family ownership, a model once beloved of European sociologists and social anthropologists, and held by them to characterise a 'peasant society'. Yet it has now been shown by Alan Macfarlane and others that this pattern was absent in England even in c.1200.[62] Even that classic text, Filmer's *Patriarcha* (written c.1630), a defence of the divine right of kings, had nothing to say about gender relations in his own day. Patriarchalism as a social formation is a construction of twentieth-century feminism. As was argued above, gender relations in the long eighteenth century displayed a range of patterns from independence to dominance, centred on a norm taught by the conduct books: companionate marriage, mutual deference, ultimate male legal authority, offset against some legal defences for female property rights. John Locke's *Two Treatises of Government* (1690) was widely regarded as having refuted Filmer, but had no measurable impact on gender relations. Indeed the bachelor Locke there twice asserted that what a wife owed her husband was 'subjection'.[63]

Reformers seldom protested. From the 1820s, the new ideology of radicalism had much to say about landlords, taxes, debt, governmental corruption and the baneful effect of the established church; but it had almost nothing to say about gender relations. Radicalism failed to make common cause with the small number of women who followed the path of Mary Wollstonecraft. As a result, the reform movements of the 1820s and 30s had almost no impact on the position of women. James Mill's *Essay on Government* (1821) ruled out women's franchise on the grounds that their interest was 'included in' that of their parents or husbands. In the eighteenth century, a few women burgage owners voted in parliamentary elections; this right was terminated by the Whigs' 1832 Reform Act.

Some historians have argued that the period *c*.1780–1830 saw the emergence of a Victorian 'domestic ideology' that divided women and men in 'separate spheres', confining women to home and family. This trend is variously linked to an Industrial Revolution, the birth of class, and evangelicalism. Against this view it has been urged that conduct books and religious teaching had described such a sexual division of labour from at least the Reformation. This teaching hardly changed over time, while other things did change: a growing expectation of women's roles in moral reform, a growing demand that men temper their aggression and pride by good manners and 'politeness'. But it seems likely that these ideals made a practical difference for only a few with leisure and money to act on them: for the majority, the growing necessities of daily life confined them to ancient roles, and ancient responses.

The debate over the 'open society' largely depends on what is being argued against. It has been claimed that the 'ancien regime' model was static, and unable to account for undoubted change in such areas as urban growth and the 'rise of the middle class'. Yet stasis has never been asserted. Change was constant, even in earlier centuries, but incremental. What is open to doubt is whether any such changes can be labelled 'forward-looking' or 'progressive': the future proved too different for there to be one set of unmoved goalposts that Locke, Defoe, Hume, Smith, Fox or Shelley all tried to reach.

Nor did the English rhetoric of progress fit Scotland, Ireland or Wales nearly as well. They remained less urbanised; more swayed by great landowners; their hinterlands less penetrated by urban culture than England. Scotland was more dominated by Edinburgh, Ireland more dominated by Dublin, than England was by London. Even the late growth of Glasgow and Belfast did not reverse this. Wales was even more lacking in substantial towns until the early nineteenth century.

Perhaps both the 'open' and the 'closed' models treat social relations as being of one kind or the other, but basically unproblematic. We should rather see social relations as endlessly contested, but for a changing set of reasons.

The wealth of nations: the economy

The keynote of the pre-industrial, commercial economy was captured by Defoe in 1724:

> The Fate of Things . . . plants and supplants Families, raises and sinks Towns, removes Manufactures, and Trade; Great Towns decay, and small Towns rise; new Towns, new Palaces, new Seats are Built every Day; great Rivers and good Harbours dry up, and grow useless; again, new Ports are open'd, Brooks are made Rivers, small Rivers, navigable Ports and Harbours are made where none were before, and the like.

There was always something new: 'new Trades are every Day erected, new Projects enterpriz'd, new Designs laid'; England was 'a trading, improving Nation'.[64] But this constant change he ascribed to the 'Fate of Things': observers did not yet identify an economic dynamic of progress. 'Capitalism' and 'the market' had not yet been reified. Change and adaptation did not entail the arrival of any single new model of economy or society. Adam Smith's *An Inquiry into the Nature and Causes of the Wealth of Nations* (1776) did not use the idea of 'capitalism' explicitly or implicitly, and attached no overriding importance to manufactures; Smith's dynamic of growth was the division of labour, the specialisation of function that had already developed within an advanced commercial economy, not any transformation in productivity about to be wrought by factory-based manufacture.

More obvious than any economic dynamic were prosperity's preconditions: political stability, the absence of war and revolution, the development of a sophisticated financial system, the absence of inflation, and the security of property. Adam Smith could take for granted 'the sacred rights of private property'; he did not elaborate on why they were sacred.[65] In 1660 the economy of the British Isles reflected the long-term consequences of the efficient monetisation of English society under the Anglo-Saxon monarchs: trade and the monetary expression of economic relationships had already progressed over many centuries to produce a sophisticated English economy with the specialisation of function that Smith was to point to as the key to maximising productivity.[66]

Behind the political disunity of the archipelago lay the economic introversion of parts of Wales, of Ireland and of Scotland, a self-sufficiency that left much scope for growth within an economy that evolved, rather than being transformed in kind, as economic integration progressed. The Union of 1707 removed tariff barriers and made England, Wales and Scotland one of the largest internal free-trade zones in Europe. Political tension and economic rivalry prevented the extension of this principle to Ireland, with profound consequences:

where the English and Scottish economies broadly converged in the long eighteenth century, the British and Irish economies did not. Ireland's integration, an obvious good in retrospect, was less obvious at the time because of the hegemony of the assumptions termed by Adam Smith 'the Commercial or Mercantile System', the political management of trade and shipping to further national strategic power, a policy in which the acquisition of wealth was seen as a zero-sum game. So trade was deeply involved in geopolitics, first in England's commercial and naval rivalry with the United Provinces; in the structured growth of trade (as with the Anglo-Portuguese Methuen Treaty of 1703); and in Britain's long rivalry with an equally mercantilist France.[67]

Yet Anglo-Irish integration was possible. In 1660, much of the British Isles already displayed diversity of employment and geographical mobility. The integration of landed and urban-professional elites dated in England from the fifteenth century, as a result of their sitting together in the lower House of the Westminster Parliament. This meant that as the trading sector developed after 1660, a sense of antagonism between land and trade did not become entrenched. Such a sense there was, strengthened by high taxes to fund the wars of the 1690s; but it tended to weaken over time, partly thanks to Sir Robert Walpole's anxiety about the landed interest. Conflict over taxation was old, but not until the agricultural boom of the Revolutionary and Napoleonic Wars, post-war protection, and the analysis of the political economist David Ricardo (1772–1823) in and after the 1810s did an idea become dominant that society was divided by the operation of the economy into blocs, each of which might have an inherent interest antithetical to another bloc. Even then, the sense of antagonism was temporary: the abolition of agricultural protection with the repeal of the Corn Laws in 1846 tended to restore the deeply etched symbiosis of land and trade, with important consequences for politics thereafter.

Everything still depended on the surpluses produced by farmers. Adam Smith, reviewing in 1776 'the manufactures of Leeds, Halifax, Sheffield, Birmingham and Wolverhampton', concluded: 'Such manufactures are the offspring of agriculture.'[68] Even England's relatively commercial economy was built on farming. In 1688 the work force was divided about 60–40 between agriculture and commerce; it took until 1800 to reverse this balance. In the 1851 census, agriculture was still the largest single employer of labour.[69] England's neighbours were even more weighted towards agriculture. Farming in the British Isles was also diverse, ranging from England's 'chalk and cheese', the productive arable and grasslands, of the South and Midlands to the Scottish Lowlands, but petering out in the undeveloped Highlands, and confronting the less advanced farming practices of much of Ireland. This diversity did not diminish; indeed the productivity gap between innovative agricultural regions and backward areas may have widened. What was unusual in Europe was that there was no productivity gap between English agriculture and English manufactures.

The success of English farming began early, but then slowed. R. V. Jackson has estimated that England's agricultural output grew by at least 4.3 per cent per decade between 1660 and 1740, but at most by 2.7 per cent from 1740 to 1790.[70] These gains in agricultural productivity had already released many people from farming by 1750, so creating a labour force for employment in trade. This early reallocation of labour calls in question how far gains in farming were due to enclosures. Enclosure – the breaking up of huge medieval common fields into a patchwork of smaller freeholds, each surrounded by hedges and ditches – was explained in the early twentieth century as the arrival of capitalist agriculture, the moment when the smallholder was expropriated, pauperised, and turned into the landless labourer. Yet although economic historians have moved on, it is still necessary to point out that this scenario is too simple. Some areas had long been enclosed. Elsewhere, the consolidation of strip holdings into fields by local agreement had been slowly progressing for many decades. It is estimated that 47 per cent of English land had been enclosed by 1600, and 71 per cent by 1700.[71]

From the 1760s into the early nineteenth century enclosure accelerated again, driven by parliamentary legislation: for the first time since Tudor enclosures shifted the balance from arable towards sheep farming, it attracted significant publicity, and hence the attention of historians. Its impact varied by region: in some, the output of grain was increased; in others, there was a conversion from arable to pasture; in others, additional land was cultivated for the first time. In some cases, common rights had been eroded and private property in land established before the passage of enclosure Acts. Yet although enclosure did not create the landless labourer, in the long run it reinforced trends, especially the late eighteenth-century rise in rents and the increasing power of the great landowners, that undermined the position of many labourers. Parliamentary enclosure did eliminate the use-rights of members of the village community who were not small landowners to begin with: such people did now become wage labourers.[72] Jackson's figures suggest that per capita consumption of foodstuffs in England 'may have fallen between 1760 and 1800':[73] the 'agricultural revolution' was not an unqualified, or inevitable, success. Population growth overtook the achievements of farming, and threatened catastrophe.

Lowland Scotland participated in the same consolidation of holdings, rising yields and rents, but this happened by the decision of landlords rather than by legislation. The same methods could hardly work in the Highlands. There, the spread of the potato contributed to sustaining the impoverished farming of the small proprietor. This had two consequences. First, a growing trend to mass emigration, especially to North America. Second, the spreading attempts of landowners to rationalise their estates by the eviction of crofters, the notorious 'Highland Clearances', to make way for cattle or sheep farming. It is debated how far these economic changes were politically motivated, part of the deliberate targeting of clan society after the battle of Culloden, and how far they were pushed through by Lowland Scots rather than by Highland landowners. Irish agriculture was least touched by 'improvement', and showed in the 1840s the consequences for a rural society of taking a route opposite to Scotland's.

Improved or not, agriculture predominated. Only when measured by state revenue did trade matter more than land. In 1693, customs and excise provided 42 per cent of public revenue against the land tax's 45 per cent; by 1705 trade had risen to 55 per cent against land's 39 per cent. By 1730, in the middle of Walpole's ascendancy, trade had risen to 70 per cent, land had declined to 24 per cent. From there, land had little further to fall: in 1760, in the middle of the Seven Years War, the percentages were 68 to 26; in 1780, during the American war, 70 to 20; in 1796, during the French Revolutionary war, 60 to 17.[74] Tax revenue was not a good guide to the relative balance of sectors of the economy, although, measured by political influence, commerce and finance still vastly outweighed manufacture.

The ubiquity of trade is striking: of the 5,034 men who sat

in the House of Commons between 1734 and 1832, 897 were associated in some way with business, rising from one in nine in 1734–61 to one in four in 1818–32. Yet of these most were financiers or lawyers; only some twenty-nine were manufacturers, twenty of whom entered the House after 1800.[75] Of all 'interests' in the Commons the dominant one was land. Reflecting this cultural dominance, a landed qualification was required to sit in the House of Commons. An Act of 1710 set the requirement for a county seat at a landed estate worth £600 per annum, and £300 for a borough seat (although this hurdle added to a sense of social difference between land and trade, there were occasional attempts to raise it). Swift expressed a lasting ideal of the 'country party' when he wrote in 1721: 'there could not be a truer maxim in our government than this, That the Possessors of the soil are the best judges of what is for the advantage of the kingdom'.[76] Only in 1838 was this qualification expanded to include non-landed forms of wealth.[77] Yet this requirement, initially expressing a rivalry between land and trade, contributed in the longer term to the tendency for successful traders to buy landed estates: symbiosis rather than conflict was the general pattern.

Britain's mixed economy grew steadily, moving away from its medieval focus on a particular sector, the export of woollen cloth. Its pattern was of productivity gains across the board, in agriculture, commerce and extractive industries; these gradually led to the rise of manufactures. Commerce rather than manufactures was still the key. Centuries of monetary exchange and social mobility had already produced a specialised, trading, financially advanced economy able to support much higher public expenditure than its continental rivals; it used this power in war to build up trade.

England's commercial prosperity was widely celebrated

from the early eighteenth century. But poverty is relative, and Defoe's praise of England's wealth may also be interpreted as Whig propaganda. In the 1790s, the artist James Gillray created images satirising English discontent amid plenty contrasted with French Jacobin self-congratulation in the midst of want; these images too need to be interpreted. Although some historians have emphasised England's growing prosperity in the eighteenth century, this wealth tended to be concentrated in few hands. By present-day (and even by eighteenth-century) standards, 'the poor' were everywhere. There is another, unrelated, debate among historians over whether an 'Industrial Revolution' at the end of the century raised or lowered the standard of living of the workers caught up in it. It is a question too simply framed to yield an answer that will fit the widely varied life experiences of workers in a diverse economy: some gained, some lost; measuring from the top of a boom to the bottom of a slump gives a pessimistic answer, and measuring from a slump to a boom seems to show a strong growth in real wages. Wales, Ireland, Scotland and England had different track records; so did different regions within each. It is not clear what experience is captured by aggregate figures.

The debate on living standards is fraught because it is still linked with another preoccupation of historians, the alleged triumph of 'capitalism' (by which they normally mean 'factory manufacturing'). The term 'capitalism' is now seldom used by economic historians. Yet even if this concept is valid (all economic systems employ 'capital', not just privately owned, free-market ones), an economy dominated by fixed capital in manufactures was not in place before 1832. The word 'industry' then meant the virtue of industriousness, not manufacturing. The earlier economy was preoccupied by 'trade' and more dependent on working capital (credit) than on the fixed capital (factories, machines) implied by Victorian 'capitalism'.[78]

What, then, made for success in commerce? The security of private property, restored in 1660 after the lawlessness of rebellion, made possible the further development of a monetised economy, with price stability, sophisticated means of exchange and credit, mobility of labour and increasingly efficient transport. Historians also debate whether an important element was a code of labour law that favoured the employer and so facilitated capital formation at the expense of wages.[79] Yet this may be a misconception: the Combination Acts of 1799 and 1800 did not upset the joint regulation of prices in unionised trades like framework knitting, but only penalised 'industrial action' to achieve such ends. Those Acts sought to preserve older practices of mediation and conciliation, the setting of wages and prices by magistrates; for that reason, they were repealed in 1824. Even after that date, it was the 'trades', like bricklayers, carpenters and shoemakers, that pioneered the development of unions, not workers in large factories: hence the term *trades union*, not *working-class union*. However low eighteenth-century wage rates are from a twenty-first-century perspective, it may be that England's system of poor relief acted to keep up wages and so to create a greater incentive to technological innovation and capital formation than prevailed on the continent. But this possibility has yet to be studied by economic historians.

Beneath this legal umbrella, industries changed and grew as technological advances were linked to production for a broadening market. This became true of several major commodities. Beer was once brewed in the household; increasingly it was produced in industrial breweries. Textiles, glass, salt and soap moved from small-scale to large-scale production. But this was not true of everything: one study has shown production in Kentish households rising to c.1750, not falling as the theory of universal specialisation suggests.[80] Moreover, the site of mechanised production, except in brewing, naval dockyards and a few other sectors, was still normally the craft workshop. This meant that although manufacturing grew, its overall share of the growing English economy was for a long time stable. What grew most was trade.

Overseas trade, in particular, supported an ever larger fraction of England's non-agricultural population. The diversification of foreign trade beyond woollen cloth, and its naval support, really took off from the 1660s. As Lord Haversham reminded the House of Lords in 1707, 'Your Fleet, and your Trade, have so near a relation, and such mutual influence upon each other, they cannot well be separated: your trade is the mother and nurse of your seamen; your seamen are the life of your fleet, and your fleet is the security and protection of your trade, and both together are the wealth, strength, security and glory of Britain.' Over time, this symbiosis strengthened still further, and export trade produced a host of connections with domestic demand and technology. How significant exports were in the overall growth of GNP is, however, still debated.

Overseas trade grew, although not as much as eighteenth-century political rhetoric suggests: 'industrial output increased fourfold over the eighteenth century, home consumption of it threefold and exports sixfold. The outcome by 1800 was that around a fifth of manufacturing output was exported compared with a third in 1700, and that whereas manufactured goods had then been up to a third of imports, by 1815 they hardly figured at all.'[81] Overall, from 1700 to 1850 English exports increased from 8 to 19 per cent of GNP. Yet there was no steady forward march: exports rose and fell, only moving ahead to about 15 per cent in *c*.1780–1800. The next decisive shift, to about 30 per cent, did not come until 1870–1914. The home market was all-important. There is little room for the argument that 'imperialism', by grabbing overseas markets, was the main engine of growth, or that 'proto-industrialisation', by creating capitalism before the arrival of the word, fulfilled that role. The fashionable demonology of the sources of economic growth is largely mythical. Those sources were mostly domestic and prosaic.

Historians now attend more to the preconditions of economic growth than to what used to be celebrated as its specific triggers, and many of these preconditions were geopolitical: political, legal and financial stability, sustainable demography, and, of course, survival in war. Whether war was good or bad for the British economy has been disputed. Some have pointed to the often larger share of military expenditure than of civilian capital formation in GNP; to the periodic disruptions to trade and to domestic demand; to the diversion of resources away from consumption and capital formation; and to the cycles of boom and slump that war promoted.[82] Others have argued that war promoted technological innovation and stimulated certain areas of manufacture; that it took up slack in the economy rather than producing a diversion of manpower from productive employment; and that capital diversion drew chiefly from house building rather than from capital investment in manufacturing or transport. This debate is not yet decided, partly because war had different impacts on different sectors of the economy; partly because different wars had different impacts; and partly because the alternatives (defeats in war and their disastrous economic consequences) are seldom made part of the calculation.

England's external wars of the seventeenth century were expensive failures: against Spain in 1624–30 and 1655–60; against France in 1627–30 and 1689–97; against the United Provinces in 1651–4, 1665–7 and 1672–4. Of these only the trade wars against the United Provinces may have yielded some economic benefit. Later wars were more mixed, notably to limit French expansion in 1702–13, 1740–8, 1756–63, 1778–83, 1793–1802, 1803–14 and 1815. The early attempts were stalemates. Britain then divested France of its North American possessions in 1763; France had its revenge in 1783, but at the cost of French bankruptcy and revolution. Against this background of disruption and hazard, Britain learned to live with war, and by the Napoleonic Wars was doing quite well out of them.

To imagine a long eighteenth century without war is to imagine a utopia that could never have existed.[83] Wars could be expected; but more adverse outcomes to Britain's wars than actually occurred were perfectly feasible. Victory in war, or at least a draw, was a precondition of prosperity less because resources spent on war per se were an economic stimulus than because some forms of war might be beneficial (raising shares of trade in a mercantilist world order) and because the devastation, disruption and death that went with military defeat were definitely adverse to growth. Nevertheless, there is evidence that Britain's wars, especially from 1776 to 1815, produced a diversion of capital and manpower away from production. The real acceleration in growth rates came in and after the 1820s, as Britain began to recover. And if the wars of 1793–1815 hindered economic growth, was the same true of other wars that followed the Revolution of 1688? Work on this question has only begun.

Recent research has established the remarkable success of

England, then Britain, in raising state revenues. Britain's share of GNP transferred to the state in taxes and loans ran second only to the United Provinces, and made Britain a formidable naval and military rival to continental states of far greater territories and populations.[84] Historians of finance sometimes interpret this as evidence for a consensual British patriotism. Yet against that argument are the political records of continuous resistance to taxation, both at Westminster and in the American colonies, and the emergence after c.1793 of a new discourse which made high taxation and national debt central to the post-1815 critique of 'Old Corruption'. Britain was never consensual, and there was never agreement, in the English-speaking world, on whether the wars promoted or undermined liberty and property. Continental European states had incurred disastrous levels of debt in an era of warfare between the invasion of Italy in 1494 and the Peace of the Pyrenees in 1659, but between 1689 and 1815 England, then Britain, did the same. Britain was a late starter, not a democratic pioneer.

An 'Industrial Revolution'?

The 'Industrial Revolution' is one of those subjects (like 'the Enlightenment', examined below) that became encased in historians' rhetoric. It was conventionally not just described but celebrated as a 'moment' of mankind's 'emancipation', both from poverty and from the social relations held to stem from poverty. It was depicted as an integrated 'process' that brought linked transformations in manufactures, transport and agriculture. Technological change allegedly set mankind on the road to vastly higher gross national products, and initiated the 'modern world'. Yet historians are now more cautious about the idea of a turning point.

For good reasons, 'the Industrial Revolution' was a concept unknown in the eighteenth century; it was a term of historical art popularised in English usage only from the 1880s. It evidently originated in France: where France had had its political revolution in 1789, Britain was said to have had its economic one, equally sudden. Even then, it was not quickly taken into English discourse (where one might have expected a quick adoption, had it matched widespread domestic perceptions). Arnold Toynbee (1852–83), a leading agent in its naturalisation, intended the idea of a fundamental divide produced by industrialisation to prove the need for moral and spiritual regeneration.[85] But others from the late nineteenth century took the idea in another direction, launching the movement that we now look back on as 'modernism', and by an 'Industrial Revolution' meant an assertion of the priority of material considerations in human affairs and of supply-side issues in the economy.

The term was intended to privilege the idea that there was an essential transition between the premodern and the modern; it pointed to industrialisation (specifically, to technology-driven manufactures) as the motor of that transition. Yet even if production determines everything (which is questionable), an economy built around manufacturing industry, with coal and steel at its heart, and producing the great industrial conurbations in which most of the population spent their lives, was not mature until about the 1880s – not coincidentally the era when the term 'Industrial Revolution' was popularised. The rate of growth of England's GNP was also substantially lower in the eighteenth century than it was to be in many continental economies that industrialised in the late nineteenth (when the idea of an 'Industrial Revolution' began to look plausible).[86] In the eighteenth century commerce and evolution, not industry and revolution, were the keys.

Until about the 1980s, available statistics of economic output seemed to bear out the idea of a sharp discontinuity and a major acceleration in the growth of GNP. Since then, economic historians have argued over these figures, intensely difficult as they are to reconstruct for past ages that made few attempts to collect the data from which they could be calculated. In general, the recent school of 'econometric' historians (those who apply sophisticated statistical modelling techniques to the data) have steadily scaled down the rate of acceleration of GNP to the point where a clear change of gear is now hard to detect. The English, then the British, economy certainly grew in the eighteenth century, but its growth had been somewhat greater in earlier centuries, and was less in the late eighteenth and early nineteenth than was recently believed.

If economic growth in England as a whole was slower than was once thought, of much older origin, and more protracted, this model of gradual evolution hardly applies to Clydeside, Belfast or the valleys of South Wales: there, industrial growth was indeed sudden and fraught, with larger consequences for the host society. Industrial development was highly localised in England also, but England's larger population, and the wide extent of trade and pre-factory manufacture, cushioned and averaged the effects. According to R. A. Houston, 'Some 9 per cent of Scotland's people lived in towns of 10,000 or more inhabitants in 1750 compared with 17 per cent by 1800, a rate of growth faster than that of contemporary England (17 per cent and 20 per cent respectively) and indeed more rapid than that of any other European country except Poland which started from an extremely low level of 1 per cent in 1750.'[87] Yet Scotland's urbanisation hardly began before the last two

Engrav'd for the Universal Magazine 1750, for J Hinton, at the Kings Arms in N°Paul's Church Yard LONDON.

The Art of STOCKING-FRAME-WORK-KNITTING.

1. Proto-industrialisation. This print records the techniques of stocking framework knitting. Before the rise of factories, the artisan workshop was often, to different degrees, dependent on machinery. How much of a difference did 'industrialisation' make?

decades of the century. Before that, Scotland was at the bottom of European tables of the percentage of population in towns over 10,000; after 1800, Scotland moved close to the top. Ireland hardly shared in this urban growth, and in 1800 still trailed behind deeply rural France.[88]

No single model of industrialisation fits all four cases. Yet the old historiography advanced just such a single model and a single chronology. It depicted a single 'take-off into self-sustained growth' in about the 1780s. Since the 1980s, this model has been largely discarded by economic historians. It tended to celebrate only a few causes of economic growth (cotton, steam engines, technological innovation, capital formation); economic history increasingly records that, when quantified, none of the 'usual suspects' can be shown to have made more than a modest contribution to the twelvefold increase in real income per head of the population in Britain from c.1780 to the present.[89] Nevertheless, assertions of the transforming and unprecedented effect of industrialisation have proved remarkably durable, perhaps because of the survival of the polemical purposes that the term 'Industrial Revolution' originally promoted.

Economic change was, of course, continuous. But against the traditional thesis of an essential discontinuity must be set evidence for change being evolutionary rather than revolutionary; for important changes across many areas of economic life, not just in manufactures; for important changes at earlier times, notably the introduction of arable farming and the widespread use of coinage; and for economic change preceding the traditional 'period' of c.1780–1830, notably in the century after 1660. The major quantifiable change was a tripling of population in 1660–1830, but the life experiences of the new millions changed less.

Nor are there just two sorts of society, 'pre-industrial' and 'industrial': many models are found, mixing sectors in different ways and with different effects. As to an Industrial Revolution being produced by technological innovation, this has to be measured by productivity growth; and over the eighteenth century, it has been argued that, for England at least, productivity growth was as great in agriculture as in manufactures. Nor was change all one way, for the prosperity of sectors fluctuated: as the iron and steel centre of Sheffield grew, the iron industry of the Sussex Weald declined; growth in the textile trades of the West Riding of Yorkshire was partly at the cost of decline in the woollen trades of the west of England.

Some have argued that the phenomenal growth in cotton manufacture at the end of the eighteenth century acted to draw other sectors like transport and machine tools into industrialisation, but the strength of the links is debatable. Others contend that a series of changes over many years produced a 'critical mass', so that no single sector was responsible; but this analysis still depends on there being a single thing, an integrated Industrial Revolution, to explain. It seems, rather, that 'industrialisation' as a logic that would link and propel the whole economy was a later concept that does not fully capture the diversity of the growth that undoubtedly happened in the eighteenth century.

The preconditions of late eighteenth-century economic growth now seem more important compared with any later dynamic, and these preconditions often prevailed in earlier eras. Even so, historians disagree over the more immediate causes of economic change in Britain. Some see the country as the first industrial nation, writing a narrative of the growth of an economy in which technological innovation, or consumption, triggered higher production. Others stress that Britain was already an advanced commercial economy with a highly developed financial system, high labour mobility and specialisation of function; that Britain developed from the seventeenth century an important imperial trading dimension; and that before the nineteenth century this broadly based trading economy still generated much more wealth than the small sectors based on factory production. This debate has often been framed as a choice between two alternatives, since it is phrased as a misleading question: what caused the Industrial Revolution? Once we cease to look for a sudden discontinuity, a *revolution* created by manufacturing *industry*, we can ask how these different components of the 'old' economy gradually promoted each other.

In that respect, some economic historians have pointed to a considerable redeployment of labour between sectors in c.1660–1760 as a source of prosperity. Others have argued that redeployment was slow enough in the following century to restrict growth to modest figures. It has also been urged that spending on war from the 1770s to the 1810s (and later, via the burden of debt) 'crowded out' investment in industry, agricuture and housing.[90] Whether or not 'crowding out' occurred, England, then Britain, preserved its prosperity through productivity gains in all sectors of the economy, from farming through extractive industries and transport to artisan-based manufactures and services. These productivity gains were by specialisation of function and the transfer of labour from agriculture to other employments more than by the use in manufactures of novel technologies; and this sectoral reallocation had been proceeding for many years.

Nevertheless, changes in manufacturing techniques were real, often building on an older base. Coal had already achieved exponential expansion in the sixteenth century. By 1700,

Britain was producing 2.6 million tons of coal a year, five times the rest of world output. Coal made possible technological innovation through steam pumping in the mining industries of south-west England in the 1680s (Savery and Newcomen) that led on (although slowly) to Watt's improvements of the steam engine in the 1760s.[91] If technological change, consumer demand, improvements in transport and the development of domestic and overseas trade were preconditions of faster growth, they were all present before *c*.1750 without producing a sharp upturn in productivity. Technological change undoubtedly occurred, but without producing a 'revolution', a marked discontinuity of growth in overall productivity or GNP. It is still a question whether expanding population thereafter provided both a growing market and a growing labour supply, or whether, by outstripping production, it threatened the continuation of the very growth with which the idea of a unitary 'Industrial Revolution' associates it.

Economic growth is often assessed in relation to its capacity to reduce poverty, yet poverty is relative and was therefore often taken for granted. In these years many people ignored the problem of the material condition of life for the great majority.[92] Daniel Defoe, in *A Plan of the English Commerce* (1728), produced an often-quoted salute to the prosperity of the pre-industrial economy. His answer turned on 'Trade'. Defoe described 'the Manufacturers and the Shopkeepers', who were the basis of this prosperity:

We see their Houses and Lodgings tolerably furnished, at least stuff'd well with useful and necessary household Goods: Even those we call poor People, Journeymen, working and Painstaking People do thus; they lye warm, live in Plenty, work hard, and need know no Want.

These are the People that carry off the Gross of your
Consumption . . . these are the Life of our whole
Commerce, and all by their Multitude: Their Numbers
are not Hundreds or Thousands, or Hundreds of
Thousands, but Millions . . . by their Wages they are
able to live plentifully, and it is by their expensive,
generous, free way of living, that the Home
Consumption is rais'd to such a Bulk, as well of our
own, as of foreign Production.

Although agricultural employment for husbands alone was
not enough to keep the poor from poverty, argued Defoe, the
possibility of employment for wives and children too, in
trading and manufacturing districts, initiated a virtuous
economic spiral.[93]

Despite the element of Whig propaganda in Defoe's
picture, it does seem to have been the case that England (but
not Scotland, Ireland and Wales) began industrialisation with
higher real wages per head than many of its continental
neighbours thanks to the achievements of the old commercial
economy. But that was not saying much: by present-day
standards, in the long eighteenth century things were
expensive, people were cheap. By European standards,
however, real wages were distinctly higher in England, and
this may have been a stimulus to technological innovation and
capital formation.[94]

The problem of poverty was more inescapable in the urban
economy that characterised more and more areas from the
end of the eighteenth century. How soon, and how far, the
benefits of economic growth 'trickled down' to improve the
living standards of the majority is debated.[95] In the long term,
a great growth in real wages is undeniable; in the short term,

some historians still argue that the first generation of industrial workers was sacrificed to buy growth. Did early industry require a shift of GNP from wages into profits and capital formation? Some increase in capital formation there was, but against this must be set the modest requirements of many early industrial technologies compared to the much larger investments in naval dockyards, or spent in war. The income of the top 1 per cent is estimated to have increased as a share of GNP from 24.5 per cent in 1801 to 34.9 per cent by 1848,[96] but of these men the great majority were landowners, merchants and bankers rather than manufacturers. 'Industry' is not the only suspect; even into the 1790s, a reformer like Thomas Paine could trace poverty primarily to high taxation and war, two results of aristocratic hegemony, and treat the interests of manufacturers and workers as being aligned.

The picture was also highly diversified across regions, across occupations, and over time; the figures for wages and prices are inconclusive, although they do show unusually wide fluctuations in the years c.1780–1840. Grain prices were especially volatile, and were the key to whether workers went hungry: Britain's was still an economy close to agricultural cycles. For these reasons, a single, simple answer to the problem is unattainable. Answers are often influenced by subjective judgements. Was a rural pattern of life preferable to an urban one? Here it was chiefly the twentieth-century bourgeois intelligentsia which developed a cult of the countryside and bought weekend cottages there; eighteenth-century country labourers, experiencing the reality of rural poverty, more often sought to migrate to the towns. Technology also weights the scales in favour of the 'pessimists', since Victorian poverty was the first to be recorded in photographs; no comparable visual record of Hanoverian or Stuart poverty survives, and readers are subtly influenced instead by the images of happy peasants that fill the canvases of George Morland (1763–1804). Similarly, Victorian commissions of inquiry gathered statistics on poverty; they had few Georgian predecessors. Georgian novelists took poverty for granted; their Victorian successors were often deeply moved by it.

Migration does not prove that labourers improved their quality of life by urbanisation, but it suggests that migration may have been the least bad alternative. Life expectancies at birth in England in 1750–99 were somewhat higher than in 1650–1749, despite a larger proportion of children in the population (death rates were higher in childhood), but there was no dramatic increase before 1871.[97] The worst-case scenario, of population growth without urbanisation and industrialisation, was a reality in Ireland, leading to the famine of 1845–7 and depressed wages thereafter: the economic achievement of the mainland economy in the first phase of industrialisation, c.1780–1840, cannot be taken for granted. Nor can the other major variable, Britain's survival of the effects of military conflict and avoidance of domestic revolution: the devastating effects of war and of revolution on large areas of the continental European economy provide a yardstick against which Britain should be judged.

Industrialisation or its absence was therefore not the only point at issue in the British economy; indeed it was still only a part of the picture. Recent figures from econometric historians suggest a more optimistic picture from c.1815 to 1830, with price falls running ahead of declines in wages, and show an opposite pattern only in the war years from the 1790s to 1815. If so, war was more important than capital formation. But these figures are aggregates: as in all recessions, the ill effects were felt most by specific sectors. Minorities suffered when particular occupations were overtaken by technological change, most famously the handloom weavers; larger numbers suffered where geographical immobility increased competition for employment and drove down wages, as in the overpopulated rural economy of parts of the south of England; more again suffered during economic slumps. Over time, aggregate figures improved. But the debate is hampered since one term, 'poverty', is used to cover many diverse phenomena: the poverty of the Glasgow slum had different causes from that of the Irish countryside; the poverty of child workers was different from that of the aged sick. These complexities can be overlooked if the object of enquiry is, implicitly, either to vindicate or to condemn 'capitalism'.

Population growth, which was undoubted, has been enlisted by some historians to prove the reality of an Industrial Revolution by taking population growth as the cause of increased domestic demand, fuelling industrialisation by a novel thirst for consumer goods. By this means a 'consumer revolution', held to be evidence of a new *mentalité*, is linked to the old scenario and made to function as a marker of a transition to an 'industrial society' more widely understood. But this argument is undermined if population growth was an extraneous variable (as it clearly was in Ireland and probably elsewhere), and if rates of growth of productivity were similar across a mobile economy, not concentrated in an industrial leading sector.

It is likely that the 'optimistic' view of the standard of living question has been appropriated by those who wish to rescue the old account of an Industrial Revolution as social and economic *transformation*. But the model of transformation is built on false economics. If all else in a society remains the same (notably per capita savings; and this was probably the case, since most of the population in the eighteenth century were too poor to spend much out of savings) then people cannot improve their standard of living by autonomously consuming more, any more than individuals can lift themselves off the floor by pulling on their shoelaces. All else did not remain the same (overseas trade and the inputs of factors of production grew); but it is doubtful whether such incremental changes were enough to *transform* the economy as a whole.

People at the time were aware of growth, but did not talk of an 'Industrial Revolution'. Formally, it is not necessary to have a name for a thing in order for the thing to exist (the absence of the term 'Industrial Revolution' in the eighteenth century does not in itself prove its absence). But such a situation would be very peculiar indeed in the real world, and seldom if ever happens.

An important reason why contemporaries did not sense a decisive discontinuity is that there was no overall breakthrough in productivity. This grew at a similar rate across the eighteenth and nineteenth centuries with a partial exception in the mid nineteenth, although some sectors clearly transformed their positions. Overall productivity growth in England, Wales and Scotland never reached 1.5 per cent per annum in these years, and was probably significantly less in Ireland.[98] Between *c*.1700 and 1851, a fairly constant 60 per cent of British economic growth was due to greater inputs of land, labour and capital, about 40 per cent to the improved productivity of the factors of production: productivity growth accelerated in the early nineteenth century, but not enough to transform this picture.[99] Much was happening in the British economy, but none of these things caused transformation.

Contemporaries, especially from the early nineteenth century, praised the shipping, commercial prosperity, towns and

manufactures, but few before 1832 argued that they had produced a fundamental social change.[100] Their localised impact
was one thing; their overall effect on the economy another.
No one hailed the arrival of 'modernity': no such concept yet
existed, and 'improvement' fell far short of that grandiose
idea. Even those who might be expected to understand their
own day best, the political economists, had no sense that
ancient constraints had been escaped, and that an era of exponential growth was beginning that would transform human
lives: Adam Smith, Thomas Malthus and David Ricardo had
no such expectation. Most political economists, on the contrary, were preoccupied by the limits to economic growth, and
sought to discern when and why a stationary state would be
reached. Consequently, they lacked any generalised optimism
about the human condition. Even into the 1870s, standard economics textbooks identified the finite nature of land as the
final limitation on economic advance.[101]

Some acceleration in the rate of growth of GNP and of
real income per capita undoubtedly occurred. Recent
quantitative economic history has merely proposed that this
acceleration was less than was once thought; that it happened
later than was once thought; and that mid nineteenth-century
growth rates look fast chiefly by contrast with a modest
eighteenth-century starting point. Other historians have
concluded that the term 'revolution' now looks implausible,
and that 'evolution' is the more appropriate. Few still insist
that the new figures, by delivering substantial growth over a
century and a half, disclose a 'fundamental change'; but the
key term here is 'fundamental'. The debate therefore goes
beyond the unanswerable questions 'how many is a lot?' and
'how rapid is fast?' What is ultimately still at issue in these
debates is whether 'being determines consciousness', and on

this philosophical (and ultimately religious) question no ultimate agreement is likely.[102] All that can be said is that everything changes, but normally so slowly that almost everything seems for most people to remain much the same.

Class: the changing nature of social images

Did an 'Industrial Revolution' create 'class'? A longer perspective permits an answer. The ways in which people pictured the identity of groups in society, and relations between them, changed greatly over time irrespective of industrialisation. In 1660 the leading categories were national and religious: the Scots, Irish, Welsh and English were all keenly aware of themselves as such, and aware too of their denominational identities. Other things mattered much less, although Scotland saw a continuing cultural divide between Highland and Lowland society that was only partly denominational. Some craft-based occupations, like stonemasons and shoemakers, had developed a sense of solidarity, but this was specific to each trade and was not generalised to create a 'working class'. The social elite was aware of its group identity but traced this to 'gentility' or 'honour', not to its location within the means of production.

The term class still meant 'group', not 'stratum'. It derived from the Latin *classis*, used within early seventeenth-century Puritanism to mean a group that met to worship separately from the established church. The same usage continued in eighteenth-century Methodism. Since it echoed the Calvinist idea of a 'gathered church', a minority of the 'elect' predestined to salvation, it could not easily be generalised to mean a whole social category, universally possessing some identity. Although gradations of wealth from rich to poor were obvious over many centuries, and poverty for the many still a grinding reality, this had not generated a picture of society in terms of strata. Since historians still try to find earlier origins for Marxist social class, it creates confusion that the word 'class' was common in eighteenth-century usage. We must instead work backwards from the discovery that 'class' (in the sense of an identity created by the mechanism of production and exchange) was a new ideology in the early nineteenth century, not a natural reflex to changing economic relations.

A key component of an adequate history of class would be a comparison between the different track records of the idea in England, Scotland, Ireland and Wales (and even within those geographically diverse areas); yet such work has not yet been attempted, partly because some aspects of the social history of England's neighbours are still overshadowed by an older and essentially English debate about conditions in industrial England. In Scottish historiography, this English Marxist tradition is modified chiefly by crediting a Scottish 'working-class movement' with nationalist desires to create a Scottish republic, a movement, visible or 'underground', pre-sumed to last from the 1790s into at least the 1820s.[103] Such theories await scrutiny from less committed researchers. It is at present equally plausible that the later outcomes, 'Red Clydeside' or the cultures of the Ulster shipyards and the Welsh coalfields, represented specifically Scottish, Irish or Welsh phenomena (including transpositions of sectarian religious discourse) more than local examples of developments more clearly and classically found in England. We do not know.

We can, however, show that before the arrival of this new language the social order had long been diverse: there were large numbers of people in England, especially in the more commercial south, with middling incomes and properties. This was less true in the north of England, and less true again in Scotland, Ireland and Wales, where social divides were starker. Yet it was not in the Welsh valleys or on Clydeside, but in early nineteenth-century England, that the idea of class was coined. In other words, neither poverty, nor inequality, nor the conflict of rich and poor, of themselves created class. Class was a novel ideology, not an objective response to long-familiar circumstances. Even when the language of class was coined, sectarian, political and status divisions within each putative class were often more important than class solidarities.[104]

This argument is not widely accepted, and most historians still write the history of eighteenth-century class relations as prefiguring the forms of the nineteenth century.[105] Those inspired by E. P. Thompson's *The Making of the English Working Class* (1963) sometimes tried to spot other classes being formed in earlier decades. The years *c*.1660–1730 have been proposed, variously, as the birthplace of the middle class[106] and the site of the 'making of the English ruling class',[107] but both arguments are open to doubt. People in middle conditions of wealth had long existed without giving rise to the ideology of class identity that was novel in the early nineteenth century; the English elite were conscious of their separate status for many centuries earlier still, without generating a class analysis either among themselves or their opponents. Even Thomas Paine, hostile as he was to the England of his day, did not invent 'class'. Indeed no social stratum did much to work out an ideology of its nature and claims.

Some have contended that the early-Hanoverian ruling group was essentially a *propertied* oligarchy, drawing on nascent capitalism, celebrated by Locke's alleged transference of divine right from monarchy to property.[108] Against this must be set the complexities of measuring who did well out of Walpole's ministry among the financial, the mercantile and professional elite. Yet a good part of this elite was bitterly opposed to him, and Walpole himself tried hardest to placate the landed interest. The diversity of social groups makes such an argument from class interest problematic. So does the fact that the idea of 'capitalism' was not coined until the nineteenth century: it clearly meant something very different from the idea of private property as such, which was securely entrenched in the English common law (although not in Irish Brehon law) from the early Middle Ages. There may, rather, be political explanations for the priority given to property in these years. Stuart monarchs were held to have threatened it, so that defending property was held to be synonymous with defending liberty.

This theme of early class formation continually recurs in the works of some writers, where it performs a variety of present-day tasks. Some wish to hasten the arrival of a well-defined but unattractive middle class in order more easily to argue for the early emergence of a morally justified working class. Others reverse the values and wish to depict a burgeoning but more appealing middle class as a sensible, pragmatic social constituency whose expansion refutes a stress either on the emergence of a militant working class or on the long survival of the power of the old elite, the nobility and gentry. Scholarship on this question is inconclusive, not least since the purposes of too many participants in the debate are still overtly presentist.

Some authors aware of the problems of objectively identifying a working class fall back on the argument that class consciousness might be present without class. Some even wish to extend this argument into the nineteenth century, as if the lasting power of the landed elite was merely synonymous with class power as later envisioned. But this is not obviously the case: style and status are not the same as class; nor were they precursors of class, but in some ways its opposites.

Crowd action, riots and conflict in the workplace have sometimes been used as keys to class formation: as E. P. Thompson wrote, 'we can read eighteenth-century social history as a succession of confrontations between an innovative market economy and the customary moral economy of the plebs'.[109] The people, in this view, appealed to old ideas of paternalist regulation; but the decline in the power of the gentry and the church, and the rise of the capitalist cash nexus, steadily eroded the 'moral economy'. These protesters eventually cohered in a plebeian, working-class culture, defined over against capitalism. Such a scenario appears to be Marxist, but it deserves consideration how far it belongs instead to a more romantic or nostalgic idealisation of a 'world we have lost'. If there ever was such a world, there is evidence that it was lost in a much earlier era. Alan Macfarlane's research on the origins of English individualism[110] finds it in the centuries after the Norman Conquest, while historians of Anglo-Saxon England have their own stories of the spread of coinage and monetary relations. Labour relations at all times may express the greed and resentment of masters and men as well as the defence or violation of paternalist decencies.[111]

Once we abandon the idea that the emergence of 'class' in an 'Industrial Revolution' is an unchallengeable end point at which history has to arrive, it becomes possible to see paternalism and altruism, profit and selfishness at work at all points on the social spectrum and in all centuries. If (as some economic historians now argue) the eighteenth-century market economy was not as dynamically innovative as was recently thought, it may also be that labourers were not as attached to the ideals of 'paternalism'. We should instead see the 'moral economy', like monarchical absolutism, not as an objective social formation but as a language that all groups could use in an attempt to achieve their ends.

Collective action needs to be examined for evidence of emerging class consciousness, but in the eighteenth century it points in other directions. It has been argued that groups of organised labourers, like the 'Waltham Blacks' in the 1720s, might see themselves as defending their own property rights, or a right of free trade, against Whig class repression; to their opponents it could seem like poaching and smuggling, undertaken also with an eye to the dynastic alternative of the Stuarts, rather than class warfare.[112]

Social protest, whether by the rural poor or by the urban employee, normally focused on ideas of constitutionalism or of rights rather than of class;[113] it targeted middlemen, like the baker who sold bread above its customary price, or the wholesale merchant who organised the collection of goods from domestic or artisan producers, or the small manufacturer whose way of life might differ little from that of his employees. These roles were central, since large factories were as yet uncommon; outwork and artisan organisation were the norms. The middleman was not the same as the 'capitalist' (understood in the nineteenth century as the great factory owner), and the ordinary daily conflicts of a diverse commercial economy were not the same as class conflict. Indeed, the growth of mass production, eroding the position of the artisan, initially had the same effect on him as ordinary economic fluctuations: they focused more resentment on the middleman rather than creating a new way of analysing society. That was owed to political economists objecting to the exactions of the landowner, not of the capitalist. The same was true of groups with elite leadership. The Independent Electors of Westminster, formed in 1741 to mobilise the wide electorate of that populous city and drawing support from tradesmen and minor professionals in a way that anticipated John Wilkes in the 1760s, were overtly Jacobite, not expressive of a nascent class consciousness.

Historians of crime, social disorder and workplace relations have uncovered much evidence for friction and conflict between haves and have-nots. But it is not clear that this was new, or different in scale, in these decades: popular discontent was probably more cogent, better organised and more violent in earlier episodes like the Peasants' Revolt (1381), the Pilgrimage of Grace (1536), the civil wars of the 1640s, the Sacheverell riots (1710),[114] the Jacobite risings of 1715 and 1745, the Irish agrarian disturbances of the late eighteenth century, or London's Gordon Riots (1780)[115] than in the Luddite disturbances (1811–13), the Captain Swing riots (1830) or the riots over the Reform Bill in 1830–2.[116] Class consciousness eventually mattered, but it was not a key that released labourers from political inaction: they had long played a part on the national stage.

Other historians have contended that consumerism is evidence of class formation, specifically of the middle class, the one group, it is claimed, that provided a market for consumer goods.[117] But the existence of such a sharp boundary has not been documented; nor has the use of consumer goods as emblems of a particular social stratum. On the contrary, much eighteenth-century comment deplored the blurring of rank and degree as all who could afford it bought the latest fashions. Consumerism confirms that the age's key concepts were hierarchy and emulation, not class and exclusion.

Class is not the only identity at issue. How deeply rooted identities in general were in the eighteenth century is a question that many postmodernists find fascinating. For example: the masquerade ball was first organised in London in 1708, and caught on: it appealed to the idea of escaping one's social status and acquiring freedom of behaviour. But it was a formal convention only: the small masks worn were token disguises, not real ones, and status was not so easily dropped. This was a small-scale society by present-day standards: identities were not easily escaped. It was a society with its own, very public, group loyalties; 'class' was not among them. Identities were arranged differently from those dominant in later centuries. Gregory King in 1688 depicted society as a pyramid with many gradations of wealth and status rather than three clearly differentiated strata. In 1700 there were about 180 English peers, 150 Irish and fifty Scottish; according to Gregory King, there were about 16,500 gentry families in England (the numbers of those thought to be of gentle status in Scotland and Ireland is unknown). The elite was tiny; poverty assimilated the great majority in material terms, but allowed their identities and conflicts to develop on other foundations.

More important than any nascent class divisions in response to exploitative pressure from above were gender divisions arising from below, and it is debated how far these really changed. Some have argued that working practices evolved to exclude women from more skilled employments (although this was least true of artisan businesses, where wives might take over after the deaths of husbands); others have observed that this division was already very ancient, but that women's employment continued to be central to the household economy.[118] Some urge that, in agriculture, more and more tasks were defined as men's, and the employment of women became a seasonal and casual addition to the employment of men. Others urge the antiquity of this division; for the poor, this was an effect not of nascent class but of the progressive specialisation of the labour force with the spread of national markets for food, and perhaps of an increase in family cohesion with the rise in life expectancy. The live-in farm servant, hired for the year, and the cottager with access to land, were slowly succeeded by the landless day-labourer whose status had been diminished by economic change; but this was a development in train for centuries.

If this scenario of women's exclusion is correct, it may have been the result of status, not capitalism: if women were excluded from economic activity, it occurred first, and most thoroughly, at the top of society, where it cannot have been produced by economic necessity.[119] Yet others have argued that leisure was the precondition not of female idleness but of female engagement in a whole range of social activities: this very activity may have reinforced differences of status, yet status diversification was not owed to the elite alone. Among male workers in expanding industries, diversification of function and technological skills created a preoccupation with status (and its attendant 'demarcation disputes'); class was an unrelated, and much later, comment on an economy which became more, not less, diversified with commercial, and finally industrial, growth. The ideology of class tried to simplify that diversity in order to mobilise blocs for political action; it is not clear that it was a result of that growing diversification.

Treating 'class' as a descriptive language has not completely solved the problem since 'class' was indeed an eighteenth-century term, but, confusingly, with a meaning that was part of the existing terminology of 'ranks', 'orders' and 'degrees'.

Some historians, not recognising this older meaning, wish to trace a transition in the middle of the eighteenth century from the old terminology to a wholly new language of 'class', but this claim is problematic.[120] Even when the term 'working classes' is first found in England, in 1789, the plural contradicted the idea of a single identity, objectively generated. The singular terms 'working class' and 'middle class' were in occasional usage from the 1790s: they could have represented a quantum leap in attitudes, but there is no evidence that they actually did so. When this leap occurred, class analysis did not derive from social observation or enquiry: even that acute social commentator Henry Mayhew, famously exploring the culture of the London poor in the 1850s, did not use the categories of class.[121] Scotland had equally lacked any sense of class identities and was slower than England to adopt the new language. Sir John Sinclair's careful social survey, *A Statistical Account of Scotland* (1791–7), compiled in the 1780s, still used the language of 'ranks and orders' and 'people of quality'; it was this that created the plural when it described the 'lower classes' and 'higher classes' in Glasgow. The same was true of Ireland. 'Class' in the nineteenth-century sense was the result of a specifically English debate, and it is to England's conflicts and polemics that we must look for answers.

This image of class as social stratum arrived only very late; the ancient realities of rich, middle income and poor had not created it. Nor was class as stratum evidently a metaphor drawn from new developments in geology, associated for example with James Hutton from the 1780s.[122] It came, initially, from political economy in the 1810s. David Ricardo's *Principles of Political Economy and Taxation* (1817) built on Adam Smith to give a clear tripartite division of society, based on function and source of income: landlords (rent), capitalists (profits) and workers (wages). It was an academic analysis of 'factors of production', those ideal types of the economists; it did not attempt to do justice to the complexities of the old economy, with its overlaps between land, extractive industries, manu-facture and urban development; its merchants; its domestic industry and small workshops; and its professionals. But it suited a developing social polemic, radicalism's campaign against the Anglican, landowning elite, and was therefore taken up and used. Only after Ricardo was the stage set for the further development in the nineteenth century: the 'working classes', a plurality of groups, was now asserted to be one bloc, the 'working class'; the 'middle classes', another diverse part of the spectrum, was redefined for other purposes as 'the middle class'.

Even Ricardo's polemic was not enough to create 'class'. An additional stream, joined to Ricardian economics, was necessary: the polemic mounted by men such as John Wade, a Unitarian, and James Mill, a religious sceptic, against what they depicted as the aristocratic order and the established church that underpinned it. Into this alleged clash of interests between the old elite and what the Wades and the Mills hailed as a new 'middle class' intruded the issues raised by nascent trades unions and by the developing ideologies of radicalism and socialism, inheritors but novel developers of Thomas Paine's polemic of the 1790s against kings, aristocrats and priests. These polemics now acted to give new meanings to an old vocabulary.

From the mid 1830s the 'middle classes', until now a diverse collection of groups with different interests and aims, came widely to be called 'the middle class' and to be ascribed its own attributes; later in the 1830s the 'working classes', an even more diverse collection, was increasingly termed 'the working class'. The singular term implied a unity of nature and goal, but was not necessarily evidence that such a unity had emerged on the ground. On the contrary, into the nineteenth century the conflicts within these 'classes' were more important than any solidarities: the conflicts between skilled and unskilled workers, between Irish, Scottish and English workers, between 'respectable' and 'unrespectable', between 'upper middle class' professionals and the 'lower middle class', between Liberal and Conservative nobility. Meanwhile, land, industry and labour showed much co-operation, failing to fulfil predictions of a necessary clash of interests. Class solidarity, in so far as it ever existed, came later, in the cultural uniformities brought by life in the mass urban conglomerations of the late nineteenth century; even then, solidarity was more solid in some areas (like mining districts) than others; more solid in communitarian Wales and Scotland than in individualist England.

Material realities were not irrelevant, for mutual antagonisms in society had always been promoted by economic change; what mattered was how those conflicts were perceived and managed. So it was in the early nineteenth century, especially when population pressure, enclosures and the decline of living-in service in agriculture eroded the position of labourers and subjected them to increasingly harsh treatment by farmers. This situation was then aggravated by the working of the poor laws, early eighteenth-century provision being eroded and finally reversed by booming rural populations for which there was too little employment. This fire was fed by a continuing growth in England's rural population into the 1850s. There is much evidence for growing social estrangement in many areas from the 1790s, reaching flashpoint in the decades after c.1810. Deference went sour; resentments flourished. In some areas rural violence, and the threat of

2. Politeness. The rise of the coffee house and the periodical, notably *The Spectator*, is sometimes held to symbolise a new polite culture, part of a secular Enlightenment. But this print shows a cup of coffee being thrown in a man's face during a heated argument. Did people continue locked in acrimonious conflict over the old issues? The year is 1710: perhaps the argument was over the trial of Dr. Sacheverell and the interpretation of the Revolution of 1688 that it raised.

revolution, could breed hatred, fear and contempt. The question is whether historians have been right to see such frictions as evidence of class. Social conflicts in industrial areas were perhaps a different thing, although lumped together with agrarian conflicts in retrospect when the ideology of class had been accepted as if it were fact. Even industry had a complex effect on identities.

At issue were differences not only of wealth, but of lifestyle. The growing alliance of the middling orders against Jacobinism, and the sudden prosperity of the landed interest during the Napoleonic Wars, acted to open up social distances when increasing wealth was translated into houses, clothes, cleanliness, carriages, furniture, paintings, silver, books, music, education and travel. Tea and shopping became social markers.[123] The wives and daughters of the newly wealthy were especially prominent both as avid consumers of luxuries and as definers of social identities around these goods. While the social hierarchy retained its old rationale, the cultural space between its members yawned in some areas. This had begun earlier for the elite: one author in *The Annual Register* of 1761 had complained how 'Politeness and taste seem to have driven away the horrid spectres of rudeness and barbarity' in the country. 'The nobleman and country 'squire no longer affect an old-fashioned hospitality', replacing the old inclusiveness in which they would 'keep open house' with, instead, 'genteel entertainments'.[124] By the Napoleonic Wars, this social withdrawal had often reached the ranks of tenant farmers: that new ideology of the 1820s, radicalism, expressed also a cultural critique of landed wealth, and provided fertile ground in which the new ideology of class as conflicting group interest could flourish. Such, at least, is one hypothesis; but proof of the link between lifestyle and ideology awaits more research. So does the effect of geographical diversity. The idea of class was invented in the early nineteenth century in the south-east of England, but took root most strongly elsewhere: it was not that industry created class, but rather that class grew up and became persuasive in areas that had been least diversified by commerce, least opened to social and geographical mobility by employment opportunities in a monetised economy, least susceptible to Anglican ideas of a seamless social hierarchy.

Historians imbued with twentieth-century ideas of class tended to read them back into the past and see class conflicts everywhere. Yet it is now by no means clear that even the Chartist disturbances of 1838–48 can be categorised as the first working-class movement, let alone Jacobinism in the 1790s or labour unrest after 1815.[125] If a study of the eighteenth century shows that class was not a thing but a doctrine, then the social history of the nineteenth and twentieth centuries needs to be rethought.

Part II
Religious Cultures

Religious pluralism as a source of armed conflict

From the Reformation into the 1640s, Europe was devastated by wars of religion. Even short of war, religion remained into the nineteenth century the most potent cause of domestic political and social conflict. Statesmen and clerics were torn between the ideals of truth and peace, and proposed a succession of solutions to the conflicts that principled commitment had sanctioned. How to order the relations of church and state was therefore the most urgent of practical problems; historians debate whether this practical dimension led to the secularisation of British society, and whether secularisation meant only separation. These debates are often inadequate, since specialist students of politics and political thought typically attend only to discourses of natural rights and contract, discourses that seem to indicate the early demise of confessional politics; these researches often ignore the related theological discourses that denominations sustained and by which they laid claim to hegemony. A programmatically secular present-day discipline like the history of political thought yields only secular results; yet in the long eighteenth century the union of church and state ensured the survival of a politico-theology well into the nineteenth century.[1]

Over several centuries, three main responses to religious diversity were worked out in England. Before the 1660s the dominant ideal was unity: a single church, rightly ordered, was seen as the appropriate and attainable solution. From the 1660s to the early nineteenth century a system of 'toleration' was developed: a dominant church was entrenched as the establishment, committed to guaranteeing freedom of worship for intolerant minorities by not granting them the political power that they were expected to misuse to persecute others. From the 1830s the state's increasing reluctance to endorse any single church created a third system of pluralism which sought to distance contests over public morality from denominational rivalries. None of these systems was 'modern'; all evolved by political contingency more than design; none was the certain antidote to conflict over ultimate values. Nor were any of them ever consensual: disagreement on whether uniformity might legitimately be imposed preceded 1660 and continued long after the Revolution of 1688. It may be that British society did not become more tolerant; it only became intolerant of different things.

England, Scotland and Ireland dealt with the issue of religious pluralism in different ways; even so, the ideal of a single national church remained powerful in all three into the early nineteenth century. Each polity had a national church, as did Hanover, of which British monarchs from 1714 were first electors, then (from 1815 to 1837) kings. Each national church had different fortunes, but each was underpinned by a sophisticated body of theory (subtly or substantially different). Everywhere, denominational structures continued to colour social life. Although Scotland had a Parliament before 1707, and forty-five MPs in the Westminster Commons after the Union, this did little to make Scottish life, in a broad sense, democratic: even in 1830, the Scottish electorate totalled only a minuscule 4,500 out of a population of some 2.3 million. In all parts of the British Isles, participation in national life (in the currently fashionable phrase, in the 'public sphere') was exercised mainly via religious denominations, primarily the national church. Despite religious Nonconformity (sometimes growing, sometimes shrinking), despite challenges to orthodox theology, and despite sometimes ambiguous support from monarchs (most dramatically James II), large majorities both of the rank and file and of the intelligentsia wished to see a close relationship between church and state. Despite what historians much later termed 'secularisation' and 'modernisation', this confessional system was eventually upset not by the Revolution of 1688 or Enlightenment secularism but by Irish Catholicism in 1828–9. Meanwhile, the ideal of Christian unity was not abandoned; instead, other denominations than one's own were blamed for violating it.

The British Isles shared in the Europe-wide problem of religious pluralism, and it was Scotland's 'Bishops' Wars' of 1639 and 1640 that triggered the 'English' civil war. At issue were attempts to take control of Scotland's national church and steer it in a particular direction; yet war soon brought to prominence in England a sectarian Protestantism that in its extreme forms rejected the validity of the state church ideal itself and sought instead to create 'gathered churches' of religious zealots. It was the revolutionary potential of this upsurge of religious feeling that made the re-establishment of the episcopal Anglicanism of 1660 so important, but also so unlikely.

Much depended on the monarch's choice. Read closely, Charles II's Declaration of Breda of 4 April 1660, issued just before his restoration, committed him only to 'the Protestant religion', not to the Church of England as such; his promised 'liberty to tender consciences' was also unspecified. The first could be seized on by Presbyterians, the second by all forms of Nonconformist. It seems that Charles's personal preference was for the policy termed 'comprehension', the inclusion of as many as possible within a more loosely defined national church. In 1660, he offered bishoprics to three moderate Presbyterians, although on the Crown's terms: acknowledgement of the royal supremacy and episcopal church order. In late 1660, the court managed to prevent the still largely Presbyterian Convention Parliament from defining the religious settlement (that task was left to its successor). Yet this body, nicknamed the Cavalier Parliament, expressed commitments that had evolved since the 1640s, under adversity and persecution, in a High Church direction: a greater stress on sacramental religion, on the divine right of episcopacy, and on a formal liturgy. These things were now enforced by a developing legal code that penalised Nonconformity; but, as with the Elizabethan laws against Catholic recusants, the official case was that the laws were safeguards against political rebellion and not aimed against religious belief as such. Yet even within the public realm, it was clear that what was at issue was not just an internal matter of church government; this was recognised to be emblematic of a whole social system. To this uneasy 'settlement' there were to be three main challenges.

Challenges to the national churches: Catholicism

Resurgent Catholicism, latterly in the person of James II, was a challenge made plausible by its international and Irish dimensions rather than by the numbers of English or Scottish Catholics. The Council of Trent (1545–63) had been the Catholic Church's own Reformation; inspired by a renewed vision and backed by armed force, Counter-Reformation Catholicism made steady gains across Europe in the early seventeenth century and continued to press forward even after the Peace of Westphalia of 1648 ended the Thirty Years War.

Historians debate whether the Catholic Church in England, Wales and Scotland was the surviving representative of the medieval church, or whether it was a new creation, inspired and organised by Counter-Reformation missionaries from the continent. The first was more true in Ireland, the second in England. In England and Wales, Catholics were a tiny minority, some 60,000 in 1660 rising to 80,000 by 1770, but, after 1688, they were shut out from public life. Scottish Catholics grew more, from some 14,000 in 1660 to 30,000 in 1779 and 50,000 in 1800, their numbers now boosted by immigration from Ireland. But this was still a Catholicism of the old world in which the lay elite had much influence.

Catholics, if given elite support, stood a good chance of making gains among the powerful, if not of converting a deeply Protestant and still more deeply anti-Catholic majority. Gentry patronage was the key at local level; at national level, what mattered most was the monarch. Rumours circulated of Charles II's private inclinations, and while he worshipped in the established church during his life he was received into the

Catholic Church on his deathbed. Meanwhile, his subjects debated whether his instincts were for toleration or 'popery'. In December 1662 Charles issued the first Declaration of Indulgence, an attempt to impose religious toleration by royal prerogative. Conspiracy theorists had free rein, and seemed vindicated when in 1672 the heir presumptive, Charles's brother James, Duke of York, ceased to take Communion in the Church of England; the next year, his resignation as Lord High Admiral was interpreted as evidence of his conversion to Catholicism, a fact openly acknowledged from 1676.

The Catholic gentry were severely handicapped by their past: the Gunpowder Plot of 1605 and the Catholic massacre of Protestants in Ireland in 1641 were public-relations disasters that made it easy for the anti-Catholic Whigs to depict James II as determined on introducing 'popery and arbitrary power'. The Church of England responded during the 1680s with a huge outpouring of anti-Catholic theological writing;[2] together with James II's deposition, it ensured that Catholicism was taboo in England, Scotland and Ulster until the 1820s. In Ireland their position was much more adverse: there the Church of Ireland mounted a sustained campaign, seeking to win what it saw as a benighted populace from 'popery' and 'superstition'. The campaign failed, and the balance of population tilted even further away from the Protestants: about three to one at the beginning of the century, it was about four to one at the end. But Irish Catholics, after 1691, failed to mobilise their full strength until the very different circumstances of 1829: the Protestant Church of Ireland, and its social constituency, was one of the success stories of the eighteenth century, holding on against impossible odds until its position began to be undermined in the 1770s when Irish Protestants' patriotism began to align them against England.[3]

Catholicism's failure to retrieve its position in England was not inevitable; indeed Catholicism was driven to accept a religious pluralism that anticipated much later ideals. In 1687 James II echoed Charles II's Declaration of Breda of 1660 in a declaration of indulgence: it had been his settled view, James announced, 'that conscience ought not to be constrained, nor people forced in matters of meer religion'. Many churchmen and Dissenters doubted his commitment to this principle, and the matter of sincerity became more pressing when the king reissued the declaration in 1688 and ordered the clergy to read it from their pulpits. Was Dissent no longer synonymous with disloyalty? Had James remained on the throne, a clear answer to that question might have been given, but his expulsion in 1688 meant that the situation remained ambiguous, different answers being offered from different points on the spectrum. Many (notably Protestant Dissenters) maintained after 1688 that Catholic Dissenters certainly were, as such, disloyal to the state; many churchmen preserved a lasting suspicion of Protestant Dissent, a fear spectacularly vindicated by the American rebellion of 1776; and in the early nineteenth century the idea that Britain enjoyed a 'Protestant Constitution' experienced a revival. The Revolution of 1688, in this respect, settled little: religious persecution declined in England (though not in New England, Scotland or Ireland), but religious exclusivism changed less. Meanwhile, political anti-Catholicism remained a more powerful political force than Catholicism itself: Whiggism remained premised on anti-Catholicism for more than a century after 1688, and in 1776 American colonists, sincerely or not, turned this virulent rhetoric against the home country.

By then, Catholicism was no longer expansionary. Only after 1789, and the arrival of émigré French priests, did an 'ultramontane' attitude begin to develop, looking to Rome for leadership. With the removal of the Stuart option in the 1740s, Irish Catholicism was a leaderless force until its politicisation by a brilliant lay organiser, Daniel O'Connell, in the 1820s. Catholicism's failure after 1688 was dictated by politics; in Ireland at least, it was politics that finally reversed the verdict. Catholicism never made mass conversions, but in 1829 it achieved what it had threatened to do after 1660: it broke up the Anglican hegemony.

Challenges to the national churches: Protestant Dissent

The second challenge to the national church ideal was posed by the aftermath of civil-war sectarianism, from the 1660s expressed as separated denominations now termed Dissenters or Nonconformists. As such, they constituted a new phenomenon, partly respectable and open, partly revolutionary and underground. The most numerous were the Presbyterians, who generally accepted the idea of a national church but rejected its governance by a separate order of bishops. Other sects rejected the idea of a national church itself: the Congregationalists (also called Independents), who held the autonomy and equality of each congregation; the Baptists, who held the necessity of the baptism of conscious believers; and the Quakers, who dispensed with an ordained ministry in favour of the individual's 'inner light'. None of these were otherwordly, looking to the next life rather than to this, though some later became so; all were interpreted by churchmen as zealots and fanatics whose ancestors had caused the civil war.

In 1660, some English clergy sympathetic to these sectarian

positions chose to leave their livings; others were pushed, forced out by popular mass action in parish after parish. An exodus of about a fifth of its clergy[4] is often held to have weakened the Church of England, though this has been debated. How many lay followers left with them? In 1676 Henry Compton, Bishop of London, organised a religious census of England that revealed only about 5 per cent of the population to be Protestant Nonconformists.[5] This was encouraging for churchmen; but sympathisers with Dissent, and occasional conformists, would have swelled this percentage. Nonconformity was more important than Compton's figures suggest.[6] Scotland and Ireland were also more divided along denominational lines than England, and their divisions contributed to the new pattern of alignments within the British Isles. Where before 1660 the leading dynamic was a 'three kingdoms' one, after 1660 it increasingly became one of tension between denominations, reinforced by the larger proportions of Catholics and Protestant Dissenters in Ireland, Scotland and the American colonies. In Ireland, the Achilles heel of the established church proved to be the dour and unreconciled Protestant Dissenters more than the Catholics.

Yet Nonconformists themselves differed in their composition and aims. English Presbyterians initially sought an accommodation with the establishment that would have allowed them to return to the national church: this option was real, and the Presbyterians were lastingly weakened when it was frustrated by the bishops and the House of Lords in 1661–2 and 1688–9. Dissenters who openly opposed the state church ideal had more scope for action, but were drawn into a formulaic and ultimately futile litany of objections to certain English church practices. Over time, English Nonconformity grew cool and declined in numbers.

English Dissenting sects lacked leadership except a London-based body, the Protestant Dissenting Deputies, launched in 1727, which took as its chief goal the repeal of the Test and Corporation Acts. Here it was unsuccessful; but this pre-occupation merely locked Dissenters into a backward-looking legalistic confrontation with the church in which Dissenters were the losers. Increasingly, Dissenting congregations tended to fragment as some ministers adopted Arian or Socinian theologies (demoting Christ from an equal partner in the Trinity to a subordinate figure, and, in the case of Socinianism, a purely human one); from the 1770s some separated from their brethren to worship openly as Unitarians. Only a few Anglicans joined them. It was to be the remaining Dissenters, revitalised in their Calvinism and Trinitarianism, who began to flourish in the new mood of evangelicalism that marked the decades from the 1790s on.

In Scotland, about a third of the clergy left the established church after the Restoration. Following 1688, this exodus was reversed, for in that kingdom, unlike in England, William III imposed Presbyterianism as the principle of the established church's government. It was this church that now organised the persecution of Scottish Episcopalians, linked as they were with Jacobitism. Again, persecution worked: although the numbers of Episcopalians and Presbyterians were probably equally balanced in 1688, the expulsion of 664 ministers from Scotland's 926 parishes between 1688 and 1716 meant that Episcopalianism was driven into an exclusive association with Jacobitism and suffered the fate of that political option: legislation of 1746 virtually proscribed the Episcopalians, and it remained in force until 1792. Yet Scottish Presbyterianism fell into schism again and again. The formation of the Secession Church (1733) and the Relief Church (1761) was only the start. The Secession itself split in 1747 into two groups, and each of these split again around 1800. From the 1790s, 'New Light' evangelicalism added to their expansionary zeal, so that by 1826 about 38 per cent of Scotland's population dissented from the Kirk.[7]

These schisms were inevitably political: in 1733 Ebenezer Erskine, leading a secession group which claimed to be the true national church, denounced the Act of Union for guaranteeing the continuance of the episcopal Church of England. Nevertheless, the Seceders of 1733 still subscribed to the ideal of a single state church. The Relief Presbytery, formed in 1761, broke from this consensus to advocate disestablishment, but not until the early nineteenth century did most of the Seceders adopt that principle. From events like the Cambuslang revival of 1742, evangelical fervour was found at least as much within the Kirk as among the Seceders. Consequently, until the 1840s, Dissent was not nearly as disruptive in Scotland as it was in England, Ulster or the American colonies.

In England, the legal position of separated Dissent was deeply ambiguous after 1660. In response to this new challenge, some churchmen advocated toleration; others, comprehension within a church whose terms of membership had been relaxed; others held that a degree of coercion was legitimate in order to encourage Dissenters to rejoin the church as then constituted. In 1689 the measure nicknamed the 'Toleration Act' permitted freedom of worship to Trinitarian Protestant Dissenters only, on condition that certain terms were met. This was not the principled charter of religious liberty that Nonconformists had sought: the word 'toleration' appeared in neither the title of the Act nor its text. Yet they soon hailed it as such a charter, and it acquired a political weight beyond its formal provisions.

Some historians claim that the Act broke Anglican hegemony, yet although the setting within which the Church of England operated changed, and the religious homogeneity of many parishes was lost, its position was still strong, as many indicators show (for example, the tiny number of Protestant Dissenters in the House of Commons). There were important changes. 'Occasional conformity', criminalised in the Tory high tide of 1711, was legalised again in 1718; from 1727, Indemnity Acts often shielded from prosecution for one year Dissenters who had 'omitted to qualify themselves for offices and employments' by taking the sacrament in the church.[8] But only some elements in the church had favoured the Toleration Act: it was the political result of a bidding war with the Catholics. Ironically, Dissent as a whole was the long-term loser in the system now established. The Toleration Act provided a framework, not a full set of answers: the relations between church and Dissent varied diocese by diocese and bishop by bishop.[9] Yet, in general, the Dissenters found themselves marginalised by the working of 'the Toleration', since it conceded freedom of worship but continued in practice to deny political power to those deemed to be threats to the state. After the Corporation Act (1661) and the Test Acts (1673, 1678) were passed, local and national office was effectively confined to churchmen. Although there was some non-implementation at local level, public life at national level was almost wholly restricted to genuine or nominal Anglicans until the 1830s. There was no Anglican 'consensus', but 'hegemony' may better capture the reality of ascendancy at the centre combined with declining, then growing, diversity in the localities. Meanwhile, much intellectual effort was poured into the defence of the established church; its adherents backed it for sophisticated reasons, not because they were backwoodsmen. By contrast, English Dissenting theology languished. So, in Scotland, did the theology of the Presbyterian Kirk.

The Dissenters' experience was generally of persecution before 1688, and sufferance thereafter. Historians have often been reluctant to admit the effectiveness of the established church, and the contribution of the two policies can be debated; but the net result was that, in the century after 1660, the numbers of Protestant Dissenters in England approximately halved. Catholic numbers held steady where patronised by gentry families, but Protestant Dissent overwhelmingly lacked gentry support and suffered accordingly in a society in which elite backing counted for much. Dissenters were excluded from the universities and from the resources of scholarship; their isolated theologians tended to fall into private heterodoxy; and heterodoxy reduced the size of congregations. In Anne's reign, High Churchmen laboured by the use of legislation to reduce the Dissenting interest. Whether or not this might have worked, the accession of the Hanoverian dynasty in 1714 meant that the policy was abandoned. Those anti-Dissenter measures the Occasional Conformity Act (1711) and the Schism Act (1714) were repealed. But the Dissenters declined anyway. Denominational affiliation had a social dimension, too; but if the decline of Protestant Dissent in c.1660–1760 had nothing to do with economic change, it is difficult to argue that the resurgence of Nonconformity after c.1790 was a response to such change.

Yet monarchs remained unreliable allies of the Church of England. In England, High Churchmen (those who interpreted the Church of England as a branch of the universal Catholic Church rather than as a Protestant denomination) were alarmed by the accession in 1714 of a Lutheran Elector of

Hanover: some saw him as an 'Occasional Conformist', qualifying himself for office by a legalistic and insincere reception of Holy Communion. Yet in a legalistic age, this was enough: neither of the first two Georges was eager to imperil his hold on the throne by alienating the church. Both conformed, and neither gave Protestant Dissent the encouragement for which it hoped.

Before 1760, English Dissent languished. Not so in colonial America, where the balance of denominations (as heavily weighted towards the Dissenters as in England it was towards the church) produced an explosive situation, ignited when the sects put their seventeenth-century resistance theories into practice in 1776.[10] Everywhere in the wider British polity, religion remained the best predictor of allegiance, especially Congregationalism and Prebyterianism. In parts of the colonies, the backbone of the republican cause in the revolution was often the 'Scotch-Irish', emigrants from Ulster and the adjacent Scottish mainland who still nurtured the Covenanting commitments of the 1640s. In Ireland, it was the Ulster Dissenters again who were the key to Ireland's attempts to break from London's control. Even in subservient Scotland, it was the evangelical Popular Party in the Kirk who in the 1770s sympathised with the American cause in opposition to the regime of the Moderates, who were enthusiastic unionists in relation to England and eager participants in the patronage system of an imperial state machine. If the American Revolution had some of the character of a war of religion, the whole trajectory of Dissent in eighteenth-century Britain must be reconsidered: if Dissent remained a significant threat to the state, the success of the church in defeating it becomes much more important.

The English Nonconformist position was gradually revived

after *c*.1760 by two developments. The first was the rise within their ranks of various forms of theological heterodoxy, especially Arianism and Socinianism; these theological positions animated a galaxy of talented figures including the philosophers Richard Price (1723–91) and Joseph Priestley (1733–1804), extending to atheism with William Godwin (1756–1836) and James Mill (1773–1836). They finally made common cause with a convert to atheism from High Church Anglicanism, Jeremy Bentham (1748–1832). It was the heterodox Dissenting intelligentsia who framed the novel doctrine of universal manhood suffrage in the 1760s; even Bentham did not accept it until the 1810s. The Deist Major John Cartwright, though a churchman, included universal manhood suffrage, the secret ballot and annual parliaments in his pamphlet *Take Your Choice* (1776), doctrines not yet heard in colonial America but justifying the author in offering a similar rhetorically exaggerated choice between 'liberty' and 'a speedy subjection to arbitrary power' or 'slavery'.[11]

These theological innovations placed a generation of Dissenters in the spotlight of politics, but did not swell their congregations. What increased numbers was the second development, one that pointed in the opposite direction: a revival of evangelical fervour from the 1770s, sometimes fed by Calvinism, which gathered pace from the 1790s. Even so it was not the 'pressure from without' of growing Protestant Dissent that forced a legislative dismantling of the confessional state in 1828–9, but the threat of civil war from Irish Catholicism, as it impacted on Westminster politics. Religious change accelerated after *c*.1790, but this does not mean that fundamental change of the sort later seen had always been immanent in British society since 1688, only waiting its opportunity to emerge.

Challenges to the national churches: internal heterodoxy

The third challenge to the idea of a national church was the most powerful: that of theological heterodoxy *within* the established churches of Ireland, Scotland and England. In Ireland this trend was least fully developed and had least impact: the presence of a surrounding majority Catholicism gave little scope for the Church of Ireland to rest its self-image on anything other than a matching claim to the apostolic succession, the Fathers, the councils and the creeds of the western church. Irish churchmen were, in theory if not in liturgical practice, mostly High Churchmen. Heterodox Irishmen like John Toland (1670–1722) were in some peril, and often had to live abroad.

In Scotland the coercive and communal nature of parish church discipline after the restoration of Presbyterianism in 1689 left little room for theological heterodoxy to take root. The execution for heresy in 1697 of an Edinburgh student, Thomas Aikenhead, was an effective warning. Scottish theological writing entered an arid age, and the talents of the most able were diverted instead into what became known from the 1960s as the 'Scottish Enlightenment'. Yet this movement had one remarkable characteristic: where similar 'Enlightenments' elsewhere in Europe were associated with anticlericalism, religious scepticism and even implied atheism, the Scots literati normally tried to steer clear of religious speculations that might explode in their faces (a partial exception was David Hume, yet even he left his key work, *Dialogues Concerning Natural Religion*, to be published posthumously). They were content to soften the Calvinism of established Presbyterianism and generally did not seek head-on doctrinal confrontations. The established Scottish church remained relatively united in doctrine, and was to fracture in the nineteenth century over the quite different matter of lay patronage, made non-negotiable by religious literalism. Heterodox Scots, from David Hume in the 1740s to James Mill in the 1820s, often found it safer to live in England.

In England the scope for heterodoxy was greater. Pre-publication censorship ended in 1695, and opportunities for theological speculation steadily widened. Dissent's threat to the Church of England gradually subsided; the church was increasingly relaxed and accommodating in tone; it was drawn from a population open to innovation in many areas of life. Curiosity, candour, and free enquiry were the passports of many Anglican theologians to private theories that now went far beyond the agenda of the sixteenth-century reformers; indeed the long eighteenth century may be seen as a Second Reformation. The initial targets of such later reformers were ecclesiastical, in the position of supremacy enjoyed by the re-established church, and dynastic, as Charles II and James II came under increasing attack for their presumed or actual commitments. In the eighteenth century, and especially after the defeat of the Jacobite threat in the 1740s, heterodox thinkers, sometimes Nonconformists but often churchmen, began to take further the implications of their beliefs.

It was from the 1760s that the heterodox generated the new idea of universal suffrage; revitalised natural-law theory; explored a critique of their society's assumptions about the claims of ancient institutions or values, and of inherited or inherent rank or worth. With William Godwin in the 1790s this issued in a position now known as anarchism, a rejection of a legitimate role for the state.[12] With others, including

Jeremy Bentham, it led in the 1820s to the new ideology of radicalism, a combination of David Ricardo's economics, programmatic atheism and universal suffrage.[13] Against successive generations of heterodox thinkers stood a long gallery of orthodox churchmen who sustained a quite different vision of the social order in terms of providential disposition, rank, order and prescription.

Modernity, secularisation, and the Enlightenment

The late seventeenth and early eighteenth centuries have recently come under the historical spotlight as some historians have tried to revive older ideas of secularisation and modernisation (questionable in the changed circumstances of the present)[14] by reasserting a picture of England as 'the first modern society', the home of 'modernity', the birthplace of 'the Enlightenment', an exemplary case of 'secularisation'. Where fifty years ago these assumptions commanded wide-spread assent in academe, they now need careful scrutiny.

First, modernity. Late seventeenth- and early eighteenth-century Britons might take sides in a literary debate between 'ancients' and 'moderns', but never understood the 'moderns' as being on the side of what we describe with the more recent term 'modernity'. This concept was formulated only in the late nineteenth century,[15] when it meant something unknown in the seventeenth: a positivist, reductionist denial of Christianity and an alternative faith in the natural and social sciences as the new matrices of human perfectibility in this world. Sir Isaac Newton, by contrast, was a churchman and a writer on religion, open to the concept of miracle. John Locke, in *Two Treatises of*

Government, depicted no watershed between anachronistic and modern doctrines of politics, presenting instead the views of Sir Robert Filmer as a very present threat. As late as 1769 the Huguenot and Anglican clergyman Louis Dutens, in *An Inquiry into the Origin of the Discoveries attributed to the Moderns*, argued that, for invention after scientific invention, the ancients had got there first. Just as the Church of England had long appealed to Scripture, reason and tradition as its grounds of authority, so in various ways did secular writers; for any of them to make a special claim to reason to validate their positions was a rhetorical device, not a self-evident historical analysis. That being so, for historians to draw up teams for their chosen 'period', some people being held to be for 'modernity', others against it, is one of the larger solecisms.[16]

The nineteenth-century idea of 'modernity' is closely related to another concept, equally problematic. Some historians have celebrated the onset of those complex developments brought together (perhaps wrongly) by the label 'secularisation', but, inconsistently, have seen this phenomenon in many different ages. This ubiquity should arouse suspicion, since if secularisation is characteristic of one age it cannot be so of all. A case was once often made for the late seventeenth century as the crucial divide between an age of faith and an age of reason: worldly, pragmatic, licentious, the restored monarchy was hailed as an era whose secular values acquired an official sanction. The rise of the new science (symbolised by the Royal Society) and of latitudinarianism within the Church of England (the doctrine that no particular form of church organisation was divinely mandated) were depicted as essentially related. From the late seventeenth century a new theological position can be found, Deism, that was to flourish in the eighteenth, and was much later to generate another historians' category, 'the Enlightenment'.

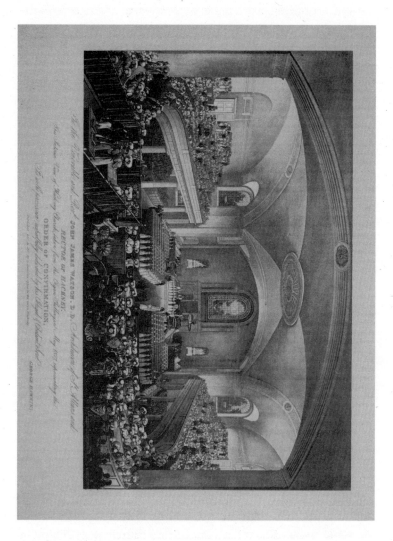

3. Secularisation? Modernisation? These ideas have often been linked in sociological explanation, but have they ignored historical evidence for continuing religious allegiance by the great majority of people? This print shows Hackney Church, London, packed for a confirmation service in 1827, and the home of the High Church 'Hackney Phalanx'.

The assumption that the new science of men like the chemist Robert Boyle (1627–91), the physicists Robert Hooke (1635–1703) and Sir Isaac Newton (1642–1727), and the astronomer Sir Edmond Halley (1656–1742) compromised religious faith is central to the scenario of secularisation. But that is not how these men saw it: most natural scientists in Britain (unlike many of their European contemporaries) entertained a fervent religious belief, if sometimes built around heterodox theologies (ironically Newton, a member of Trinity College, Cambridge, was not a Trinitarian). They saw no contradiction between faith and reason: Newton used reason to show how his cosmos could only be sustained by the intervention at every moment of God, and used astronomical calculations to establish a more exact Scripture chronology.[17] The main challenge to religion came not from natural science but from the Deists, men who generally knew little of physics but read the Bible avidly to reveal what they saw as its contradictions or absurdities; they argued that God (often only an abstract idea in their thinking) related to Creation by invariable general laws that precluded 'special providences', miracles, and (by possible inference) an Atonement exercised in favour of some individuals but not of all.

Historians have sometimes used this scenario of secularisation to explain a change in mass behaviour. It is argued that the conflicts of the seventeenth century discredited zealotry and eroded popular religious commitment. The ability of the church courts to enforce moral behaviour was in decline: the Toleration Act was used not only by Dissenters but also by the lukewarm or sceptical to avoid hitherto mandatory church attendance. On the other side, there is also much evidence of religious zeal and the conflicts it inspired, sometimes denied by the elite, as in 1776 in the American colonies or 1780 in London's Gordon riots.

Religious zeal, or bigotry, was more entrenched in Scotland, Ireland and Wales, and even more vivid in New England. In England many of the moral functions of the church courts were taken over, more efficiently, by JPs (who were Anglican gentry and increasingly, by the early nineteenth century, Anglican clergy). Much evidence for a powerful mainstream religiosity is now being uncovered, and the receptiveness of English-speaking populations to revivalism can be interpreted as a manifestation of this mainstream religiosity rather than a disproof of it: from Methodism through to early nineteenth-century evangelicalism, religion was the common coin of mass discourse.

The popular mind of the eighteenth century was shaped less by rationalism than by a growing evangelicalism. This was an international movement, spontaneously manifesting itself in Germany, the North American colonies, Scotland and England at the same times from the 1730s, its followers growing markedly in numbers and influence from the 1790s. An evangelical idiom spanned denominations, from High Church Anglicans like John Wesley in Oxford and London, to Congregationalists like Jonathan Edwards in Massachusetts, itinerant preachers like Howell Harris in Wales and Baptists like Robert Hall in Cambridge. It also spanned theologies, from Arminian beliefs that Christ died for all (again, Wesley) to Calvinist doctrine that He died only for the elect (George Whitefield). This movement ignored parish boundaries, and often denominational boundaries, to reach individuals with a message of personal sinfulness and the possibility of atoning grace; the 'new birth' demanded of converts was often experienced, sometimes at mass open-air revival meetings like that at Cambuslang, near Glasgow, in 1742.

The most famous practitioner of this new style was John Wesley (1703–91). Why did he succeed? One interpretation sees him as essentially counter-cultural, speaking directly to the people, condemning the somnolence of the established church and appealing to those unmoved by Nonconformity's routine condemnations of establishment. An alternative explanation sees him as a more typical churchman, expressing the strength of that tradition. He profited from his High Church background to flourish within an established church that was already receptive to his literalistic interpretation of Scripture. By contrast, where an episcopal religiosity was lacking, as in Scotland, Methodism did not take root. Wesley himself insisted that he was not a Dissenter, and only local hostility towards his followers led many of them from the 1760s to apply for licences under the Toleration Act to protect their preachers and places of worship.

Wesley was not alone within the Church of England: its evangelicals reached larger numbers and had more impact by deliberately targeting the social elite. This was the strategy of Selina, Dowager Countess of Huntingdon (1707–91), who used her wealth to sponsor her own 'connection'. Yet even she resorted to the Toleration Act to shield her followers in 1779, and they formally became a Dissenting church in 1783 over the issue of unauthorised ordinations. John Wesley began to ordain his own ministers in 1784, although without acknowledging the implications of this act; Methodist independence became a reality after his death in 1791. George Whitefield's followers had tended to become Congregationalists after his death in 1770; in Wales, Howell Harris's followers left the church in 1811. Their supporters believed themselves to have been expelled from the church, but the rising tide of Anglican evangelicalism calls this explanation into question.

Methodism developed in many different environments: in economically changing and insecure places that were growing up outside the Anglican parish structure, but also in traditional centres of Anglican strength, like York, where it has been argued that evangelicalism stimulated an appetite for vital religion that the church was organisationally bad at meeting. Nevertheless, Methodism was a minority movement until it developed into a substantial denomination in the nineteenth century: membership of the Wesleyan Connection was still only 87,000 in 1801, rising to 305,000 in 1841, by which date the Primitive Methodists added another 76,000.

As yet, the mass movement was evangelicalism within the church. Wesley carried into his denomination a key principle of the Church of England: resistance to 'enthusiasm', the pretence of private revelation and private exemption from the moral law ('antinomianism') that had caused revolution in the British Isles in the 1640s and did so again in North America in the 1770s. In their English social teaching, Anglicanism and Wesleyan Methodism were essentially in harmony; it has been urged that this partnership was important in the avoidance of revolution after 1789, and again in the turbulent years after 1815. Anglican evangelicals were also reformers, especially prominent in the anti-slavery movement, but their humanitarianism went with support of the government in all other respects: in the 1790s the 'Clapham sect' backed William Pitt, in the 1820s Lord Liverpool.

In Wales, evangelical revivalism stemmed very directly from a nearly ubiquitous Anglican church, labouring for education and popular literacy in Welsh: this early Methodism was no rejection of the established church, but a development of it. Only much later did Welsh-speaking Calvinistic Methodists and Baptists sweep the board. Wales, which in the seventeenth century had been a stronghold of royalism, became in the nineteenth heavily associated with the Liberal party and in the twentieth with Labour: this reorientation may have had a constant element in the principality's religiosity. In Scotland the regime of the 'Moderates', associated with a softened Calvinism and the use of lay patronage to defend the political order, was revitalised during the French Revolution. It was challenged 'from below' less by democracy than by popular protests against the right of private patronage which allowed many landowners to nominate ministers rather than their parishes to elect them. This dispute became central when Thomas Chalmers, a leading evangelical, became Moderator of the Church of Scotland in 1832; massive conflict followed the 'Disruption' of 1843, the secession from the Kirk of a third of its ministers, opposed to lay patronage.

In Britain's Thirteen Colonies, the situation was different again. If John Wesley stood for social order in England, in America his fellow Methodist George Whitefield, on successive preaching tours the length of the seaboard, acted as an important catalyst of a new consciousness, spanning denominations and linking very different colonies, that perceived a threat to religious liberty in metropolitan policies; his revivalistic fervour was an important element in political mobilisation. In 1776 these colonies collectively experienced a 'new birth', to create a 'redeemer nation'. Historians who debated the question of whether Methodism saved Britain from revolution in the late eighteenth century overlooked the central test of their thesis, that of North America. There, its role in promoting revolution was clear.

Secularisation and modernisation run together in the idea of 'the Enlightenment', a term unknown in the eighteenth century, coined in the late nineteenth, popularised only from the mid twentieth. After the 1960s the idea was developed as shorthand for values held to be antithetical to Nazism, enjoyed enormous vogue, and still carries heavy normative overtones. Confusingly, like 'class' and 'race', the word can be found in these years, but meant something different: not 'the Enlightenment', a *movement* with members, goals and values, but 'enlightenment', the *intellectual apprehension* of truth. In that sense the latitudinarian Whig Edmund Burke, on the reforming wing of English politics, objected against Richard Price that the seventeenth century 'appears to me to have been quite as much enlightened' as the eighteenth: he mocked the pretensions of 'this enlightened age', as some wished to call it.[18] American politics, too, was anything but secular.

'Enlightened' was a familiar adjective (light as a metaphor for truth being often found in Scripture) but not yet reified as 'the Enlightenment'. A range of people at all points on the political and social spectrum pursued 'enlightenment' without imagining themselves to be forwarding 'the Enlightenment'; to draw a line around the commitments of only a few of these people and call their goals 'the Enlightenment' is merely normative. It is especially normative to imply, by such a misuse of evidence, that a project of secularisation was at the heart of intellectual activity in these years. The British Isles demonstrated a variety of religious commitments; 'secularisation' is a poor explanation of that diversity. Many people pursued 'enlightenment' in its familiar form, spiritual truth; none invented the term 'the Enlightenment' to describe a social movement built on the premise that religion was anachronistic.

Theology as a model of the social order

Every social order is supported by a rationale; at this time it was still profoundly theological. Accounts of English universities in this century too often take at face value small anecdotes that suggest the contrary, like Edward Gibbon's picture of his teaching at Magdalen. In 1775 a visitor noted: 'A gownsman of Oxford thus painted the fellows of All Souls – They lived so luxuriously & indolently that they did nothing but clean their teeth all the morning & pick them all the evening.'[19] But this was not the norm. Elsewhere, the university intelligentsia was active in supporting the hegemony of a public ideology in such subjects as theology, history and law.[20] Even so seemingly secular a work as William Blackstone's *Commentaries on the Laws of England* (1765–9) derived the specific content of English law from divine command: 'Upon these two foundations, the law of nature and the law of revelation, depend all human laws'; the law of nature was 'dictated by God himself'.[21] From these divine commands could be deduced the structure of the state and of the church, two aspects, as many claimed, of a single body. In defining the position of the church, the key elements were 'ecclesiology' (the theology that described the essential nature of a church) and 'ecclesiastical polity' (the branch of theology that explained a church's proper organisation). Between them, they accounted for a vast printed output.

Throughout the ten thousand parishes of England and Wales, clergy taught obedience to 'the powers that be' as a Christian duty; theologians expounded the legal institutions entailed by such a doctrine. Judges on circuit were greeted with assize sermons that enforced a similar lesson, and from the bench the judges acted on the familiar common law doctrine that Christianity was part of the laws of England. The Lords, the Commons and countless congregations were taught the same lesson on occasion of the state sermons of 30 January (the execution of Charles I), 29 May (the Restoration of Charles II) and 5 November (the Gunpowder Plot).

Blasphemy was a common-law offence, and was still punished by the civil courts after the church courts shrank in their role.

In England and Wales, no clergy sat in the House of Commons, but two archbishops and twenty-six bishops sat in the House of Lords. Dissenters could vote in elections and sit in Parliament; but although many voted, few stood for election. Of the 2,041 MPs who sat in the House of Commons in 1715–54, only fourteen were Dissenters.[22] This hardly changed: of the 1,964 men in the House in 1754–90, only nineteen were Dissenters.[23] Social leadership was overwhelmingly in the hands of churchmen. To be a member of the political and social elite it was almost essential to be a member of the church. The elite had, moreover, a powerful set of defences designed to exclude those hostile to it. These defences were successful: the old elite survived, to be eclipsed in the twentieth century by the wealth and numbers of new groups, rather than being destroyed by them as happened in France after 1789.

Debate among historians continues over the nature of this order. Some maintain that it was 'Erastian', i.e. that the church was subordinated to the state. Few think it was 'theocratic', with the state dominated by the church (although this could be argued in the case of Presbyterian Scotland and Congregational New England). A third and more persuasive alternative points to the wide acceptance of the doctrine worked out under Henry VIII in which church and state were held to be aspects of a single body. This created an extremely durable state form in England, although its status was highly ambiguous in respect of the composite polity created by England's steadily closer relations with Scotland and Ireland.

This world, deeply structured by theology, fell into schism with the expulsion of James II in 1688. A substantial part of the established churches in England and Scotland (but much less in Ireland or Wales) refused to swear allegiance to the new monarchs, William III and Mary II. People who so refused were termed 'Nonjurors'. They became a disaffected intelligentsia that not only underpinned the Jacobite movement, but called into question the legitimacy of the national church from the position of those who had formerly been its chief supporters. The size of this group is unclear, but its leverage was considerable.

Nor is it established that social life was developing in an opposite direction. As patriarchalism was denounced in political thought following 1688, there is evidence that it strengthened in family life and in social organisation with the administration of the poor law:[24] families grew in size, and servants became more widely affordable to the middling sort. Into the nineteenth century, women were progressively excluded from manufacturing, often by unionised male labour. The new evangelicalism that swept the late eighteenth century in England, Wales and Scotland (in southern Ireland moral reform arrived later, via the Catholic Church) stressed reciprocities and the moral duties of the rich in a way that was strange to eighteenth-century attitudes. It has been conventional to say that the church was weakened in the late eighteenth century when the parish clergy moved closer to the gentry in origin and life-styles. This is not obvious, however: elite backing was still the precondition for the success of many political movements, and gentrification may have worked both ways. In 1800 religion played a changed role in the English state, but still a central one.

Wales was at least two cultures: a moderately anglicised south, where the established church contended with some success against the survivors of civil-war sects, and a Welsh-speaking north, where a Welsh-speaking church gave voice to a stubborn royalism. Welsh Nonconformity in the nineteenth century was a child of the church in the eighteenth. Revivalism had a long history, and its eighteenth-century manifestations were nursed by Welsh-speaking Anglican clergy like Griffith Jones. This movement tended to be Calvinist, and few Welshmen yet had much to do with southern Welsh heterodox Dissenters like Richard Price, more at home as he was in the London salons. Not until 1810–11 did Welsh Methodists in the north turn away from the established church; even then in order to vindicate their Calvinism, not because they were expelled.

Scotland had been a society fractured by religion from the sixteenth century onwards. There the conflict between Episcopalians (who advocated a 'top down' idea of authority) and Presbyterians (who championed a 'bottom up' principle) was decided only by outside intervention: Charles II established the former, William III the latter. This did not end the conflict: Scotland remained a divided society whose identity was weakened by having at its heart a quasi-theocracy that did not command sufficient support to sustain it, especially from the intelligentsia that developed from the mid eighteenth century.

In Scotland, 1660 saw the restoration of the ascendancy of the Episcopalian interest over the Presbyterian (the third element, the Catholic, was much smaller in comparison). It was only a temporary victory. Although the two parties were evenly balanced, William III's coup in England tipped the scales towards the Scottish Presbyterians. They marked their insecurity by the expulsion and persecution of Episcopalian ministers who, in turn, became the intelligentsia of the Jacobite cause. The political threat kept the established Kirk, now Presbyterian, defensively Calvinist. But with the failure of the Forty-five Jacobite rising, the old polarity weakened.

Now Scottish Presbyterianism itself divided between the Popular Party (literalist, pro-American, anti-Catholic and harshly Calvinist) and the Moderate Party (patrician, unionist, anti-American, pro the toleration of Catholics, with softened Calvinist or sometimes even freethinking views in theology). The Forty-five, again, had the effect of finally breaking the Episcopalian interest: subject to increasing persecution, it was eclipsed as a political force. When the penal laws against Episcopalians were repealed in 1792, nothing happened.

The Scottish church had no formal presence within the Edinburgh Parliament, and when this was abolished by the Union of 1707 the Kirk acquired no formal share in the Anglo-Scottish Parliament that met at Westminster. It did, however, exercise a much larger role in local government than its English counterpart. Where Anglican clergy became JPs in larger numbers only after c.1760, in Scotland the Kirk Session was already the core of local government. In practical terms, the Scottish church was strong; theoretically, it produced little to defend its established status, and the Union of 1707 was defended chiefly by the literati who are today identified as part of the Scottish Enlightenment.

Ireland was different again. Catholic Ireland was a culture in touch with the sixteenth-century Counter-Reformation, but too poor and oppressed to be transformed by it. Irish Catholicism was ubiquitous, but lacked spiritual dynamism. If Daniel O'Connell in the 1790s looked for inspiration to the French Revolution, things later changed. In the early nineteenth century Ireland finally caught up with the Counter-Reformation,[25] with results that echoed the sixteenth century more than they foreshadowed the twentieth: denominational self-awareness became the matrix for what looked, from continental Europe, like 'nationalism'.

Meanwhile, the problem for London governments was the latent threat posed by Ireland's Catholic majority. William III avoided draconian action against Irish Catholics: he was too concerned about retaining the sympathy of his European Catholic allies in the struggle against France. It was under Queen Anne, when the Revolution was more secure, that most of the 'penal laws' against Irish Catholics were passed by the Dublin (not the London) Parliament. Yet this code embodied more than mere persecution: it expressed the belief (the mirror image of the Catholic belief) that the opposite denomination could be made to wither away in the face of the progress of divine truth. Until the 1790s, there was much evidence that religious persecution worked in Ireland as everywhere else; it may be debated whether the return of Irish sectarian conflict in the early nineteenth century was the result of the unwisdom of the penal laws, or of their progressive abandonment to secure Irish support in the wars that followed 1776.

In Ireland, the amendment in 1780 of the Irish Test Act of 1704 to allow Protestant Dissenters to hold public office was probably a ministerial effort to head off the Irish campaign for legislative independence; if so, it failed. In England, a concession to Protestant Dissent passed in 1779, which removed the requirement on the part of Dissenting ministers and school-masters to subscribe most of the Thirty Nine Articles in order to qualify under the Toleration Act. This did not reconcile English Dissenters to the state: they continued to trumpet the American cause, mounted from 1786 a new campaign for the repeal of the Test and Corporation Acts, and in 1789 almost secured a majority in the Commons for such a repeal. But by the time they renewed their application in 1790, the French Revolution had demonstrated something to British observers, and the Dissenting attempt was voted down by a two-to-one majority. These Acts still remained as symbols of the church's precedence, and debate continued to rage around them.

With colonial rebellion about to turn into a European war, Lord North's government backed a Catholic Relief Act for England in 1778. It recognised (what was already a fact) Catholic freedom of worship, but now put Catholics on the same footing as Protestants in the ownership and inheritance of land (provided they took an oath to renounce the Stuart claimant, styling himself Charles III, and the papal deposing power: 1745 did not seem as far away as it now does). The same year, the Dublin Parliament also began the relaxation of the penal code with respect to Catholic landholding. North's main concern was evidently recruiting to the armed forces. However necessary, the bill passed the Dublin Parliament only in the face of strong Ascendancy hostility that may have stimulated both the Volunteer movement, an unofficial Protestant militia, and the parliamentary campaign that led to the attainment of Irish legislative independence in 1782. The same year two more Acts of the Dublin Parliament were passed, pushed through by the Lord Lieutenant, that effectively extended to Ireland all the concessions in the English Relief Act of 1778. Only in Scotland did a bitter anti-Catholic outburst coerce the London government into abandoning plans for a similar Act.

Ireland's divisions were even greater than England's and Scotland's. First the Church of Ireland (the episcopal sister church of the Church of England), then Ulster Presbyterianism threatened to become the vehicle of a national consciousness. This phase ended with the rebellion triggered by Jacobin aspirations in 1798, for it turned into a war of religion and had the effect of lastingly preventing a united Ireland. It was Catholicism that subsequently became the mould for Irish national identity, not the Church of Ireland, the Irish equivalent of the Scottish Moderate Party. Unionism and what came to be called the Enlightenment were to be strong in Scotland, weak in Ireland.

Race: the extent of racialist ideas in Britain

Ireland's direction after 1798 was not unusual, however, since religion still played a large part in shaping identities throughout the British Isles; and this role was important in explaining the lateness in Britain of the emergence of ideas of racial difference. 'Race' was a known but uncommon term in Britain in *c*.1660–1832, but, like 'class', it signified something very different from its later meaning.

'Race' then meant chiefly 'descent', and could be synonymous with 'family'.[26] In that usage it could be attached to a historical group, the Jews, who were later to be stigmatised with very different nineteenth-century meanings of the term 'race'. During the crisis over the general Naturalisation Bill of the 1750s, one representative pamphleteer set out his case as a defence of 'Liberty and Property' and of Christianity, not of any supposed English racial purity.[27] 'Race' could be political, as when an anonymous author anticipated the Hanoverian succession, or another celebrated the Stuarts.[28] Usually its context was historical, when national histories were organised around the succession of monarchs, identifying a ruling 'house'.[29] Subsequently, the meaning of the term changed to denote certain characteristics allegedly determined by inherent genetic composition. In and before the eighteenth century, this usage was almost unknown.

Since the church taught that humanity had originated in common parents, Adam and Eve, the word 'race' was normally found in the phrase 'the human race', which implied the opposite of nineteenth-century ideas of inherent, indelible group exclusiveness. George Burges used the phrase in that way, synonymously with 'mankind', to preach against war in 1797.[30] The theory of 'monogenesis', asserting the descent of humanity from a single stock and the unimportance of minor variations in skin colour, was loudly championed by British anthropologists, ethnologists and theologians; it was the dominant view until its opposite, 'polygenesis', arose in the mid nineteenth century to claim that mankind originated in many, essentially different, stocks which would naturally have indelibly different characteristics.

The intellectual dominance of the Church of England within England may therefore have had a major role in ensuring that, by the twentieth century, England was less receptive than many continental European societies to the new ideology of racialism. Whether Ireland and Scotland were more receptive to such doctrines is a question that historians have not been eager to ask, and no research addresses that point. Yet in 1773 James Boswell wrote: 'I observed how curious it was to see an African in the north of Scotland, with little or no difference of manners. A man is like a bottle, which you may fill with red wine or with white.'[31] English speakers in the long eighteenth century were inclined strongly to nurture rather than nature, subscribed to ideas of the common origin of humanity, lacked scientific ideas of genetic difference, and were, instead, intolerant and aggressive over other matters, notably religion and culture.

Part III
Political and National Cultures

The political life of this era set up seemingly familiar landmarks, but each is the subject of intense historical debate: none is now secure from reinterpretation. In 1660 the English republic failed, and Charles II was restored as a champion of the church. In 1688 his Catholic brother, James II, was expelled by the invading troops of Willem van Oranje, who seized the throne as William III; by about 1714, this episode was hailed by the Whigs as 'the Glorious Revolution'. In 1714 a Whig *coup* installed the Elector of Hanover, Georg Ludwig, as George I; in 1776–83 thirteen of Britain's colonies dissented from the libertarian claims of this Hanoverian monarchy so strongly as to trigger a world war to secure independence. Far from collapsing in the face of this major defeat, the British state strengthened and even emerged triumphant after years of war (1793–1802, 1803–15) against revolutionary France. Despite this success, Britain's constitution was challenged and underwent a transformation in 1828–35 the extent of which is still disputed. Moreover, this fast-changing domestic political scene was played out within a European state system that was itself dynamic. Throughout, problems of interpretation are major ones.

The parameters: foreign policy, 1660–1832

Three 'grand narratives' have shaped understandings of England's, then Britain's, history. One sees the story as essentially insular, the largely domestic working-out of a series of practices or episodes (the common law, Parliament, the Industrial Revolution) that were very different from anything seen elsewhere, and would long sustain an English, or British, exceptionalism. The second, rejecting this self-sufficiency, emphasises England's, then Britain's, close involvement with continental Europe as far back as the Romans, finding its policy alternatives in c.1660–1832 in a Dutch state model, adopted in 1688, and in two French ones: Louis XIV's centralised state and the revolutionary ideals that found expression in and after 1789. The third historical tradition defines itself against the first two, emphasising instead England's, then Britain's, unique creation of a vast world empire and the orientation of the 'English-speaking peoples' in transoceanic directions. Although each of these schools has its present-day equivalents, each is also very old; and in the years covered here they created an unresolved tension in foreign policy between isolationism, continental involvement and colonial enterprise. It was also the case that none of the three options could ever be pursued, or assessed, in its pure form, unmixed with the others.[1]

Some observers, like Samuel Johnson during the war of 1756–63, condemned overseas conquest (whether European or colonial) as a vain pursuit of glory, urging a moral and prudent restraint in national conduct; but such voices were seldom dominant. Others (especially Tories after 1689) urged the prioritisation of naval power as a defence against threats from Europe and as a means of acquiring wealth, first through capturing other countries' trade, then increasingly by acquiring colonies. A third position, associated especially with certain Whig ministers from 1689 to 1763, argued that continental states could outbuild the Royal Navy and overturn English naval superiority unless those states were forced to commit resources to warfare on land, and that only by involving Britain in systems of continental alliances (often subsidised from London), and by land campaigns, could command of the sea be maintained.

These arguments were, and are, difficult to quantify: colonies could cost more or less than they returned in trade. Alternatives could seldom be embraced in a pure form: coalitions could be fragile, with interests different from Britain's, and might collapse at crucial moments, as in 1754–6. Alliances might be difficult to secure, as in the 1770s. These three alternatives also simplify a diplomatic picture of extreme and changing complexity, one in which outcomes could seldom be foreseen. The results of wars in these years were often ambiguous, making simple lessons difficult to draw. 'Continental' and 'blue water' elements were also present in each major conflict. The greatest victory, in 1756–63, was in a war most associated with colonial conquest, but the greatest defeat, in 1776–83, coincided with a failure to sustain a system of continental alliances, so that both options had some apparent support; debate in and out of Parliament was therefore sustained and sometimes bitter. Many wars were indecisive, like 1689–97, 1740–8 and 1793–1802; the War of the Spanish Succession in 1702–13 failed to achieve its major objective, and the Napoleonic War of 1803–15, although the most spectacular in its outcome, was also the most perilous.

In recent decades historians have echoed these old alternatives. Some have explored the domestic, self-sufficient strength of the 'fiscal-military state' that permitted first England, then Britain, to play a part on the European stage beyond the size of its population. Others, in what is often termed the 'new imperial history', have stressed the dominance within domestic society of the questions of race, class (and even gender) that were raised by increasing colonial possessions. Others, again, perhaps echoing the UK's recent closer association with the European Union, have recovered the closeness of English ties to the Dutch after 1689 and to the Electorate of Hanover after 1714, with the intricate involvement in the defence of the Low Countries and in the internal politics of the Holy Roman Empire that this entailed.

Within these three broad options English, then British, foreign policy was shaped in these years by four key problems: by England's small size vis-à-vis major continental states, this balance only slowly changing through the progressive incorporation of Scotland and Ireland and as a result of population growth; second, by the ingrained Protestantism of England, Wales and Scotland, which tended to demonise some but not all Catholic states; third, by successive struggles for national survival in the face of far more powerful enemies, chiefly, from 1689 to 1815, France; and fourth, by the long-running race in Europe for naval supremacy. By comparison with these struggles to survive, any independent drive to overseas expansion was arguably secondary.

In retrospect, the dramatic conflict with France that was to last well over a century was made to seem inevitable, but this was not obvious in 1660. In 1657 Cromwell's regime had concluded an alliance with Louis XIV to facilitate war against Spain in Flanders. From the 1670s it was the Whigs (swayed by Dutch propaganda in the Third Dutch War of 1672–4) who saw in Catholic France an immediate threat to England, but it is debatable how real this was: Louis XIV was not Hitler. Louis sought more defensible borders, partly at the expense of the United Provinces, but may not have planned the conquest of western Europe and its forcible religious reconversion, goals with which Whigs and anti-Catholics credited him. Not until after the expulsion of James II did Louis intervene militarily against England, backing James with an army in Ireland. In this interpretation it was William of Orange more than Louis XIV who ignited a century of Anglo-French conflict. But the Whigs were not the consistent men of principle they claimed to be in retrospect. From the 1670s, it was not only Charles II who took French money; Louis bribed the Whig opposition also (including its later heroes William, Lord Russell and Algernon Sidney) to prevent them leading England into war with France. How far the Whigs really did perceive a unique French threat is open to doubt. France was one rival among several.

In one respect France did come to pose a greater threat than the United Provinces. The hyperbole surrounding the Royal Navy obscures the fact that it was only one of the major navies of Europe, and seldom enjoyed a dominant position. France's rise was, initially, unexpected. In 1660 the English navy was four times the tonnage of the French. But the phenomenal naval building programme undertaken by Jean-Baptiste Colbert, finance minister from 1665 to 1683, meant that France achieved superiority by 1670 and held it until *c*.1700. It was to be a naval expansion as momentous in its implications as Tirpitz's creation of a major German battle fleet in the years before 1914; yet this was not as quickly grasped.

In 1660 the United Provinces still seemed England's major problem, and they responded to Colbert with a huge naval expansion of their own.[2] The Commonwealth's commitment to naval power was therefore continued after the Restoration, and the second and third Dutch wars (1665–7, 1672–4) revealed a conscious plan to diminish a trading rival. This was not easy. England lacked the overseas trading bases that her rivals had collected, and was slow to catch up. Charles II acquired, as part of his Portuguese bride's dowry, Tangier on the African coast and Bombay Island in India. The first was intended as a major naval base, but after massive investment it was abandoned in 1684 (the conquest of Gibraltar in 1704 was unforeseen). In 1668 the East India Company was made to shoulder the burden of the maintenance of Bombay, and struggled to do so: it did not aspire to the conquest of a continent. It was only from the 1740s that the English and French companies were drawn into territorial expansion by the decline of the Moghuls: the Indian empire was not planned from London. James II was seriously interested in the reorganisation of England's North American possessions, but this was successfully resisted by colonial elites. Some historians have depicted a sudden reorientation to a crusading Protestant imperialism after 1688, but this is doubtful. War with France in 1689 was not inevitable, and it meant that England's commitments became more continental, not less.

Once France was demonised as the national enemy, it posed a formidable challenge. France had three times England's population and far greater military resources, hardly yet counterbalanced by English (let alone Scots or Irish) wealth. Two main responses to this threat were possible: first, to ally with France and seek to restrain French expansion; second, to seek to assemble a coalition of European states willing to counter French power by war. Whigs claimed their interpretation of French intentions was proved by Louis' annexation of the Spanish Netherlands in 1667. With Spain ruled from 1665 to 1700 by the mentally retarded and childless Carlos II, the future of the Spanish empire would be in doubt on his long-anticipated death. Louis XIV may have long intended to engineer an alliance of the two kingdoms, creating a powerful Catholic bloc. This threat became a reality with the accession of the Bourbon Philip V (ruled 1700–46); it was confirmed in the Bourbon Family Compact of 1761, creating a Franco-Spanish alliance that was to have disastrous consequences for Britain after 1776.

Both of these possible responses to French power were explored by ministries in London whatever their party complexion. The first option, pursued from the 1670s, was made unpopular by the Counter-Reformation Catholicism of Louis XIV's France, which grated on England's militant Protestantism. The Anglo-French alliance effected by the Treaty of Dover (1670) was an agreement to wage war against the United Provinces; for this war, a French subsidy secured to the English Crown independence from parliamentary finance. Sensationally, Charles secretly promised to declare his conversion to Catholicism 'as soon as the welfare of his kingdom will permit' in return for an increased subsidy and for 6,000 French troops to aid in the reconversion of England. Charles never kept this promise, and it is doubtful that he ever intended to do so; he was nothing if not a politician. The second option, military confrontation, was pursued by William of Orange, who seized the English throne primarily to secure English backing in the struggle for survival being waged by

the United Provinces against France. French support for the
Stuarts then dictated the same alignment in the war of Queen
Anne's reign.

Which of these two options was more perilous is debatable.
By 1688 the English navy had not caught up with the French;
indeed the peak of French supremacy at sea came in c.1695
after a second great building programme that even transcended
Colbert's. This French navy was a formidable one in large
ships, technological excellence and professional skill:[3] the
possibility in the 1690s of France's reversing the Revolution of
1688 was real. Had Louis XIV not ordered his fleet to fight at a
tactical disadvantage in 1692, leading to its defeat at the battle
of La Hogue, its numerical superiority by 1693 or 1694 might
have been decisive, and made a restoration possible. Anglo-
Dutch naval co-operation was only just sufficient to avert
invasion until co-operation on land had led France to divert
resources from its navy to its army. By 1714, the European
balance of power had greatly changed. France had been
drained of resources by war: its great navy was no more, cut
to a quarter of its peak strength in 1695. The United Provinces
too had suffered badly; although they had defended their
territorial integrity, their predominance in European shipping
was over. It was Britain's navy that emerged as the leader in
Europe, not dominant in numbers but the largest and the
most consistently resourced.

After 1714 the problem became France's steady revival.
With a French Bourbon on the Spanish throne, which Anglo-
Dutch efforts during the War of the Spanish Succession had
failed to prevent, Spain now began to build a navy on Colbert's
model. By 1740, France and Spain combined were little short
of naval parity with Britain; Britain's naval dominance only
lasted from 1714 to c.1740. The two alternatives in foreign

policy – alliance with France, or military conflict – therefore persisted. By the time a French alliance was again in place from 1716 to 1730, after the death of Louis XIV, religious animosities had cooled to the point where Sir Robert Walpole, Britain's prime minister in 1721–42, gained more from the low land tax that peace secured than he lost by association with a Catholic state. Even so, peace was fragile: during the war of the Polish Succession (1731–5) Walpole kept the navy in readiness and used diplomatic pressure to deter France from invading the Austrian Netherlands; France, for the moment unwilling to resume war with Britain, complied. Nor was France the only possible enemy in war. British colonial conflicts with Spain, and Spain's intermittent interest in playing the Jacobite card, meant that Spain, with its revived fleet, now became a regular opponent. Such conflicts were tactically dramatic but strategically indecisive: the Royal Navy never succeeded in cutting off Spain's supply of gold and silver from the New World, or in seriously damaging Spain's position in Europe.

As long as France could be induced not to back the exiled Stuarts, France and Britain might be at peace. But global rivalry, especially in India and North America, was eventually resumed between Britain and both France and Spain; the Franco-British alliance was dead by 1731, having lasted barely fifteen years. Anglo-Spanish friction over trade, and conflicts between Spanish Florida and British settlers to the north, led to war in 1739. This eventually tempted Louis XV again to support a Stuart restoration as a way of destabilising the possessions of George II; the result was the French invasion attempt of 1744 and another Anglo-French war. The invasion ended in failure when a storm seriously damaged the French landing craft assembled at Dunkirk, and when Walpole's secret service uncovered the Jacobite plan for a domestic rising to coincide with the French landing. The failure of this serious project led Charles Edward Stuart into the quixotic gamble of his rising in 1745. Landing on the west coast of Scotland with only a handful of men and private financial backing, he nevertheless scored a series of military victories against uninspired government forces and in December 1745 reached Derby, only 127 miles from London. The Hanoverian regime was seriously shaken, and after the Duke of Cumberland's victory at the battle of Culloden (April 1746) his forces embarked on a campaign of repression designed to end the military capability of the disaffected Highland clans. This might be described as an act of genocide; even at the time, Cumberland acquired the nickname 'the Butcher'. Yet repression worked.

Invasion in 1744 would have been sensational, but even the unresourced rising of 1745 served French interests well: the diversion of troops to suppress the rebellion helped to ensure the French army's victories in Flanders that tipped the military balance against Britain. Whether in India, North America, or on continental European battlefields, France was the more successful from 1714 to the 1750s; the image of Britain as an effective, militaristic, expansionist, Protestant power, its triumphalism expressed by the newly composed 'Rule Britannia', is far from the reality of draws, reverses and insecurity. After the inconclusive war of 1739–48, France and Spain again expanded their navies: from 1746 to 1755 the Bourbon powers launched some 250,000 tons of naval shipping against Britain's 90,000, and by 1755 they had regained parity.[4] The Seven Years War began with significant naval reverses for Britain, and the French invasion attempt of 1759 was a genuine threat. This dire situation was suddenly and unexpectedly reversed by a string of British military victories in that *annus mirabilis*, 1759; but British astonishment at these victories reflected relief at having succeeded against the odds.

In January 1762 Britain declared war on Spain to pre-empt a Spanish attack. Efficient British expeditions now seized Manila, key to the Philippines, and Havana, key to the Caribbean. At the peace, Spain bought back Havana by the cession of the whole of Florida. Some commentators urged that Britain return at least part of Canada, conquered four years earlier, to France at the peace as a way of ensuring the allegiance of the British colonists and of justifying a British garrison, but this was not done. The entire eastern seaboard of North America was now in British hands; France, to win support in a future war of revenge, ceded Louisiana to Spain. The failure of the Forty-five, and unprecedented military success in 1756–63, left the Hanoverian dynasty far more securely established and elevated it to be a symbol of national unity. But triumph in 1763 also isolated Britain in a Europe apprehensive of Britain's sudden accession of power, and would deprive Britain of continental allies in the next war.

In ceding these territories the French minister César Gabriel de Choiseul probably laid a trap for Britain, isolating her internationally and setting the scene for future rebellion in North America.[5] Triumph in 1763 was short-lived. France and Spain embarked on renewed naval building programmes, consciously aimed at worldwide theatres of war, to which Britain responded too late: by 1770 the balance of naval advantage had swung in favour of the Bourbon powers. From 1770 to 1785 all the major naval powers engaged in the greatest naval building programme seen in the age of sail.[6] Colonial rebellion in 1776 was bad enough, but the war was made unwinnable by the entry on the side of the Thirteen Colonies

first of France in 1778 and then of Spain in 1779; by Britain's
pre-emptive declaration of war on the United Provinces in
1780; and the same year by the League of Armed Neutrality
between Russia, Sweden and Denmark, intended to secure
their trade with Britain's enemies. British dominance of the
Channel was temporarily lost in 1779, and control of the
American seaboard became intermittent: in 1781 the navy's
failure to displace a superior French fleet led to the army's
defeat at Yorktown and the independence of thirteen of the
American colonies.[7]

Military defeat in the American war of 1776–83 did not
unseat George III: Britain's political system, like its financial
one, was acquiring an ability to survive catastrophe that it had
lacked as recently as the profoundly destabilising rebellion of
1745. Yet one key problem was not resolved. The naval lead of
the Bourbon powers was reduced, but not eliminated, by the
mid 1780s; by 1790 France and Spain had opened up another
distinct lead. Britain's survival in a future European war was
no foregone conclusion.

The French Revolution accidentally reversed Britain's isolation of 1778. Initially it created an anti-French coalition of
absolute princes with which Britain was reluctant to ally; but
France's declaration of war on Britain of 1793, identifying
Britain with the princely states of continental Europe, created
a host of potential allies and clients. Survival now depended as
directly as ever on naval victory. Once more, France and her
coerced allies, the United Provinces and Spain, launched more
naval tonnage than Britain, but lost far more in ships captured
or sunk. Successive naval victories steadily tilted the balance in
Britain's favour. In c.1795–6 France and her allies had an
advantage in ships of the line over Britain of about 40 per cent;
by 1800 this had returned to approximate parity; after Trafalgar

in 1805, Britain enjoyed a superiority of about a third. Even so, France and the Netherlands engaged in large building pro-grammes in 1804–8. Napoleon's ambitions at sea were real, and continued after Trafalgar; but his great battle fleet was not ready before his defeat on land in 1814–15.[8]

The leading theme of British diplomacy from 1793 to 1815 was a series of attempts to hold together fragile coalitions to counterbalance the extraordinary dynamism of revolutionary France. In 1815 this strategy finally triumphed; but victory left Europe dominated by crowned heads and by an ultramontane Catholicism. These were not Britain's war aims, and into the late nineteenth century Britain tended to side with nationalism, seen as it still was as a liberal phenomenon, in wars of national liberation and unification in Greece (1821), Italy (1859–61) and Germany (1866–71).

War, then, was an increasingly common phenomenon. Charles II fought the Second Dutch War (1665–7) and the Third Dutch War (1672–4). William III launched what has been called the second Hundred Years War against France in the War of the League of Augsburg (1689–97), continued by Anne in the War of the Spanish Succession (1702–13). After a brief Anglo-French alliance (1716–30), enclosing the War of the Quadruple Alliance (1718–20), a war with Spain (the 'War of Jenkins's Ear', 1739–43) escalated into the War of the Austrian Succession (1740–48). Anglo-French rivalry again precipitated the Seven Years War (1756–63), which led in turn to French revenge in the American Revolutionary War (1775–83). War with revolutionary France (1793–1802) was separated by only a brief peace from the war against Napoleon (1803–15), who in turn drew in the United States (1812–15). Thereafter, wars tended to be briefer, and colonial, until 1914. England or Britain was at war in more years than were spent wholly at peace between 1660 and 1815; between 1689 and 1815 war years were substantially more numerous than peace years. Moreover, this calculation addresses only major wars, formally declared: other armed conflicts, especially at sea, were endemic. Rebellions against established governments were common in the American and West Indian colonies and even at home, notably a series of risings against the restored Stuarts after 1660 and in their favour after 1689, and the Irish rising of 1798. After 1848, the assumption spread that domestic revolution was inconceivable, and after 1945 that major international war was an aberration: no such assumptions were plausible before 1815.

War was frequent; was it total? Military historians have debated whether, by the 1790s, a new form of total war was developing which involved every aspect of life, including mass mobilisation and economic warfare. Against this was the extensive scale of wars in earlier centuries, for which comparable statistics do not survive. It is not clear, for example, that the civil wars in the British Isles from the 1630s to the 1650s, or the Thirty Years War on the continent, do not qualify as 'total wars' when related to the smaller populations then involved. National survival was certainly an issue in 1793–1815; but so it had been in earlier conflicts, the war of 1776–83 included.

The rejection of the republican ideal: the Restoration, 1660–1685

The Restoration could be hailed as a 'Glorious Revolution'.[9] Charles II appeared wildly popular on his return, yet by the late 1670s his rule seemed in deep crisis. Historians debate whether this was a consequence of the unwisdom of his policies, of a royal bid for 'absolutism', or of the surviving antagonisms of the civil wars. Yet Charles won. He dealt far better than Charles I with the Westminster Parliament, and never allowed it to determine its own times of sitting. The Covenanter rebellion in Scotland in 1679 was smaller than the Scottish rebellion of 1637–41, but Charles II succeeded in suppressing it by military force where his father failed. In Charles II's reign there was no military crisis in Ireland, as there was in his father's: where Charles I had been undone by the problems of ruling Scotland and Ireland, his son's more secure hold on those kingdoms preserved his authority in England. Yet none of this proves that England was essentially stable.

A contrasting interpretation stresses the collapse of the revolutionary impetus. What was most remarkable about the revolutionary upheavals of 1640–60 was their modest long-term legacy. In 1660 Pandora's box was closed with greater success than could have been foreseen. The collapse of the English republic and the restoration of the monarchy became a defining moment; but it was largely the army's doing. Parliament, inviting Charles to return, set no conditions, and did not elect him to the throne; Charles dated his reign from the moment of his father's execution. It was as if the English republic had never existed. The army had no commitment to a greater role for Parliament, or to a restoration of episcopacy in the national churches; these were unintended consequences of the army's actions. The Restoration may have marked the triumph of an idea of the ancient constitution (ironically, since many had seen Charles I as working to undermine it), but this did little to solve the host of problems surrounding the church.

Some historians have argued that the civil wars proved to the political elite that Parliament was indispensable; but this

4. The Restoration. This famous image of a rump suspended from the gallows over a blazing fire suggests the popular reaction to the Rump Parliament and the crowd's rejection of republicanism and religious sectarianism in 1660. But how much of the Commonwealth legacy was rejected, and by whom?

needs qualification. Parliaments had hardly distinguished themselves after an initial reforming phase in 1640–1; their descent into extremism, and the failure of successive puppet parliaments to check military dictatorship in the 1650s, left few in the 1660s who claimed much for that body. Nevertheless, Charles I had agreed to triennial general elections, and this provision, together with Charles II's need for money, meant that a somewhat greater role for the institution gradually emerged. Parliaments now sat regularly enough to merge in their understanding and the public's into an institution, Parliament. But the stark fact of the executions of the surviving regicides meant that initially no one could claim that Parliament was the place where sovereignty resided. The 1664 Triennial Act abolished the Triennial Act of 1641, which had created a procedure independent of the Crown to trigger general elections every three years, and replaced it with a statement that the king *should* call a new parliament every three years: Charles II was to ignore it at the end of his reign.

Charles's chief advisers in exile had often been constitutionalists and reformers under his father; they did not intend to create a new monarchical absolutism for the son. The reforms of the first two years of the Long Parliament, accepted by Charles I, still stood: feudal financial survivals like ship money and forced loans were now things of the past. The Prerogative Courts that had been central to the Tudor monarchy, Star Chamber and High Commission, were abolished. Even the clergy surrendered their ancient right to tax themselves in 1664. The chief constitutional point at issue in the civil war, the king's claim to raise taxation without parliamentary consent, was tacitly abandoned and never re-emerged. In 1678 the French ambassador, Barillon, wrote to Louis XIV that Charles II preferred to be left in peace to 're-establish his affairs, that is to say, a good revenue; and I do not believe he cares much for being more absolute than he is'.[10] Historians still debate whether Charles II intended to create a new absolutism, or whether the persecutions of opponents in which his ministries engaged were forced responses to the extremism of civil-war activists still surviving in later decades; the former position is one that may rely on the propaganda of Charles's Whig opponents.

The Westminster Parliament's position was unformulated. Entrenched interests there carried weight, and Charles's ministers feared to offend them. Yet if the Convention Parliament set no conditions for a restoration, Charles appeared to make commitments. These concerned religion: he thought that major concessions would have to be made, especially to Presbyterians, to smooth his return. Charles was probably committed to toleration and religious pluralism as the solution to Europe's wars of religion, and there were enough groups in the British Isles that wanted to embrace this prospect for his restoration to be unopposed. Yet where Charles secured 'comprehension' in the state, appointing many former republicans to office, he failed to secure it in the church. Churchmen adopted a more familiar position: only unanimity in religion could secure peace. The king was in many respects the prisoner of the royalists: it was they who drove through the Cavalier Parliament the 'Clarendon Code', legislation setting the framework for the legal supremacy of the Church of England. It was not royal policy but the refusal of some groups to accept the content of this settlement in doctrine and church government that produced a new phenomenon from the 1660s, the separated Dissenting denominations. These created the real 'plural society', and how to deal with them occupied some of the best minds for the next two centuries.

If religious dissidents did least well out of the settlement, the supporters of the republic got off lightly. Only eleven were executed, men who had signed Charles I's death warrant; only royalist estates that had been confiscated outright were restored. There was no massive act of revenge in 1660. In the financial settlement, the Convention Parliament tried to preserve the ancient principle that the king should 'live of his own', now understood as living on a fixed parliamentary revenue rather than on the revenue of the Crown's estates. It granted taxes expected to produce a generous £1.2 million p.a., intending that this would cover the ordinary expenses of government. In familiar fashion, MPs miscalculated: receipts produced only two-thirds of anticipated revenue in 1660–1, while government expenditure proved higher than forecast. Parliament soon had to vote more taxes, but the initial shortfall was not deliberate. This suggests that Parliament did not yet see itself as a sharer in the executive conduct of government, and was not yet seeking to use the 'power of the purse' to seize such a role. This was an unintended consequence; Charles summoned the Westminster Parliament every year except two between 1660 and 1681, and parliaments learned to demand redress before supply.

Some Interregnum financial experiments were continued, like the excise (a tax assessed at the point of production, first levied, on beer, in 1643).[11] The burden of taxation was steadily shifting from land to trade, whatever the regime. Excise and customs were to be the keys to future national revenue. In 1660 a Navigation Act repeated provisions in an Act of 1651 that restricted trade with England's colonies to English ships: the image of England as a trading, maritime nation was now securely in place, but it was one that Scotland, Ireland and Wales hardly yet shared.

Scotland, not England or Ireland, had triggered the civil

war; but Charles II had been crowned at Scone in 1651, at the price of signing the Covenants, and his restoration in 1660 was popular in Scotland. Charles, moreover, gave high office to moderate Presbyterians as well as royalists; it was this group of Scottish nobility who steered legislation through the recalled Edinburgh Parliament that restored the situation in church and state as it stood in 1633, repealing the legislation of subsequent parliaments to 1648. In Scotland as in England, there was enough of a reaction against militant Presbyterianism to allow the reimposition of episcopacy, the remedy chosen by royalists in the three kingdoms to a civil war now attributed by the Anglican intelligentsia to Presbyterianism alone.

Militant Presbyterians and Covenanters, in whose direction the pendulum had swung far further than in England during the 1640s, were more bitterly and militantly unreconciled. In response, 700 individuals were excluded from the Scottish Act of Indemnity (against thirty-three in the English Act) and often suffered heavy fines. With a large Presbyterian element unreconciled, Charles refused to call a General Assembly of the Kirk and reimposed episcopacy by prerogative, followed by statutory ratification. This, and a statutory requirement to renounce the National Covenant and the Solemn League and Covenant, led to the departure from the Kirk of about a third of its ministers, a higher proportion than in England. Concentrated in the Covenanting areas of south-west Scotland, this element was to pose a continuing challenge to the regime. Financial penalties on Nonconformists, and Covenanting resistance to government attempts to collect fines, escalated in the 1660s into armed clashes, judicial torture, military repression, and a lasting consciousness of victimisation. When Charles put this policy into reverse in 1669, seeking to reinstate willing Presbyterians by royal prerogative, few accepted this outcome. Into the 1670s, the screw of persecution was tightened, and the gross bullying by the Earl (soon Duke) of Lauderdale, Secretary of State for Scotland and a favourite of the King, rendered the Scottish nobility increasingly subservient. In 1675 the Westminster Parliament even moved to ask Charles to dismiss Lauderdale, on the grounds that he sought to impose arbitrary government. Charles refused, but if arbitrary government existed anywhere in the British Isles it was in Scotland.

If England had suffered badly from civil war, Ireland had suffered far more: the Catholic massacre of Protestants of October 1641, exaggerated by propaganda, led on to Cromwell's ruthless conquest, a mortality of perhaps 20 per cent of the population,[12] and a land settlement that reduced the Catholic share from about 60 to about 20 per cent.[13] A new class of speculators and opportunists, professing Protestant purity, was the beneficiary. The Church of Ireland was reformed along English Presbyterian lines; Catholic clergy were hunted down, imprisoned or executed. The Kingdom of Ireland was merged into the republican Commonwealth; the Dublin Parliament was abolished, Ireland securing in return thirty MPs in Cromwell's puppet parliament at Westminster. In this situation of fragile Protestant domination it was the Protestant interest that staged a coup in 1660 and declared for the king, even before General Monck in Scotland decided to act. What they secured was the restoration of the constitutional situation in church and state before 1641, but with the Cromwellian land settlement temporarily intact. The price of securing their lands was, thought the Protestants, their acceptance for the Church of Ireland of episcopacy; but this only meant larger numbers of Dissenters.

The Irish settlement took longer: the Irish Act of Uniformity was not passed until 1666. But its effects were less rigorous towards Protestant Dissenters, for there was no Irish equivalent of the Conventicle Act, which penalised Dissenting worship in groups of more than five people, or the Test Act. Protestant Dissenters held office, and were not imprisoned. There was also a lax de facto toleration of Catholic worship. None of this solved the land question. The Protestant Ascendancy secured the omission of Ireland from the English Act of Indemnity of August 1660. Yet Charles's government now showed itself unwilling to endorse the confiscatory Cromwellian redistribution of estates. The king failed to impose, by declaration, a body to redistribute land; the Dublin Parliament acted instead, but the mandate of the court of claims it set up expired in 1663 with only a fraction of outstanding claims settled, and an Act of Explanation in 1665 gave justice to only a few individuals more. Eventually the Catholic share of the land rose, but this still left widespread grievance, uncorrected expropriation and Protestant fears that more redistribution might follow. They were right to think that Charles II sought to conciliate all sides. From the 1670s English policy allowed Catholics and Presbyterians to hold local office by the royal dispensing power, and in 1672 Charles II set up an inquiry into the recent Irish redistribution of estates. The stage was being set for the Catholic counter-revolution of 1689.

In England, the moderate first phase of the Restoration settlement was the work of the Convention Parliament (1659–61). Its successor, nicknamed the Cavalier Parliament (1661–79), reflected a more militant royalism. It was responsible for a series of acts that remained on the statute book until the early nineteenth century, and became symbolic of Anglican ascendancy. The bishops were restored, together with the ecclesiastical courts. The Corporation Act (1661) set a sacramental test for local office holders. It required of them the oaths of allegiance and supremacy, an oath condemning the taking up arms against the king, and another condemning the Covenant: its aim was to confine local office to churchmen. The Act of Uniformity (1662) imposed clerical vestments (a symbol of orthodoxy) and a prayer book that had been revised in a more episcopal sense; it again required of all incumbents oaths renouncing the Covenant and condemning taking up arms against the king. For some, these were unacceptable conditions.

All ministers ordained and installed during the Interregnum had now to seek episcopal re-ordination. All had to subscribe the Book of Common Prayer and make the declarations required by the Corporation Act, on pain of deprivation. Some 1,760 clergy refused, and lost their livings. The result was a more unanimous church, clearly identifying the challenges to it. Further legislation gave the state sanctions against the sects, like the Quaker Act of 1662 and the Conventicle Act of 1664 (which expired in the same year, but was extended indefinitely in 1670). The Five Mile Act (1665) provided that ejected ministers were not to come within five miles of their former parish, or of any city or town without subscribing the oath condemning taking up arms against the king. Enforcement varied, but many extremists, notably Quakers and Baptists, faced imprisonment.

With much of this, Charles had no problem. The tone of the regime was set by his symbolic sacred function, curing the 'king's evil' (scrofula) by a thaumaturgic gift in the church service of 'touching'. His prerogative powers were not trimmed in 1660: at his disposition were all titles of honour and appointments to the judiciary, to bishoprics and deaneries, to the commission of the peace and Lord Lieutenancies, to naval and military commands, and to government office. Many areas of political conflict were contentious exactly because they were within the sphere of the prerogative, like foreign policy.

But with some of this, Charles did have a problem. Debate was polarised by the legacy of the civil wars, and the private but rumoured conversion of his brother James to the Catholic Church in 1669. The policy of 'comprehension', or inclusiveness, was resisted most bitterly by churchmen aware that it would dilute the criteria for church membership in an age which increasingly feared the spread of heterodoxy from within, and was afraid to give up its means of defending itself from its enemies without. Charles attempted to counter this in ways never anticipated in the controversies that had led to the civil war: he tried to use the prerogative to secure religious toleration. In the late 1660s Charles began courting the Dissenters with the aim of building an alternative power base in the Commons. But this only produced a backlash: Parliament passed a bill to renew the Conventicle Act, and Charles was pressured into consenting.

Charles's financial position was increasingly weak. Parliament had not paid his or his father's debts. An economic depression followed by plague in 1665 and the Fire of London in 1666 cut customs revenues, as did war with the Dutch (1664–7). Parliament became apprehensive about Charles's alleged proclivities to Rome, and the reflection of this in the French alliance of 1670. The 'Stop of the Exchequer' of 1671, a decision to defer the repayment of part of the government's debt, was a major blow to its creditworthiness.[14] Charles now gambled on a renewed war with the United Provinces, partly financed by a secret French subsidy.

The second Declaration of Indulgence (March 1672), issued to coincide with the outbreak of war, provided for the suspension of laws against Nonconformists and Catholic recusants, for licensed public worship by Protestant Non-conformists and for private worship by Catholics. This met with widespread resistance; when lack of money in the hard-fought and inconclusive war led Charles to recall Parliament, it forced the king to abandon the Declaration and coerced him into assenting to the Test Act (1673). The Act obliged the holders of all offices to subscribe a declaration against tran-substantiation and take the sacrament yearly in the Church of England; it became a watertight seal against Catholic participation in public life until its repeal in 1829. Although Protestant Dissenters did not object to the first provision, and many (called 'occasional conformists') brought themselves infrequently to receive Communion, no Catholic could do so. The Catholicism of James, Duke of York, was now clear: he and others had to resign their offices. Political opinion was deeply alarmed: to secure parliamentary revenue, Charles had to end the Dutch war in 1674, and dismiss much of his ministry.

Charles's reverse over his pro-French policy led him to choose as his next Lord Treasurer an Anglican Tory, Sir Thomas Osborne, created Earl of Danby in 1674. Danby pushed through further reforms of the Treasury and Customs and Excise, creating an efficient tax-raising bureaucracy that served England well in the enormously more expensive wars of the eighteenth century. Danby also pioneered the arts of parliamentary management, using handouts, contracts and honours in a systematic fashion to sustain a loyal voting bloc: it worked not least because of Danby's close alliance with the church. Rumours of the existence of the secret clauses of the Treaty of Dover, France's success in the war against the United Provinces and the growing power of Danby as a parliamentary manager reawakened fears of 'arbitrary power' and created an explosive setting. This had two immediate consequences.

First was the creation of an opposition, in which a key leader was John Locke's patron, the 1st Earl of Shaftesbury. One source of Shaftesbury's concerns was practical: fear of what Lauderdale was doing in the government of Scotland. Another was theoretical. In the 1670s Locke, Shaftesbury and the Commonwealth survivor Andrew Marvell developed a doctrine for the opposition, soon nicknamed Whiggism, that was to prove immensely influential; it was fixated on the perceived growth of royal power and on what such men saw, or said they saw, as a conspiracy against liberty. Shaftesbury classically depicted the Whig nobility interposing to secure the liberty of 'the people' against the tyrannical designs of the Crown. He claimed to see a plan by the 'Church-Men' to '*have the Government of the Church Sworn to as Unalterable*, and so Tacitely owned to be of Divine Right . . . Then in requital to the Crown, they declare the Government *absolute* and *Arbitrary*, and allow Monarchy as well as Episcopacy to be *Jure Divino*, and not to be bounded, or limited by humane Laws.' In this 'Project' the legislation of the 1660s was seen as linked: the Corporation Act, keeping many worthy men out of local office; the Militia Act, which 'swears Us into a *Military Government*'; the Act of Uniformity, crucial 'in throwing out a very great number of *Worthy, Learned, Pious, and Orthodox Divines*', that is, the Dissenters.[15] As Marvell began a key pamphlet of 1677, 'There has now for divers Years, a design been carried on, to change the Lawfull Government of *England* into an Absolute Tyranny, and to convert the established Protestant Religion into down-right Popery.'[16] So was launched a political rhetoric that was to culminate in 1776 with the American Declaration of Independence.

About this time Locke began his extremist *Two Treatises of Government*, arguing for an 'appeal to heaven' (a euphemism for armed rebellion) against the monarch whenever 'the people' chose; prudently, he did not publish it until after the Revolution of 1688, and even then did so anonymously. Whiggism claimed at its outset to be the philosophy of the honest 'country' interest against the corrupt 'court'; in reality, Whiggism too had its share of corrupt politicians and intellectuals with self-interested purposes, sometimes republican in politics, often heterodox or Dissenting in religion. There was some basis to the Whig critique. There was also the unscrupulous management of paranoia.

This was revealed in the second consequence: a nationwide panic, centred on claims of the existence of a 'Popish Plot'. It was ignited by the accusations in September 1678 of a lying informer, Titus Oates, that he had evidence of a Catholic plot to foment rebellions in Ireland and Scotland, assassinate Charles, burn London, replace him on the throne by his Catholic brother, James, and bring to England a French army for the country's forcible reconversion. This triggered a frenzy of paranoid fears of popish conspiracy, the persecution of Catholics, a second Test Act in 1678 that removed all Catholics except James, Duke of York, from Parliament, and a series of show trials after which twenty-four innocent men were executed. It was then discovered that Danby had indeed been negotiating secretly with the French. Charles II was now turned from the potential victim of assassination into the agent of 'arbitrary power'. When the Commons voted to impeach Danby, the king in 1679 dissolved the Cavalier Parliament, which had sat since 1661. But the Whigs won by a landslide.

This triggered the 'Exclusion Crisis', the attempt to exclude by statute James, Duke of York, from the succession to the throne on the grounds of his Catholicism. Those seeking exclusion were nicknamed Whigs, a Scottish term for an

extreme Presbyterian; their royalist opponents were nicknamed Tories, an Irish term for a Catholic cattle thief: the
'three kingdoms' dimension still set the terms of debate.
Locke was not typical of Whig argument: most Whigs argued
not from natural law, as he did, but from historic legal
precedent that the Crown in Parliament had often regulated
the succession in the past, and might do so again. Even this
legal argument could end in the same extreme conclusion that
ultimate sovereignty lay with the people, who chose governments by contract. Tories tried to press Whig doctrine to this
conclusion; Whigs resisted. Basic to the Whigs' popular appeal
was a widespread, visceral, unthinking English anti-
Catholicism, plus a better-informed, if paranoid, concern
about the growth of 'arbitrary power'.

Whigs put Protestantism before monarchy, or, as Tories
claimed, favoured a republic. Tories placed monarchical
succession first, looking beyond James to the succession of
his Protestant daughters Mary (1662–94) and Anne (1665–
1714); or, according to Whigs, sympathised with popery. The
Tories looked to the whole polity, since the exclusion of James
by an Act of the Westminster Parliament would leave him
still heir in Scotland and Ireland, whose parliaments would
pass no such Act, and this would threaten civil war on
Charles's death. The Whigs' strategy was an Exclusion Bill;
but when this threatened to pass the newly elected Commons
in 1679 the king first prorogued, then dissolved it. The result
of this second election in 1679 was another Whig victory, but
the king delayed Parliament's sitting until October 1680. A
second Exclusion Bill then passed the Commons and was
rejected in the Lords; again Charles dissolved Parliament.
After a third election, a third parliament was summoned to
meet at loyal Oxford in March 1681. When it still insisted on

pursuing exclusion, Charles dissolved it and did not call another during his reign, like Charles I in 1629–40. Again, the heavens did not fall. Rather, Charles had effectively taken sides, and now purged the judges, the administration and borough corporations of the disloyal. But the Whigs, whose numbers were considerable, were to have their day in 1688.

These three general elections, the first since 1661, crystallised Whig and Tory doctrines, but did not transform the position of Parliament. Rather, they sharpened the definition of monarchy. Charles realised correctly that it was not just his brother who was aimed at, but kingship itself. Now the theorists of monarchy bent every effort to define a strong regime. Sir Robert Filmer's *Patriarcha* had been refused a licence by Charles I in 1632, perhaps as too extreme; in 1680 it was at last published. Debate was polarising. Growing royal revenues steadily gave some substance to what the Whigs feared: a royal design to do without parliaments. Trade grew strongly from the 1670s; England profited by withdrawing in 1674 from the war between France and the United Provinces, which continued without her. A new subsidy of £125,000 p.a. from Louis XIV helped, as did economies in royal expenses, but the basic cause of Charles's growing wealth was trade. At last, it paid for standing armies in England, Scotland and Ireland. In Scotland the need for troops was clear in May 1679 when a group of Covenanters murdered the Archbishop of St Andrews, went on to gather an army perhaps 6,000 strong, and launched a rebellion against 'popery' and 'prelacy'. A royalist victory at the battle of Bothwell Bridge temporarily halted them, but the publicity advantage to Charles II was considerable. When the English Parliament, meeting at Oxford in 1681, refused to abandon exclusion, Charles summoned the Edinburgh Parliament: it passed an Act explicitly disavowing the idea. England could not now pass over the Duke of York without risking civil war: it was Scotland that took exclusion off the English agenda.

In 1681–5, Charles re-established royal control over boroughs and counties by purging Whigs from the commissions of the peace and town governments. But he now prudently operated in close alliance with the Tory–Anglican interest. This successful formula provoked the Whigs into a fatal gambit, the 'Rye House Plot' of 1683 to kidnap and murder Charles and James. By overstepping the line between opposition and resistance, the Whigs alienated that large part of English opinion unwilling to see 1641 return. The Whigs had come too close to appearing as crypto-republicans maintaining a right of rebellion; even 'exclusion' implied that sovereignty lay with Parliament or 'the people' (that is, Whig gentlemen) rather than the monarch. This was a frightening prospect, made worse when it gradually became clear that there had been no Popish plot, and that many Catholics had been unjustly executed after rigged show trials. First Shaftesbury, then Locke, fled into exile; Algernon Sidney and William Lord Russell were convicted and executed. When Charles II died unexpectedly in 1685 (the result of mercury poisoning contracted in his private laboratory)[17] his brother succeeded on a wave of Tory support.

Toleration or Anglican hegemony? James II and the Revolution, 1685–1688

Budgetary pressure on the monarchy now steadily eased as customs and excise revenue grew: by the early 1680s the monarch could almost, or just, 'live of his own'. The Revolution of 1688 was not a response to claims of extra-parliamentary taxation, no longer an issue as it had been in the 1640s. In 1685, James II inherited this steadily strengthening financial position. His first parliament voted him the same taxes as his brother enjoyed, perhaps unaware of their higher and growing yields, plus a sum to put down rebellions. This parliament, too, set no conditions, despite its Anglican concerns at a Catholic monarch.[18] By chance rather than calculation, James was able to contemplate independence from Parliament, and could spend about £300,000 p.a. on military forces beyond the ordinary establishment. This combination of financial prudence and novel military power was to place James's reign in a quite different light.

In Scotland, James had ruled since 1679 through a growing group of loyal Catholic converts, notably John, 1st Earl of Melfort, and James, 4th Earl of Perth: this strategy became a model for James's reign in England and Ireland also. In Ireland, James's hold on power was firm. There he displaced the long-serving Protestant Duke of Ormond as Lord Lieutenant and replaced him with the Catholic Earl of Tyrconnell, who proceeded to remove many Protestant office holders in civil government and to fill the army with Catholic officers. Ireland remained loyal to James in 1688, except in Ulster. Only Scotland, where the Presbyterian interest was strong, was a problem for him in 1688. In England the law courts were to become even more of a political arena, and James systematically promoted Catholics to the bench and to army commands.

In England James inherited the Tory–Anglican ascendancy that triumphed in the last five years of his brother's reign: the persecution of Dissenters had once more worked. His accession saw two small rebellions, led by the Duke of Monmouth in the West Country and the Earl of Argyll in

Scotland, but these were easily defeated. James's position at the end of 1685 was secure. As long as he stood well with his major power base, the church and the Tory gentry, no domestic challenge could unseat him. Charles II had earlier tried to play off this power base against a rival, the Protestant Dissenting interest, but abandoned the attempt and retrieved his natural supporters. James II alienated much of this goodwill; but it is still a question whether this made his exile in 1688 likely, or whether the outcome was the result of an unpredictable contingency. Despite James's unpopularity, which was no greater than that of other monarchs in the seventeenth century, there was to be no domestic uprising in 1688, nor any prospect of one. Yet English Whigs and Scots Covenanters had not disappeared, and were bent on revenge.

The parliament elected in 1685 after James's accession demanded the enforcement of the Test Acts and protested against his decision to retain a standing army, including its Catholic officers, after the suppression of Monmouth's and Argyll's rebellions; James prorogued it in November 1685, and did not summon it again in his reign. The decision to maintain a regular army in time of peace, even after the initial rebellions had been put down, aroused fears of military rule; these fears increased when James used his dispensing power to nullify the Test Act and institute religious toleration by prerogative means, opening the way for Catholics to serve in the armed forces and government office. He then put this arrangement on a more permanent basis by using his suspending power to nullify the 'Clarendon Code', and in 1687 he issued a Declaration of Indulgence, effectively instituting religious toleration. Perhaps James aimed at little more than the reinstatement of a Catholic diocesan structure, as happened in 1853, and the exemption of Catholics from an Anglican ascendancy; but this required 'positive discrimination' from which there were many Anglican losers.

In order to repeal the persecutory legislation against Catholics, James tried to influence Parliament in the same way that Danby had done in the 1670s and Charles had sanctioned in the early 1680s, but he went further. The systematic management of boroughs and corporations was designed to return MPs willing to support the Declaration of Indulgence and repeal the Test Acts, but the campaign met little encouragement. It took the form, for the first time, of excluding unco-operative Tories from lord lieutenancies, the commission of the peace, civic corporations and university posts. James's strategy of seeking an alternative power base among the Dissenters was not implausible: Sir William Petty estimated that 160,000 freeholders in country seats (dominated by Tories) returned ninety-one MPs, but 40,000 electors in the boroughs (where the Dissenters were strongest) returned 418 MPs.[19] The policy was devised by James's chief minister, the 2nd Earl of Sunderland, an experienced politician. Many Protestant Dissenters co-operated, but others, including elite families, did not; nor were Catholics numerous enough, outside Ireland, to complete this alternative power base. It meant that James had unseated the dominant Anglican group from their positions without securing an alternative.

Working through a new body, the Ecclesiastical Commission, James tried to coerce the bishops to support his policy of toleration by prerogative, but without success. The Commission even suspended Henry Compton, Bishop of London; other prelates feared for the future. In 1688 James ordered the clergy to read from their pulpits the Declaration of Indulgence, which granted freedom of worship to all denominations by using the royal prerogative to suspend laws that penalised non-attendance at the established church or set religious criteria for appointment to civil or military office. Most clergy refused to read it. Seven of the bishops challenged the dispensing power in a public petition, were prosecuted for seditious libel, arraigned in a show trial but acquitted amidst massive popular celebration. Even so, the 'Seven Bishops' did not intend by their protest to dethrone James II; after 1689 a majority of them conspired for his return.[20]

In Ireland the pendulum swung far further in the Catholic direction. In 1686 the Catholic adventurer the Earl of Tyrconnel was appointed lieutenant general of the army; by 1687 two-thirds of it was Catholic, and by 1688 nine-tenths. In January 1687 James appointed him deputy Lord Lieutenant, leaving the senior office vacant. Tyrconnel now purged Protestant sheriffs, cancelled every borough charter, and, under the new ones, appointed Catholics. Catholic judges were installed, giving them a majority on the bench. Tyrconnel's long-standing goal of reversing the land settlement in the Catholics' favour now seemed attainable. James's claim in England that he sought merely to remove Catholic disabilities was contradicted: in Ireland, Tyrconnell's rule more clearly pointed to Catholic ascendancy. Early in 1688, James accepted Tyrconnel's plan for a major revision of the land settlement; although it might have left some 60 per cent of Irish land in Protestant hands, Protestants expected the worst. In October 1688, four Irish Catholic regiments were transferred to England: English Protestants realised that Ireland was no longer an island. Irish Catholics were euphoric with expectation, and Irish Protestants increasingly fearful. Still there was no rebellion.

One man made revolution possible in 1688: Willem Hendrik, Prins van Oranje-Nassau, since 1672 Stadtholder of the United Provinces. Son of Charles I's daughter Mary, and married to Mary, Protestant daughter of James II, Willem was in line to succeed to the throne of England in his wife's right if James II should die without a legitimate male heir. This seemed likely. James's marriage in 1673 to Maria d'Este, daughter of the Duke of Modena, had produced nine children: five were stillborn, four had died. The birth of a son and heir to James and Mary on 10 June 1688 displaced Mary and Willem; it created the prospect of a continuing Catholic monarchy, one that would align England with France in the war for survival being fought by the United Provinces. James's policies might now mean long-term Catholic ascendancy rather than the mere removal of disabilities. The acquittal of the Seven Bishops shortly afterwards was widely hailed as a repudiation of this option. Willem therefore arranged to be invited to intervene in England by a group of opposition figures, six English and one Scot. These, later vaingloriously termed the 'Immortal Seven', were a collection of men with grudges, clearly unable to deliver a domestic response to match Willem's invasion, and promising only that there would be mass desertions from James's forces; but they gave his intervention a show of legality. James, at last seeing an invasion pending, reversed his policies and reinstated the expelled Anglicans. It was too late.

Historians debate whether 1688 was more an act of resistance by 'the people' in James's kingdoms, or an episode in European power politics. Although few of his subjects rose in rebellion, the international odds were against him. James was allied with Louis XIV, determined to dominate the French church (a policy known as 'Gallicanism') as a means of strengthening the monarchy. Against them in Catholic Europe were aligned the Pope, Innocent XI, the Holy Roman Emperor and the King of Spain, all with reasons to fear France. In 1688 these three backed Willem van Oranje, seeking to deprive France of an ally: in this they were spectacularly successful. Even so, it is reported that the emperor and the King of Spain offered James to withdraw their backing for the planned expedition if James would terminate his alliance with France; James, from a scrupulous sense of honour, refused.

At this point Louis XIV made Willem's military intervention possible by directing his own armies in September 1688 against the Rhineland fortress of Phillipsburg in the Palatinate rather than against the United Provinces: was this a blunder, as Whig historians claimed, or did Louis tacitly condone Willem's invasion, seeing it as a way of destabilising the British Isles? If so, the wisdom of that policy may be debated. Willem's invasion was far more successful than could have been foreseen: on 5 November 1688 he managed to land his troops in Devon while James's navy remained in the Thames estuary, held (or claiming to be held) there by adverse winds and without the intelligence that would have permitted a pre-emptive strike on the Dutch fleet. Willem had many more troops under his command than used to be estimated, perhaps as many as 40,000, far more than James could assemble;[21] English deserters added little to this strength, although they sapped James's will to resist.

James, outnumbered, avoided a decisive battle. There followed weeks of shadow-boxing with no serious clashes between the rival armies: perhaps both sides doubted the security of their own positions. Here James had most to fear. First, high-ranking commanders began to cross to Willem's support; then, when James mobilised the militia, parts of it too began to join the invader. This phase ended on 22 December when James II was taken under Dutch military escort to Rochester and compelled by armed force to depart.

Few in England had foreseen a military coup and a deposition. Until a late date, Willem professed that he did not seek the crown. His declaration of 10 October had complained of James's 'evil counsellors', who had 'overturned the religion, laws and liberties of those realms, and subjected them, in all things relating to their consciences, liberties and properties, to arbitrary government': it was a formula that would have allowed Willem to secure his objectives without usurping the throne, but via a 'free and lawful parliament'. Such a parliament, Willem promised, would defend the Protestant succession, presumably by having James's son excluded from it, or by having him educated as a Protestant. Willem did not at first call for James's deposition, but once in England and in touch with English politicians (including a deserter, General John Churchill, later Duke of Marlborough) he began to see that he might secure much more. After arranging James's expulsion, Willem began to insist that unless he was made joint sovereign with Mary, and sole head of the executive, he would withdraw, so leaving England to fall into civil war. Whigs now began to speak of James's 'flight' and (a legal fiction) his 'constructive abdication'.

Willem shrewdly associated Parliament with this step, calling new elections on his own authority. These were rigged by his supporters. One MP, John Milner, estimated that 170 Dissenters sat in the new House of Commons. He exaggerated: the real number was closer to sixty-five, but it was still far higher than it was to be again before 1832.[22] This 'Convention Parliament', whose legality was denied by many, agonised over the significance of what was occurring, produced some ambiguous legal formulae to describe and justify events, and finally recognised the anglicised William, and Mary, as joint sovereigns. In the Commons debate on settling the succession,

5. The Revolution. This print, published only in 1790, shows William III being offered the crown together with a document intended to represent the Declaration of Rights; it implies that accepting the second was a condition of receiving the first. But is there any evidence that this occurred? If not, the picture, and others like it, may be evidence for the later Whig myth rather than for what happened in 1689.

it proved impossible to agree on the proposition that James II had violated an original contract, partly because such an idea was unknown to English law, partly because it was urged by survivors from the Commonwealth; as Colonel Birch put it, 'concerning King *James*'s deposing himself, 'tis the hand of God. These forty years we have been scrambling for our Religion, and have saved but little of it. We have been striving against *Anti-Christ*, Popery, and Tyranny.'[23]

Such were the preoccupations of the time. Only later developments made it plausible to argue that the Convention Parliament was clear in seeking to make government contractual, or in redefining the throne as held on conditions. The circumstances of the revolution seemed to confirm not contract theory (there was little active resistance) but passive obedience (many did nothing to defend their unpopular monarch). Some historians (especially from the United States) read the Declaration of Rights (1689) as a code of fundamental law and as a contract between monarch and people, as well as the moment when the English state adopted economically rational institutions like property rights, private enterprise and freedom of contract that paved the way for an industrial market economy, but this argument is unsustainable: economic and financial innovation had long preceded 1688, and Parliament's control of the budget long remained circumscribed.[24] The text of the Declaration, converted into statutory form as the 'Bill' of Rights (formally, an Act), contained no such constitutional claims; the circumstances of the Declaration's framing suggest deliberate ambiguity rather than clear purpose. William III resorted to ambiguity when presented with the Declaration at his coronation: in no sense was he willing to accept it as a contract limiting the Crown. A few Whig extremists saw 1688 as the deposition of the monarch and an exercise of the sovereignty of the people; but they argued uphill. For the great majority, the Bill of Rights did not override hereditary right.

Throughout its sitting, the Convention Parliament generated no outpouring of reforming initiatives, like the French Estates General in 1789; the Commonwealth initiative was muted. Parliament made no claim to have inherited sovereignty (recent historians have made that claim for it, but on doubtful grounds). The only formula for which there was a majority in both Houses was the claim that James II had abdicated and that William and Mary were king and queen (not that they had been elected to that position). This fell far short of John Locke's sensational argument in *Two Treatises of Government* that a breach of the original compact dissolved all government and returned men to a state of nature. The revolution was, in its events, neither radical nor conservative; it was rushed, un-thought-out, and ambiguous.

Locke may have published his subversive work as an attempt to recall the revolution to the more extreme course of the Whigs during the Exclusion Crisis (when the *Two Treatises* was written as a call to armed resistance); if so, in 1690 it failed. People in the middle of the political spectrum insisted that little had changed. Surviving Commonwealthmen on one wing, and Jacobites on the other, argued that everything had changed, one wing praising, the other condemning, the deposition of a monarch and the election of successors. This disagreement lasted long into the eighteenth century. With the new monarchy defending itself by treason trials, proscription of the disaffected and the suspension of habeas corpus, much was at stake. More Jacobites fled the British Isles after the Revolution than Huguenots left France after the revocation of the Edict of Nantes. In Ireland, the departure of a large section of the elite, and continued financial transfers to support exiles abroad, represented a significant drain on the kingdom's capital.[25]

Locke relapsed into the role of celebrated author, minor functionary and shareholder in the slave-trading Royal African Company. The Revolution did not create a world in which the Whigs were the natural party of government: they often did badly in peacetime general elections, and did well only in elections held in wartime. Extreme Whig political theory (emphasising contract and a right of resistance) did not sweep the board: opinion remained fixated on ideas of divine right (which the followers of both James II and William III claimed), English (or Scottish, or Irish) law, and the idea of the 'ancient constitution'. Only in Ireland did the prospect of the extinction of the English interest in 1688 prompt the clergy of the established church to a pragmatic assertion of a right of resistance in extreme necessity.[26] This was always a problematic argument. English Whigs often claimed instead that the child born to James II and his queen on 10 June 1688 had died, being replaced by another smuggled into the bedroom; and that James II had abdicated the throne. As late as 1749 Lord Chesterfield wrote:

> The idle story of the Pretender's having been introduced in a warming-pan, into the Queen's bed, though as destitute of all probability as of all foundation, has been much more prejudicial to the cause of Jacobitism, than all that Mr Locke and others have written to show the unreasonableness and absurdity of the doctrines of indefeasible hereditary right, and unlimited passive obedience.[27]

Since James denied his abdication, and since his son grew up to bear a clear resemblance to his father, Whig ideology was left looking like an evasion to disguise self-interest or more extreme republicanism. The Whig account of what had happened in 1688 came to pieces in subsequent controversy.

In England the outcome was ambiguous; in Scotland the Revolution, like the Reformation, went much further. There the covenantal theology of Calvinists had disposed people since the sixteenth century to understand civil government far more in terms of a contract. This was latent during the Restoration: in Scotland, the monarchy was firmly in charge, but undermined by opposition to its remodelling the Scottish national church on episcopal lines. James pushed through the toleration of Scottish Presbyterians in 1687; they were to turn against him the next year.

Scottish allegiance was now blown wide open: argument was eloquent and sophisticated.[28] After the expulsion of James from England, a Convention Parliament met in Edinburgh, initially divided between supporters of James and Willem. James mishandled the situation, calling it an unlawful assembly and obliging his strongest supporters to withdraw. It was then easy for the extremist Whig remnant to resolve that James had 'forefaulted' (forfeited) the crown. The Edinburgh Convention Parliament, dominated by Presbyterians seeking redress, went far beyond its English counterpart, passing a series of resolutions in the Claim of Right and the Articles of Grievances. Together with these constitutional statements, the Edinburgh Convention legislated on religion, returning the Kirk to Presbyterian polity. The resulting purge of the church and of Scottish universities created an expropriated Episcopalian intelligentsia committed to the doctrine of divine, indefeasible hereditary right. A similar purge of the Nonjurors happened in England also, with similar results; but there the issue was often evaded, and the scale of the problem was smaller. In Scotland the debate was polarised between extremes. Although William III tried to stop persecution, the General Assembly of the Church of Scotland, meeting in 1690, encouraged the mob action that drove more than 500 Episcopalian ministers from their posts.

Yet Scotland did not get all that its zealots sought. The Scottish Convention had intended to offer the throne of Scotland to Willem and Mary on condition that they accept Scottish constitutional demands, including the Claim of Right and Articles of Grievances; but when the Scottish commissioners met Willem on 11 May 1689, Sir John Dalrymple, a commissioner, altered the order of business so that the offer of the throne did not have to be interpreted as conditional.[29] Despite Scottish Presbyterians' fixation on the idea of contract, Scottish society remained much the same.

On the Jacobite side, a brilliant commander, John Graham of Claverhouse, Viscount Dundee, scored a spectacular success at Killiecrankie, but after Dundee's death in the moment of victory the cause disintegrated. Nevertheless, Scotland had to be fought for. With few troops available William III's hold on the country was disputed until 1691 when Jacobite exhaustion, and the bribery of clan chiefs by the new government, brought a temporary cessation. It did not prevent William from ordering the massacre of the MacDonalds of Glencoe to overawe those still loyal to James. Scotland's history was now to be one of ambush, massacre, betrayal and war until the rebellion of 1745 and its savage aftermath. Scots were quickly disillusioned with William III, seeing in his administration an attempt to preserve much that was most objected to about the rule of James II and VII.[30] Emancipated from a Stuart monarchy, but unwilling to be committed to an English solution to the problem, Scotland steadily distanced itself from English politics: the English political elite finally appreciated that they needed to prevent an independent Scotland, and the result was the Union of 1707.

Without control of Scotland, William III would have stood little chance of consolidating his position in Ireland. There James's Catholicising plans had a natural constituency, and there he landed in March 1689 with a French army to assert his claim to the thrones of the three kingdoms. Yet James's aims were not identical with those of his Irish Catholic supporters. James wished to use Ireland as a springboard to regain England and Scotland, and so needed to conciliate Irish Protestants. Irish Catholics wanted above all to undo the Cromwellian land settlement, and to secure a Catholic monarchy for Ireland. Their aims came to dominate the scene when the Dublin Parliament, newly elected and meeting in the shadow of James's Catholic forces, proceeded to assert its independence from the Westminster Parliament, to veto appeals to England from Irish courts, and to undo the land settlement of 1662. An Act of Attainder condemned and confiscated the estates of some 2,400 Protestants who had fled. The fears of Protestant landowners that they would in turn be expropriated by a Catholic majority were now realised. Although the lands of the Church of Ireland were untouched, religious toleration was enacted; landowners were freed to pay tithes only to their own churches. This was the full-scale Catholic backlash that had been feared in England, going beyond what James wished; but he was now the prisoner of his supporters. Arguably it was the Irish dimension that cost James a restoration in England.

Whether this legislative programme would last depended on the war, fought between two claimants in person as it had not been in England. Later Whig legend portrayed William's triumph as sweeping and inevitable; at the time, either side might have prevailed, or a lasting stalemate emerged. The battle of the Boyne (July 1690) did not complete a Williamite triumph; the Treaty of Limerick (1691) consequently contained terms favourable to Catholics, not a draconian settlement. It provided for the safe passage to France of both the French and Irish troops: at once some 11,000 of the 14,000 Irish in arms for the Stuarts left, so depriving Ireland of its elite. Whatever the terms of the treaty, what mattered was how its terms would be interpreted by the re-elected, and now Protestant, Dublin Parliament. This body implemented a Protestant backlash as severe as its Catholic precursor, steadily eroding the land settlement. The Catholic share of the land has been estimated at 59 per cent in 1641, later cut dramatically; by 1688 it had recovered to about 20 per cent; by 1703 it was only 14 per cent. As the century wore on, this percentage fell further.

The religious articles of the Treaty of Limerick were similarly eroded. They provided for Irish Catholics to enjoy the same liberties that they had enjoyed in the reign of Charles II. But this de facto toleration after the Restoration had depended on the non-enforcement of Elizabethan anti-recusancy statutes. These remained on the statute book, and from the 1690s the Dublin Parliament added to them legislation termed the 'penal laws'. In 1692, Catholics were debarred from the Dublin Parliament by an oath against tran-substantiation, and in 1727 from voting in elections to it. Successive acts prevented Catholics buying more land; divided Catholic estates among all the children unless the eldest son became a Protestant, in which case he inherited the whole; forbade Catholics to bear arms; forbade mixed marriages; excluded Catholics from the legal profession and the armed forces; criminalised Catholic schools, and the practice of Catholics sending their children abroad to be educated. As a system of persecution, it worked: by 1749 only eight of 114 Irish peers were Catholics. Equally, however, the Ulster Presbyterians received little for their efforts in the war: the sacramental test excluded them also from civil or military office and from the Dublin Parliament. Emigrating in large numbers to the American colonies, the 'Scotch-Irish' became important supporters of the revolution of 1776.

Even the members of the Church of Ireland were ambiguous victors in 1691. Ireland was now seen from London as a ticking bomb, and London made control of Irish politics a priority. This produced by reaction a classic of Irish political thought, William Molyneux's *The Case of Ireland's Being Bound by Acts of Parliament in England, Stated* (Dublin, 1698), at the time an unavailing protest against Ireland's subordination, but never forgotten. The constitutional relations between England and Ireland now became a focus of controversy. The Dublin Parliament was run, corruptly, by a series of 'undertakers', Irish fixers who delivered compliance to the Lord Lieutenants, but an Irish sense of independence could still be affronted by sensitive issues. In response to one such controversy the Westminster Parliament passed in 1720 the Declaratory Act (repealed in 1782) reasserting its legislative supremacy over Ireland. This in turn became a model for the Declaratory Act of 1766, restating the same principle for the American colonies: the revolution of 1776 saw these Irish issues played out again. Meanwhile, whatever its claims to ultimate authority, the Westminster Parliament rarely sought to legislate for Ireland after 1720.

In the North American colonies, the denominational situation was even more fraught than in the British Isles. New England especially saw its own revolution in 1688–9 as militant

Congregational majorities deposed and expelled James II's administrators. It was a series of spontaneous acts that registered the development of an essentially Dissenting political culture in North America, with results to be clear in 1776. For Ireland especially, the Revolution meant a massive drain of men and capital, with large numbers of émigrés, supplemented from England; Scots joined them after the failure of the 1715 Jacobite rebellion ('the Fifteen'). This Jacobite diaspora, more damaging to Britain than the departure of the Huguenots from France, is only now beginning to be studied.

English Whigs often averted their gaze from these consequences in Scotland and Ireland, and later described the Revolution as 'bloodless' (if 'the Revolution' includes Scotland and Ireland, or the European war in which it involved England, the claim itself needs explanation). In England, Whigs tried to depict 1688 as ordered and rational (it is now debated whether it was either). Most Whigs, like all Tories, still appealed to a divine sanction; now it was the Whigs' turn to claim 1688 as a providential deliverance. Later historians again sometimes identified 1688 as a decisive divide between the early modern and modern eras; only recently has it been asked whether there are any such clean breaks. In some ways, 1688 was even a backlash against reforms later called modern: it was deeply anti-Catholic; it was intended to keep the lid on latent Commonwealth sentiment and any potential for populist rebellion; it preserved power in the hands of local gentry elites rather than a central bureaucracy until the nineteenth century. England, Scotland and Ireland had often seen invasions, depositions, and manufactured rationales for new regimes; they had often invoked God to defend widely different outcomes; they had often sanctioned the repression of those who disagreed. All this survived 1688.

The constitutional balance

England, Scotland and Ireland were monarchies, but how monarchy was to be understood was already a problem of long standing. One answer among several was the idea of 'mixed monarchy', already old in English and Scottish history (but not found in Ireland): the idea that the executive could be tamed by notionally dividing sovereignty between various social constituencies or institutions in the state. Historians debate whether this idea triumphed in 1688, leading to the eighteenth-century idea of the 'mixed and balanced' constitution whereby authority was supposed to be divided between the sovereign, the Commons and the Lords, its components held in a mechanical system of opposing forces, or whether the idea of mixed monarchy failed in the late seventeenth century, and, by its failure, led to the stronger, more centralised states of the present day with their unified conceptions of sovereignty (including the USA).

In favour of the second interpretation are the facts that Locke ignored mixed-monarchy theory in *Two Treatises of Government*, assuming instead a unified sovereign, 'the people', and that William III and succeeding monarchs similarly looked to the sixteenth-century notion that the legal sovereign was a unified trinity, 'the Crown in Parliament', not to a division of sovereignty between three independent players. Yet either idea could be used by opposition to argue that political power was unbalanced; the two rhetorics of 'checks and balances' and 'the Crown in Parliament' came to seem synonymous. Relations between Crown and Parliament developed significantly after 1689; but it is debatable whether they developed primarily because of war rather than of revolution. English history was already littered with attempts to restrain the executive; but like the Test Acts, which told the king whom he could not employ, most formal restrictions on the prerogative were in the sphere of religion.

Other restrictions were less effective. The 'Bill' of Rights (1689), passed after the Revolution, is often hailed as instituting a limited monarchy. In reality, the Act made its assertions in the name of 'the estates of the people of this realm', not 'the people'. The political compromises needed to ensure it a parliamentary majority meant that its initial list of new rights had to be dropped; the Act as passed only restated old rights. Even so, its provisions were often too vague to be legally enforceable (e.g. 'That election of members of Parliament ought to be free.' But what was 'free'? The succeeding century was marked by widespread corruption.) By contrast, the Act's really effective provision was that no monarch could henceforth be a Catholic.

If England, Ireland and Scotland were monarchies, they also possessed ancient representative institutions; but their powers have often been overstated. In the years 1660–1832, these powers continued to evolve, in ways that were a matter for contemporary debate. Just as the Westminster Parliament developed a system in which the king worked through a chief minister who could organise support, suppress dissent and deliver votes of taxation, so the London government came to manage the Dublin and Edinburgh Parliaments in the same way. English historians have tended to disparage these neighbouring Parliaments for submitting to this system of 'undertakers', but it is debatable how far a similar convention compromised Westminster's independence too. When this system of parliamentary management broke down, the results were the same: the incorporation of the Edinburgh and Dublin Parliaments into their Westminster neighbour (in 1707 and

1801), where management and manipulation had been raised to a higher power. The alternative was demonstrated in 1776, when the long-standing metropolitan failure to control colonial assemblies produced a breakaway tradition of institutions beyond metropolitan control, oligarchical but speaking the language of representation.

A strong ministry, and parliamentary management, were responses to the common problem of rebellious assemblies. This was the major political issue in the British Isles in the seventeenth century, and many theorists and men of affairs reacted to it by preferring control to civil war. Control of parliaments came at the price of a strong executive in general: it provided a more effective customs service, a more intrusive excise, the abolition of local privileges and legal jurisdictions, larger armed forces, effectively used to suppress rebellion or disorder. The Stuarts were made to take the blame; but the state continued to strengthen, whether the monarch was James II or William III. The early eighteenth century saw the rise of a political rhetoric which ascribed a growing role and importance to Parliament. Yet this paralleled the development of techniques of political control which rendered Parliament increasingly subject to the executive. If the executive was increasingly dependent on Parliament to fund ever-larger wars, the ministry found ways of ensuring Parliament's compliance. Over time, parliaments voted sums ever larger than their more wilful seventeenth-century predecessors. The executive therefore summoned them on a regular basis and kept them in being.

Whigs often claimed that the Revolution of 1688 created a wholly new polity, and some historians have echoed this rhetoric. Whether such transformations are common in human affairs is debatable, for monarchs after 1688 had to

cope with problems not dissimilar to those of their predecessors. It is questionable whether the Revolution made the
state much less monarchical. Because the legal fiction was that
James II had abdicated, no principles were established about
deposing monarchs or calling them to account. William had as
authoritarian a personality as James. William, too, was a
monarchist, and before 1688 had feared that James would
provoke civil war in England ending in a republic, so denying
William the throne on James's death. Like James, William had
a religious mission and preferred centralised government to
achieve it. Both were soldiers of God: William, like James, was
an active military leader; the last sovereign to command in
battle was George II, at Dettingen in 1743. Even afterwards,
younger sons of the royal family continued to have military
careers, and it remained a truth decorously expressed that the
Hanoverian regime was ultimately secured by armed force.

What made most difference was not legislation by the
Convention Parliament of 1689 but the fact that the exile of
James meant that the natural friends of monarchy, the Tories,
were now cold or hostile to William III. After 1697, they had
their chance to restrict his power in what had angered them
most. The Act of Settlement (1701) not only fixed the
succession; it provided that in case a foreigner came to the
throne, 'this nation be not obliged to engage in any war for
the defence of any dominions or territories which do not
belong to the crown of England without the consent of
Parliament' (it became a dead letter); that no future monarch
leave England, Scotland or Ireland without consent of
Parliament (it failed after the accession of the House of
Hanover); that no foreigner be a member of the Privy Council,
or either House of Parliament, or hold any civil or military
office, or receive any grant of lands; and that no salaried

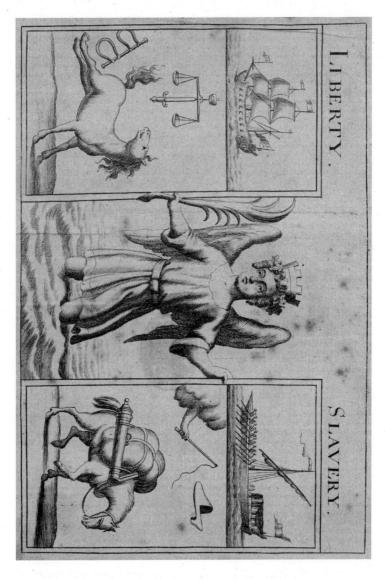

6. Political discourse. This image captures the Whig antithesis, dating from the Exclusion Crisis of 1679–81, between 'Liberty' and 'Slavery'. But how many were convinced that this really was the choice? And why did some see it like that, others not?

government officer sit in Parliament following Anne's death (a provision repealed by the Whigs in 1706 in order to safeguard themselves under a Hanoverian successor). After 1714 many considered, with some cause, that these provisions had been flagrantly violated.

Some people therefore continued to see the Crown as a threat that needed to be limited; in the eighteenth century, many came to talk of a tripartite balance between Crown, Lords and Commons. But how was this to be gauged? There had been no normal and identifiable balance in the seventeenth century that could be used as a yardstick. The civil wars of the 1640s were not caused by any drive for supremacy by the House of Commons, as was once thought. No such bid for power was present before the war; none can be traced after 1660. The Crown was still the central feature, and its powers were, if anything, enhanced: (1) In 1660 the king was recognised to have command of the militia, a point disputed before the war. (2) In 1664 the Crown was effectively released from the obligation, imposed by the Triennial Act of 1641, to summon Parliament at least every three years, with consequences evident in the 1680s. (3) In 1668 the terms of the judges' appointments were changed from 'quamdiu se bene gesserint' (as long as they behave well) to 'durante bene placito' (during the king's pleasure). But these prerogative powers were not widely resisted; prerogative was a recognised part of government. If Parliament was not trying to seize sovereignty, equally Charles II was not trying to effect a constitutional revolution, however much he may have admired Louis XIV. All government was absolute, as Sir Robert Filmer had argued in the 1640s: men well remembered that this was true of Cromwell's. During the Exclusion Crisis of 1679–81, the Whigs implicitly acknowledged that the Crown could not be bound by conditions; an unacceptable monarch could only be replaced by an acceptable one.

Republicanism was not, in origin, a functional comment on monarchy. Its origin was religious, a conviction that since God alone was the supreme monarch, and Christ the head of the church, the position claimed by worldly sovereigns was blasphemous. Republicanism was therefore a 'default position' rather than a thought-through programme for the structure of civil government. The years 1763–76 saw a sophisticated debate in the American colonies on the nature of American grievances, but blueprints for a republican future were notable by their absence. Even Thomas Paine, in *Rights of Man* (1791–2), remarkably treated a republic as any government that was directed towards the public good. British republicanism had a poor record after 1660 chiefly because it was so lacking in intellectual content.

In the 1660s, parliaments behaved more like their Tudor precursors than their Hanoverian successors. MPs were still close to their localities, and few displayed a wider vision. Information available to them on many detailed matters of national finance, trade and administration was scanty, and their position vis-à-vis the executive was weak. On foreign affairs they knew more; on constitutional law and religion they knew a great deal. What built up the role of Parliament was neither informed involvement in the business of government, nor any plan to secure a larger role, but the unplanned emergence of two groups, 'Whig' and 'Tory', each dedicated to their opponents' destruction and each pursuing knowledge and power to that end. The impetus for their formation was electoral division, but none such occurred while the Cavalier Parliament sat without a general election as it did in 1661–79. It was the dissolutions and general elections in the midst of the Exclusion Crisis (1679, 1680 and 1681) that transformed political life.

Both Whigs and Tories appealed to 'the people'. This term was commonly used in political rhetoric, but meaning the political elite, not everyone. Universal manhood suffrage was not on the agenda until the election for Westminster in 1780. Until then, politics might be populist, but was not (in a modern sense) democratic. In 1688 about 2.6 per cent of the English population voted in general elections; by 1716 about 4.6 per cent, roughly one in four adult males. Participation then steadily dropped as turnouts declined, falling to about 2.6 per cent again by 1830, and the earlier peak was not regained until after the second Reform Act of 1867. Some historians have written of 'exclusion'; but it was the first Reform Act of 1832 that was explicitly restrictive, excluding women from voting for the first time. Before 1832, another scenario links low turnouts and a general lack of widespread demand for popular involvement that made Walpole's political manipulation feasible. 'Radical politics', the mobilisation of the poor, was not an ever-present possibility, codified in 'radicalism': popular engagement was episodic; radicalism was the proper name for a new political ideology, coined in the 1820s, and a doctrine devised for the people, not by them. Popular politics was generally organised and elicited by the elite; it was not spontaneously generated by the masses.

The dynastic framework

The British Isles, like almost all of Europe, was composed of a series of polities that were assembled, and understood, in dynastic terms and in a dynastic age.[31] After *Calvin's Case* (1608), a legal test case used to define what we call 'citizenship'

after the Union of Crowns in 1603, national identity was
defined in terms of personal allegiance to the natural person
of the sovereign, not to an abstract 'state'; indeed until the late
eighteenth century, monarchical allegiance was the dominant
way of defining and picturing national identity. This usage did
not reveal some immature or subservient attitude. Rather, like
the later doctrine of popular sovereignty, monarchical
allegiance was a language that all could use in an attempt to
secure their ends.[32] The nobility and gentry, bishops and clergy
professing extravagant loyalty to Charles II retained much
power in their own hands; more, indeed, than had those who
rode the tiger of the Commonwealth in the 1650s.

Religious duty overwhelmingly reinforced this legal code
and national symbolism. It was plausible in an age of text-
centred Christian literalism that men should appeal to a
doctrine of divine, indefeasible, hereditary right; most supporters of William III disagreed only with 'indefeasible', the
idea that the succession could never be changed. Most Whigs
conceded the claims of hereditary right in seeking a successor
to Queen Anne by tracing a family tree and disqualifying only
the Catholic claimants: when this ruled out fifty-seven
individuals, the resulting choice, Georg Ludwig, Kurfürst von
Braunschweig-Lüneburg, anglicised as George I, still claimed
an hereditary title. There was nothing 'modern' about the
Hanoverians, nothing 'anachronistic' about the Stuarts: each
was a dynasty in a dynastic age. The Stuarts were unsuccessful
as a dynasty not because of personal failings, which they
shared with all dynasties and all politicians, but because they
had to deal with exceptional challenges to their rule in the
form of Protestant Dissent, the resistance theories that went
with it, anti-Catholicism, and their adverse medical histories.[33]

In 1689–92 the Whigs won the war in the British Isles, but

not the argument: the debate about dynastic ideas went on into the 1750s. The Revolution had happened, but what did it mean? The challenge was to vindicate one's own interpretation of the events of 1688–9. This was not easy, and political allegiances were not black and white. Historians consequently dispute how many Stuart sympathisers there were. There is no simple answer to this question, for political commitment was a matter of degree, varied over time with the available options, and was often concealed; but it is clear that Jacobitism was a more potent force in the early eighteenth-century British Isles than Marxism was to be in the early twentieth.

The threat had a geographical embodiment. Louis XIV gave James II the use of the former royal palace at Saint-Germain-en-Laye, near Paris; there the Stuart court numbered between 750 and 1,000 people, a substantial operation, generously funded by Louis. In 1713 the Treaty of Utrecht obliged James III to leave France; he re-established himself at the chateau of Bar-le-Duc in Lorraine. In 1716, after the failure of the rising of 1715, he moved to Avignon, and in 1717 to Italy, eventually to Urbino; then to Rome in 1718, settling at the Palazzo Muti from 1719.[34] Here members of the British elite on the Grand Tour might pay a discreet visit to what was now the Palazzo del Re.

The hard core of Stuart supporters were the Nonjurors. Samuel Johnson, in his *Dictionary* of 1755, defined Nonjuror as 'One who conceiving James II unjustly deposed, refuses to swear allegiance to those who have succeeded him': he used the present tense to describe a persisting commitment. Historians formerly identified 'Nonjuror' with that minority of clergy who declined the oath of allegiance in 1689 (and later the oath of abjuration, specifically disavowing the title of James II or his son), were ejected from their livings, and

7. Jacobite propaganda, 1721. The medal's inscription, *Unica Salus*, 'the only security', carried a double meaning in the age of the South Sea Bubble; on the reverse, the white horse of Hanover tramples the British lion, with London and fleeing British subjects in the background. The inscription is *Quid Gravius Capta*, 'what worse than captivity'. How effective such Jacobite propaganda was is a matter of debate.

thereafter worshipped in separated congregations. This usage was too limited: far more laymen never faced demands to take the oaths, and the separated Nonjurors were probably only the tip of an iceberg whose size is impossible to determine. What is clearer is the insecurity and lack of zeal with which England and Scotland responded to major European war in the 1690s; Catholic Ireland was openly hostile. In 1770 the Tory Samuel Johnson wrote of William III that 'half the nation' had denied him their allegiance. In 1776 the Whig Edmund Burke spoke of 'half of the kingdom' attached to 'their exiled Prince' in William's reign.[35] Whatever the numbers, men on opposite sides like Johnson and Burke could express the same sense of the scale of the problem.

Some people (Nonconformists and heterodox Anglicans) nevertheless tried to escape from the intellectual framework of monarchical legitimacy, chiefly for religious reasons. This had been one point at issue in the civil wars of the 1640s; but with the Restoration a monarchical understanding of society was reasserted. At the Revolution, this legal and political system was preserved, and a Commonwealth option rejected: even Locke dedicated his *Two Treatises of Government* (1690) to William III. In a dynastic age, the only security from the claim of the Stuarts was another dynasty.

Yet William III had no children: as a patriarchal deliverer his shelf life was short. At his death in 1702, the same was true of James II's daughter Anne, martyr to an illness that killed all her children in infancy. Everyone knew that on her death the revolution would be re-fought. This indeed happened: 1714 saw a Whig coup when their candidate, the Elector of Hanover, was proclaimed, but this verdict was at once contested in the Jacobite rebellion of 1715. A precedent was set in 1660: restorations were possible. Recent work on the Fifteen has emphasised how plausible another reversal now was.

The ideologies of two rival royal houses only made it more essential for the supporters of each to lay claim to dynastic propriety, and this competition for ownership of the dynastic idiom was intensified with the accession of the House of Hanover in 1714. Supporters of William III, George I and George II had to hail their monarchs, however implausibly, as bulwarks of liberty because lawfully entitled to the throne, and the same idiom was in full repair at the accession of the young, idealistic George III in 1760. Jacobites replied in kind: James III (1688–1766) too claimed to respect the laws, and promised to rescue his country from an illegal regime.[36] Some historians argue that Jacobitism stood no chance because it was 'romantic' and therefore impractical; others point out that Romanticism took root only in the early nineteenth century, and reconstruct the world view that made dynastic allegiance a viable and powerful framework for public affairs.[37] The exiled Stuarts were supported for somewhat different reasons in England, Scotland, Ireland and Wales; yet those reasons combined material advantage, libertarianism, national pride, religion and political ideology in durable combinations.

Where the exclusion of the Tory–Jacobite half of the nation from political office under George I and II had strengthened the monarchical idiom, both sides bidding for a monopoly of it, the removal from office in the 1760s of the old corps of parliamentary Whigs by George III's chief minister, Lord Bute, had a different effect: with no other dynastic option to fall back on, and despite being eventually compelled to accept the patronage of the Hanoverian Prince of Wales (to reign as George IV in 1820–30), the Whig opposition gradually developed a far less dynastic attitude to politics. Open republicans were few in the British Isles before the French Revolution, and the American war gave little impetus to anti-monarchical thought at home. But 1789, and the execution of Louis XVI in 1793, became symbols of which the disaffected made use. This was especially true in Ireland and Scotland, where the failure of Jacobitism left large areas of local society politically decapitated, without a symbolic personal focus. In England the challenges of 1776 and 1789 led to a reassertion of the monarchy as a national symbol, but there were counter-currents too: in treason trials the state came to be defined in more impersonal legal terms.[38] Edmund Burke's defence of the whole social order in *Reflections on the Revolution in France* (1790) paradoxically meant that the spotlight moved away from the person of the king.

The last two decades before 1832 saw a reassertion of the church over the monarchy via the formula of 'the Protestant constitution': Catholic demands for 'emancipation' initially strengthened the Protestant component of the state's self-image. Yet this doctrine narrowed the foundation of the state, for it applied most obviously to England. A powerful challenge to it came in the threat of armed rebellion in Ireland, and Scotland too now began to slip away from the unionist commitments that the men of the 'Scottish Enlightenment' had championed. After the reforms of 1828–35, especially the 1832 Reform Act, Robert Peel redefined the doctrine of the party of order and so, by implication, the nature of the state that it defended. Out went the old 'Toryism' focused on church and king; in came the new 'Conservatism', a secular, pragmatic defence of property and power. Queen Victoria still headed a Europe-wide family, but for her British subjects dynasticism mattered less.

Securing the revolution: William III (1689–1702) and Anne (1702–1714)

Political stability did not arrive in 1689, as used to be asserted. The 'growth of political stability' in England had been the achievement of James I, not William III. Treason trials had slumped to a low point after 1605; following the Revolution of 1688, treason trials were frequent again into the 1740s as society in three kingdoms failed to come to terms with the change of dynasty. William's regime was ambiguously supported in England and Wales; in Ireland and Scotland it faced substantial hostility. That he was able nevertheless to arrange the participation of his new kingdoms in a European war was remarkable. This may be evidence for the anti-Catholicism that made plausible William's claim that war was the only way to counter Louis XIV's France, or evidence for the degree to which the Parliaments of Westminster, Dublin and Edinburgh could be swayed by the executive: the Westminster Parliament in the 1690s was indeed packed with Williamite placemen, pensioners and contractors. Ironically, the large parliamentary grants to payroll William's continental wars were steered through by Danby, Charles II's most successful parliamentary fixer. Ironically again, it was Charles II and James II who had looked to trade; William III needed to rely on the land tax also. John Wesley echoed the resentments this caused, writing in 1776:

> It had ever been his [William's] wish, to humble the French, whom he considered as the most formidable enemies of the liberty of Europe. Many of the English, on the other hand, had neither the same animosity

against the French, nor the same terrors of their increasing power. These, therefore, considered the interest of the nation as sacrificed to foreign connexions; and complained that the war on the continent fell most heavily on them, though they had the least interest in its success . . . Patriotism began to be ridiculed as an ideal virtue, and the practice of bribing a majority in Parliament became universal.[39]

Many of the Revolution's consequences were unforeseen or unintended by its participants. One consequence was a burst of activity by representative institutions: from the parliaments of Westminster, Dublin and Edinburgh, through the Church of England's Convocations of Canterbury and York, the Convocation of the Church of Ireland (from 1704) and (from 1689) the General Assembly of the Church of Scotland, to (in 1702) Cornwall's 'Parliament of Tinners', institutions reconvened after periods of abeyance, met more often and for longer, transacted more business, and developed their procedures and bureaucracies.[40] This was no democratic triumph. William's regime needed the sanction of such bodies. Yet the widespread rejection of his legitimacy that these exercises in consultation uncovered compelled a greater resort to techniques of management and manipulation, practised before but now brought to a fine art. The Westminster Parliament was summoned more often chiefly because it was more effectively controlled by the executive. The Dublin and Edinburgh Parliaments were increasingly subjected to the London government, and when the Edinburgh body threatened to break free its existence was terminated in 1707. When England's Convocations challenged a spokesman of the new Hanoverian regime, Benjamin Hoadly, they were prorogued in 1719 and had only a token existence until 1852 and 1861. In 1752 even Cornwall's Convocation of the Stannaries became politically inconvenient to the Whig ministry, and was suspended.

The Revolution soon became anything but bloodless: it was fought for on land in Ireland and Scotland; at sea, a French naval victory at the battle of Beachy Head (June 1690) made possible a French invasion attempt, frustrated only by the English fleet's victory at the battle of La Hogue (May 1692), although the allegiance of the English admiral, Edward Russell, was in doubt. Stuart attempts at a restoration were repeated in the 1690s. A second French initiative followed in 1695, but was abandoned on doubts of the willingness of English Jacobites to organise rebellion. France would not act before an English rising; English Jacobites would not rise until French troops had landed. The fate of Monmouth's and Argyll's rebellions in 1685 was unforgettable. William III had broken this impasse by landing a substantial army in 1688; the French, in successive attempts of which the last was not until 1759, never quite managed to do so. Yet the Jacobite option was one among many in French foreign policy; France was the Stuarts' greatest asset, but was never an unequivocal ally.

William's attention quickly returned to the continent and his crusade against France; in the 1690s he consistently failed to win over English opinion. Scotland and Ireland seemed worlds away. The king did not even give his Whig friends his wholehearted confidence. Among his inner circle, his position was further undermined when in 1692 it was discovered that John Churchill, then Earl of Marlborough, had been in contact with James II in case the times should alter. Marlborough was not alone: many of England's elite wished to hedge their bets. Nor did men need to be theorists to judge the regime. In circles close to the court, the moral standing of government saw a decline from James II's pious austerity: Whigs like Thomas Wharton matched the lifestyles of Charles II's rakes. A class of profiteers and nouveaux riches gained most from the war: financiers, contractors, stock-jobbers, merchants, lawyers, military men. Others outside this charmed circle denounced 'corruption' and lamented the loss of 'liberties'.

Even the Whigs did not always share William's sense of mission against France, and often gave precedence to eroding the position of the Crown. Conflict with the Crown continued under William as it had under James, though on different issues. In 1691 Parliament established Commissioners of Public Accounts to scrutinise government expenditure. In 1693 William vetoed a Triennial Bill that would have limited the duration of parliaments and ensured general elections every three years, but in 1694 he was forced to accept it. In 1693 he vetoed a Place Bill that would have blocked holders of ministerial office from sitting in the Commons. But the political elite were complicit in the 'creative accounting' that led to the Bank of England and the national debt: war meant profit for the financiers, contractors and placemen on an unprecedented scale, at least in England.

Historians have often taken for granted the military survival of William's regime, preferring eulogies of the financial innovations that war encouraged: the extension of the excise and the tightening-up of customs duties; the establishment of a funded national debt, taxes being specifically appropriated to pay the interest on it; the creation of the Bank of England in 1694. In England (but not Ireland or Scotland) loans could now be raised at lower interest rates than Louis XIV paid. Historians have termed these changes the 'financial revolution', and they made a difference.[41] Yet many of the changes began under Charles II or the Commonwealth.[42] William's wars were almost the ruin of the English economy: higher taxes hampered growth, war at sea hit trade, and the recoinage of 1696–7, intended to restore economic confidence, precipitated a damaging slump.[43] The financial drain of the war in Flanders followed a symbolic insult: the Westminster Parliament was made to pass an Act reimbursing William for the cost of his invasion of 1688. Meanwhile, the Jacobite menace was serious diplomacy, not sentiment.

However well funded, the European alliance against France lost battle after battle. From this situation the allies were rescued by Louis' lack of money; he sought peace in 1697. William's regime narrowly survived a financial war of attrition rather than winning a decisive military victory. At home, the costs of war produced a Tory backlash in the 1697 election. John Wesley, echoing a pro-Hanoverian Tory perspective, commented:

> In the general pacification, her [England's] interests seemed entirely deserted; and for all the treasures she had sent to the continent, and all the blood which she had shed there, the only equivalent she received was, an acknowledgement of King William's title from the King of France.
>
> Such was the issue of a long and bloody war, which had drained England of her wealth and people, almost intirely ruined her commerce, debauched her morals by encouraging venality and corruption, and entailed upon her an immense debt, which has gradually increased to an intolerable burden.[44]

There was no Revolution 'settlement' in Britain, but lasting uncertainty. William's insecurity is shown by his offer to James

in July 1696 to allow the Stuart Prince of Wales to succeed if
he, William, were allowed to retain the throne until his death
(evidently James's queen, Mary of Modena, vetoed the idea).[45]
With James so well provided for in France, his chances of
restoration might have seemed stronger than those of Charles
II in the 1650s. In the summer of 1700 Princess Anne's one
surviving child, the Duke of Gloucester, died, and the succession question in the British Isles was once more wide open.
There was no European settlement either, despite William's
wars: in the autumn of 1700 Carlos II of Spain at last died, and
the Spanish problem was back on the agenda.

In 1701, Anne being unlikely to bear more children, the Act
of Settlement provided for the crown to pass on her death to
the nearest Protestant heir of James I's youngest daughter (at
that time, to Sophia, Electress of Hanover, or her children).
Anne may have had other ideas. Recent historians argue that
in William III's last months, Anne secretly promised her father,
James II, that if she were allowed to succeed on William's
death, then the son born to James in 1688 would eventually
succeed her.[46] But such matters now depended on European
power politics. After Anne's accession in 1702, war returned
when Louis XIV broke the Treaty of Ryswick to recognise his
grandson Philippe de Bourbon as heir to the Spanish throne,
and he also refused to remove Philippe from his place in the
succession to the French throne, a condition laid down in the
will of Carlos II of Spain. Louis broke the treaty again to
recognise the Stuart Prince of Wales as James III on his father's
death in September 1701.

At stake was the succession to the thrones not only of
Spain, but of England, Scotland and Ireland. Consequently,
the War of the Spanish Succession was the setting for renewed
French invasion attempts to restore the Stuarts. In 1708, a

French fleet almost landed an army in Scotland with James III in person in command, but failed to do so. The war was therefore fought on the European continent. Unexpectedly, England now produced a general of world class, the Duke of Marlborough, on whom a contemporary historian bestowed a memorable accolade: it 'could not be said of any other General, either Ancient or Modern, *That he never sat before a Town, which he did not take; nor ever fought a Battel which he did not win*'.[47] But even Marlborough had contacts with the rival court at Saint-Germain as insurance. He secretly contributed £4,000 to Jacobite funds as late as 1715, the year of a rising which might have reversed the dynastic verdict that his desertion of James II in 1688 and Marlborough's victories had secured in his lifetime.

Abroad, the dominant issue of Anne's reign was the war; at home it was the church, and the church implied the Revolution. The Tory ministry with which Anne began her reign sought to move against occasional conformity, the practice of some Dissenters qualifying themselves for office under the Test and Corporation Acts by occasionally taking Communion in the church; Whigs responded with a militant defence of Toleration and an attack on High Churchmen. Both sides failed: the political elite was too divided for a consistent response to the problem of Dissent, whether toleration, 'comprehension', or coercion. The Test and Corporation Acts remained, the latter softened by annual Indemnity Acts and inconsistently enforced, but the church retained a substantial monopoly on public life.

The Whigs' *raison d'être* was increasingly the war, which they claimed was essential to preserve the Protestant succession and check France's drive to dominate Europe. Marlborough's initial victories consolidated Whig power, but French victories in Spain secured that kingdom for Louis' Bourbon candidate;

public opinion in Britain finally turned against the awful casualties and mounting expense of Marlborough's campaigns. For France, war meant near bankruptcy and negotiations for peace in early 1709; for England, war weariness meant a swing in public opinion and a Tory ministry that signed the Treaty of Utrecht in 1713. This change of mood was catalysed by the Whigs' decision to use parliamentary impeachment against a Tory clergyman, Dr Henry Sacheverell, who sailed provocatively close to the wind in his interpretation of the Revolution and his severe comments on Dissenters. But this show trial exploded in the Whigs' faces. Its published proceedings, subjecting the Revolution to searching legal analysis, became a best-seller. Anne's private interventions ensured that Sacheverell, although convicted, received only a token punishment which amounted to a vindication. The trial of the Seven Bishops in 1688 was now repeated, with similar results: a Tory landslide in the general election of 1710.

From 1711, the ministry began peace negotiations with France that produced the Treaty of Utrecht. From the outset, Whigs and Tories were locked in controversy: was it a sell-out, accepting a French candidate on the Spanish throne, or did its provisions on trade and colonies, including retention of Gibraltar, set the scene for Britain's prosperity and growing naval power? If the second, was it the achievement of the Tories, or the Whigs, or both? At the time, the Elector of Hanover felt abandoned by the Tories and convinced that the treaty was a preliminary to a Stuart restoration on Anne's death. His fears became self-fulfilling: more Tories now began to look to James III.

Anne's aim in 1710 in dismissing, one by one, the great Whig lords who had monopolised her council was to return to William's system of ministries mixed in their party composition. But although her new chief minister, Robert Harley, Earl of Oxford, shared this goal, the Tory electoral triumphs in 1710 and 1713 led strongly in the other direction. Tories in the country wanted to win the peace by instituting their vision of a more homogeneously Anglican society and receding from the experiment of the Toleration Act. An Act against occasional conformity passed in 1711; the Schism Act of 1714 penalised Dissenters who kept schools. The Tories thus framed a persecutory code at just the moment when Anne's declining health brought nearer the prospect of Nonconformists' deliverance (as they hoped) by a second William III in the person of the Elector of Hanover, and at the moment when a significant number of the Tories might have preferred the restoration of the youthful James III, especially if he renounced his faith. This was the moment when a *politique* conversion might have tipped the political balance, but James, for reasons of private conscience, declined to renounce his faith. In April 1714 Anne, ailing, promised the Duke of Ormonde to do something to ensure the succession of James III; but nothing was done. When Anne discovered that Oxford was in touch with both claimants to the throne, uncertain which would triumph, she dismissed him. On her deathbed she appointed as Lord Treasurer (or was said to have appointed) the Whig Duke of Shrewsbury, one of the seven who had invited Willem van Oranje in 1688. In 1714 Shrewsbury ensured the succession of Georg Ludwig.

Centre and periphery

The British Isles, and their overseas possessions in North America, experienced a perpetual tension between definition as a federal or as a confederal polity, between centralisation and devolution; indeed the same unresolved conflicts were inherited by the United States after 1783. This is a recent way of putting it; at the time, many Europeans saw their polities as either multiple monarchies (a single sovereign ruling simultaneously over several kingdoms, the sovereign being the sole point of unity) or as composite kingdoms (a unified polity created by a dominant core kingdom absorbing neighbouring kingdoms or principalities). It was the ancient autonomy of the kingdoms of England, Scotland and Ireland that created the potential for future tensions. This was especially true when England's growing power encouraged the country to see itself as a 'core' to which Wales, Scotland and Ireland were 'peripheries'.

One tangible expression of this was commercial. The Union of Crowns in 1603 had threatened commercial integration: England's Navigation Acts, which from 1651 restricted the use of foreign shipping in English trade, initially applied against Ireland and Scotland just as much as against the United Provinces. Scotland's attempt to catch up economically in the 1690s took the form of a scheme for a trading company to Africa and the Indies, but in the face of London's hostility its outpost at Darien (near present-day Panama) withered and collapsed, involving a massive loss of the capital subscribed by an impoverished homeland. The independence of the 'peripheries' had an economic price.

Between centralisation and devolution there was continuous tension. Cromwell's regime had adopted the military conquest of the peripheries and their assimilation into a centrally directed godly commonwealth. Charles II, re-establishing the autonomy of the thrones of England, Scotland and Ireland, necessarily reversed this. James II, pursuing bureaucratic efficiencies, moved back towards centralisation in a way that offended the localities, yet William III and his successors, whatever else they disavowed in James's policies, continued this trend towards centralised control. The first two Georges, aware of the fragility of their hold on power, found it prudent not to arouse the regional loyalties that the Stuarts could exploit, and not to provoke the sensitivities of Dissenters to rule from the centre; theirs was a policy accidentally captured by a phrase of the 1st Duke of Newcastle, 'salutary neglect'. The end of the Stuart threat allowed a trend to central direction to reassert itself in the 1760s in the shape of metropolitan policies on colonial taxation, with atavistic consequences in 1776; the new republic then trod the same path of devolution to the thirteen states, followed by the reassertion of federal control. Some historians have seen a distinctively new state form emerging in Britain after 1689, especially measured by a higher percentage of taxation in relation to national income than can be measured in Britain's continental rivals; although these tax contrasts are well evidenced, the tension between centralisation and devolution was an older problem.

Centralisation was not necessarily a bad policy. James I and Charles I had pursued the integration of England and Scotland, notably the creation of a single national church, and the religiously based resistance that this evoked may be evidence either of the need for that strategy or its imprudence. It was the Westminster Parliament that refused an incorporating union after 1603 and later insisted that the Navigation Acts be applied to exclude Scottish trade, even with England's colonies. Scotland gained little economically from the Union of Crowns in 1603, as became clear in the wars of the 1690s. London politicians rightly saw that Scotland threatened to break away from England after the Revolution of 1688: the Edinburgh Parliament steadily gained control of its business and its composition in the 1690s, escaping from its old subordination to the Crown. In the 1690s, William's regime failed to find Scottish grandees who could deliver local compliance, as was to happen in Dublin. The Edinburgh Parliament even refused to ratify the English Act of Settlement (1701). Its Act Anent [concerning] Peace and War (1703) instead provided that foreign policy decisions made in London after Anne's death would need the consent of the Scottish Parliament. The Act of Security (1704) provided that the Scottish Parliament would choose Anne's successor on her death (by implication, a Stuart, implying a French alliance), unless London conceded free trade.

This was effectively a delayed declaration of independence, and compelled English intervention to secure Scottish participation in the war. The English ministry's first response was the Alien Act (1705) which provided that if Scotland refused to accept a union it would be legally an alien nation. This finally decided an old Scottish dilemma, and commissioners began to negotiate. According to Sir John Clerk, one of the Scots who negotiated the terms, his fellow commissioners debated among themselves 'whether they should propose to the English a Federal union between the two nations, or an Incorporating union'. They recognised that 'The first was most favoured by the people of Scotland, but all the Scots Commissioners, to a Man, considered it rediculous and impracticable' since 'in all Federal unions there is behoved to be a supreme power lodged some where'; nor would the English commissioners accept it.[48] The terms agreed on were nevertheless anomalous: an incorporating union, creating a single government and armed forces, was to leave Scottish law and Scottish religion untouched. It was an inconsistent compromise, but it worked because the Scottish Parliament was absorbed in and swamped by its Westminster cousin and because the Presbyterian coup of 1689 was preserved: just as, for the Frenchman Henri IV, Paris was worth a Mass, for the Dutchman Willem van Oranje Edinburgh was worth a General Assembly of the Kirk. But in the French-backed Jacobite invasion attempt that followed in 1708, James III promised to restore the Edinburgh Parliament: this remained a possibility, if the times should alter.

The Union was unpopular in Scotland. Sir John Clerk confessed in his memoirs that of the Scottish people 'not even one per cent approved' of what the Edinburgh Parliament was doing in agreeing to that measure. The Scottish commissioners had asked for the whole of the Edinburgh Parliament to be absorbed at Westminster; the English commissioners offered only thirty-eight seats in the Westminster Commons (later raised to forty-five, but falling far short of the 159 constituencies of the Scottish Parliament) plus sixteen representative Scottish peers in the Lords, arguing that representation should reflect property, not population or the size of existing institutions.[49] Yet although these sixteen peers were 'elected' from the whole body of the Scottish nobility, control from London meant that they became largely official nominees: the Scottish contingent at Westminster was henceforth usually subservient to the government of the day.

The Union was unpopular in England, too. Scottish dissatisfaction with its working led to a motion by a Scottish peer in the Westminster Parliament in 1713 to repeal the treaty: it attracted much English support and failed by just four votes. When rebellion followed in 1715, the Union was secured by military force. Only slowly did its economic benefits emerge. Under its terms, Scotland was brought within the ambit of England's Navigation Acts, evaded many of the duties under those Acts by widespread and flagrant smuggling, shouldered a disproportionately small share of the land tax and excise burdens, and retained its own church and legal system. From the mid 1720s, Walpole built up a patronage machine in Scotland, run by the Earl of Islay, later 2nd Duke of Argyll, to parallel that in Dublin; these political arts brought stability, of a sort, to the Union of 1707. Scotland retained a large degree of self-government, but via an oligarchy. Nor was it invariably subservient: when Walpole's agent Argyll turned against him following the Porteous riots of 1736, his following at Westminster tilted the balance and helped ensure Walpole's fall in 1742. But control was re-established via the 3rd Duke of Argyll, who held Scotland for the London government from 1743 to 1761 and weathered the rebellion of 1745.

Union with Ireland, however, was resisted by the British government throughout the eighteenth century: it came in 1801 only as a result of the Irish rebellion of 1798. Englishmen often looked on Ireland as a kingdom already subordinated: union was deemed unnecessary. In 1764 the American patriot James Otis drew a distinction between the extensive liberties to which his fellow colonists were entitled and those of the Irish, since 'Ireland is a *conquered* country'.[50] Ireland was seen as a trade rival, where Scotland was not. Ireland was also more populous than Scotland, and could not have been as easily assimilated at Westminster. An Irish unionist elite, dedicated to moderating old religious passions and to promoting scientific, technological and social change, therefore did not emerge, as it did in Scotland. Irish opinion oscillated during the eighteenth century, sometimes for a union, sometimes against.[51] Union came in 1801 when both Irish and English elites agreed simultaneously.

Neither union was, therefore, self-explanatory. Was 1707

an episode in state formation, part of a drive by England to assimilate surrounding cultures? Or was it a bid for security, an attempt to arrange political co-operation by concession to the peripheries where no easy military dominance was possible? In favour of the second interpretation was London governments' preoccupation with dynastic instability after 1660, 1688 and 1714, and the resolute focus of William III and the first two Georges on continental European politics. None of these leaders had any record of 'state formation' in their native countries (the United Provinces was a ramshackle coalition, Braunschweig-Lüneburg a petty princedom among petty princedoms); the idea would have been above the head of Queen Anne.

Despite the Union, Scotland remained, for the English, a remote and strange country until the reign of George III. From 1688, Scotland had a substantial disaffected intelligentsia, inward-looking and unreconciled. From the mid eighteenth century, however, more and more professional careers in England and overseas opened up for the graduates of Scotland's efficient universities, and the disaffected intelligentsia gradually evaporated. Change was not immediately obvious, but by the 1780s was undeniable: in 1763, one stagecoach a month left Edinburgh for London, which it reached in twelve to sixteen days; twenty years later, sixty stagecoaches a month were making the same journey in four days.[52] Even more than the professional middle orders, the Scottish elite increasingly left for careers in England. Consequently, the Scottish nobility was largely anglicised by 1760. Short of a Stuart restoration, undoing the Union was inconceivable. After the 1760s, Scots began to hold high office in England in substantial numbers, and to fill more and more posts in the East India Company: by 1776, the empire had a distinctly Scottish look.

Something similar happened in Ireland, though to a lesser degree: more of the Irish elite stayed at home, or joined the Jacobite diaspora on the continent, than engaged in empire. Yet whereas the Scottish nobility and gentry had been in a time warp before 1707, reversing that stance dramatically only after *c.*1760, Irish patricians were already more cosmopolitan, the result of conquest, mobility and intermarriage over many centuries. Whatever the image of self-sufficiency devised by nineteenth-century Irish nationalism, the eighteenth-century Irish elite was assiduously part of an Anglo-Irish cultural world, as their magnificent houses still testify.[53]

Scotland and Ireland came to be ruled from London in similar ways. Managers who could deliver local compliance (in Ireland nicknamed 'undertakers') were recruited from local elites. Colonial America differed in that such local 'undertakers' tended not to emerge, and direct rule by royal governors, backed by inadequate patronage and weak military force, failed long before 1776. In subservient Scotland, by contrast, the system of 'undertakers' continued successfully into the 1790s with the ascendancy of Henry Dundas. In Ireland the presence of an English Lord Lieutenant, appointed by London, meant a divided elite and encouraged the emergence of anti-unionist sentiment that secured its fullest expression during the American Revolution. Partial siding with Catholic opinion meant that a united unionist bloc was never born, and Ireland was prone to stresses which erupted in rebellion in 1798.

Centralisation did not go unchallenged. For the Thirteen Colonies, 1776 saw a rebellion against centralisation, a reaffirmation of the idea of creating a more libertarian polity by dividing up sovereignty. But no sooner had a confederal republic been born than much of its own political elite began to denounce it as dangerously weak, a trend that resulted in the establishment of a centralising, incorporating union with the American constitution of 1787. This in turn was only the precursor of a series of legal disputes in the American courts over states' rights that ended in civil war in the 1860s. In constitutions, no settlement is ever permanent; indeed ten years is a long time.

National identities

England, Wales, Scotland and Ireland were ancient societies: each in 1660 had long-standing, complex and continually developing ways of describing their identity that seldom strongly anticipated the new ideology, 'nationalism', that was to be coined in continental Europe after Napoleon. 'Nationalism' would later appeal to blood and soil, to nineteenth-century scientific ideas of racial difference, and to the allegedly separate and characteristic nature of folk culture, literature, art and music. Earlier ages had different attitudes to these things. Before the nineteenth century (as noted earlier), 'race' meant family lineage rather than indelible genetic identity, and related to family pride rather than to ideas of popular commonalities. Elite culture in any European society that possessed elites was saturated in the classics of Greece and Rome, and seldom regarded popular vernacular culture through the eyes of the Romantics as a guide to the unchanging inner essence of a 'people'. Before the nineteenth century, elites were far more cosmopolitan than they later became. But the societies of the British Isles were well aware of their special characteristics, and had other ways of picturing themselves that did not depend on 'nationalism'.

The English had a well-developed historiography that traced the deeds and achievements of Englishmen (and some women, notably Boadicea and Queen Elizabeth I) over many centuries. The cult of the English common law was already ancient, and was revitalised by texts like Matthew Hale's *The History of the Common Law of England* (1713) and William Blackstone's *Commentaries on the Laws of England* (1765–9). But the biggest body of literature outlining a shared experience concerned the English church. It was here especially that an image of a free, Protestant people was worked out and sustained, whether in best-sellers like John Foxe's *Book of Martyrs* (1559 and many later editions) or in heavyweight theological texts like Richard Hooker's *Of the Laws of Ecclesiastical Polity* (1593; first complete edition, 1662). Between them, these texts kept alive the interpretation long ago placed on English history by the Venerable Bede (d.735) in his *Historia ecclesiastica gentis Anglorum* that its unifying theme was providential destiny and survival in the face of overwhelming odds.

The identity of Wales, lacking universities and a major capital city, was far weaker. The Welsh in the seventeenth century, like the Welshman Judge George Jeffreys, often tried to be more loyal than the English loyalists. At the dawn of the eighteenth century, Wales was a stronghold of Stuart allegiance. The failure of this option, and the rise of the evangelical movement, provided Wales with a different idiom. A growing body of books printed in Welsh, especially works of devotion, laid the groundwork for revivalist Methodism, eventually outside the framework of English and Anglican culture.[54] From royalism in the seventeenth century, Wales turned to liberalism in the nineteenth and socialism in the twentieth. But neither liberalism nor socialism created a strong national identity: even in the Romantic era, Welsh 'nationalism' was hardly a political force. 'Wales' was partly invented by expatriates in London, founding in 1751 the

Society of Cymmrodorion to celebrate a unified native culture; Wales itself was still riven geographically between north and south, confessionally between church and Dissent. Cultural entrepreneurs like Edward Williams ('Iolo Morganwg') had some success, but not as much as London-based Scots like James Macpherson, author of the poems of national idyll he presented as having been written by an ancient Gaelic bard, 'Ossian'. Macpherson had no Welsh parallel. In Wales it was to be Protestant Dissent that unified the country, but generally with an orientation opposed to the culture of London.

Scotland in the seventeenth century was divided between Gaelic and English speakers, between Highlands and Lowlands, between clanship and market economy, between Presbyterian, Covenanter, Episcopalian and Catholic. Lasting rivalry meant that the victory of Presbyterianism in 1689 was hollow: the abolition of the Edinburgh Parliament by the Union of 1707 was a major symbolic loss, and Scottish resentment long outlasted the Jacobite option. Unionism was always of more importance to the Scottish literati than to the English, and what is now called the 'Scottish Enlightenment' was oriented more to an English Whig myth about the centrality in English history of Parliament, print and Protestantism than to supporting a tenable rival account of Scotland's past and identity. Appropriately, Hume chose to write a *History of England* (1754–62). Lacking a more intellectually defensible account of their homeland, Scottish imaginations were captured in the late eighteenth century by the fictions of 'Ossian', and in the early nineteenth by fake tartanry and biscuit-tin Jacobitism. Macpherson's 'Ossian' was overwritten in Scotland by the powerful mythmaking of that convert to Hanoverianism Sir Walter Scott, notably in his novel *Waverley* (1814). Scott created a cultural image of his country that unified Highland and

Lowland cultures in the Hanoverian interest. It had few immediate political consequences. Engineering and empire later proved much more compelling images.

Ireland's identity was the most bitterly disputed of these four societies. Protestant Ulster necessarily subscribed to a powerful version of the English Whig myth. Memories of the Protestant defence of Londonderry (1689) and of William III's victory at the battle of the Boyne (1690) long retained their potency in Ulster society. Yet this was a self-image that owed most to the Covenanting tradition of south-west Scotland, and so offered only an uneasy basis for co-operation between Ireland and England: many Englishmen remained ambiguous about the Whig myth that others of their fellow countrymen had invented, and were uneasy about the literalistic implementation of that myth to oppress the Catholic majority in Ireland. If Scotland's identity was weakened by its Union of 1707, Ireland's as yet had not benefited from the absence of a union. The Irish Commons in 1703 petitioned for just such a union, although unsuccessfully. Only from the 1770s did the Church of Ireland's adherents begin to construct a patriotism defined against England, but this belated flowering was first frustrated by Westminster, then swamped by the passions unleashed by the French Revolution. Meanwhile the south of Ireland sustained an unmobilised identity, latently built around its Catholicism.

This basic Irish loyalty to the exiled Stuarts was a more potent force than the official adherence of the Ascendancy to the Hanoverians revealed. Jacobite allegiance was driven into a Gaelic culture that was extensive but cut off from anglophone contemporaries and present-day historians alike. Yet it prevented the emergence of a popular cult of loyalty to the wider polity (as the Scots came to celebrate their Union by the

1760s) with long-term consequences: a transition from Jacobite in the 1740s to Jacobin in the 1790s, the movement of the 1820s for Catholic Emancipation, and the eventual reversal of the settlement that followed 1688.[55] This national consciousness was slow to arrive partly because Catholicism functioned in Ireland as a peasant church without significant gentry leadership: the political activation of Catholics was difficult, and when it happened was often conducted by Protestants from Wolfe Tone (1763–98) to Charles Stuart Parnell (1846–91). For a Catholic politician of genius, Ireland had to wait for Daniel O'Connell (1775–1847). Meanwhile, Williamite conquest in 1689–91 meant that the Old English in Ireland could now confidently depict themselves as Irish, look forward to the withering away of Catholicism, and use English constitutionalist arguments against England itself.[56]

If English, Welsh, Irish and Scottish identities were ancient and deep-rooted, much debate has recently turned on when, why and how far a shared 'Britishness' emerged or was promoted after the Unions of 1707 and 1801. The thesis of the shallow roots of Britishness has seemed most persuasive to historians who use the term 'nationalism' as timelessly valid and who find their postmodern preferences for claiming 'nationalism' to have been recently 'constructed' to be confirmed by the weakness of eighteenth-century 'Britishness'. Those who recognise the novelty of 'nationalism' in the early nineteenth century have reservations about the inclusiveness or acceptance of 'Britishness' in the eighteenth. Certainly, the term 'Britain' was used, though often for polemical purposes. Where Scottish Whigs after 1707 made much of it, sometimes rechristening their nation 'North Britain', the Irish elite, increasingly rejecting an image of themselves as colonists and affirming their Irishness, made fewer such bids for inclusion in a shared identity. The term 'British' was problematic for most Irish not least because it implied a common identity with Ulster Protestant Dissenters.[57] Not until the 1830s did Daniel O'Connell offer the Whigs at Westminster the prospect that the Irish, if treated with justice, would 'become a kind of West Britons';[58] it is unclear when such gestures were too late. After 1714, however, the Irish Ascendancy less and less felt threatened by a Stuart restoration; even during the Fifteen and the Forty-five, the Catholics in Ireland were quiescent. As a result, Catholicism was strangely unimportant for national identities before O'Connell, whether by its affirmation or negation.

Protestantism has been proposed as the main foundation for a shared Britishness, but this is a simplistic generalisation. True, England, Scotland and part of Ireland predominantly described themselves as 'Protestant' and at times showed strong populist anti-Catholic sentiments, notably at the time of London's Gordon Riots (1780) but also when the 'Catholic question' was brought forward in Westminster politics after 1805. Yet despite its negations, Protestantism was never able to create a strong shared identity, for it covered a range of mutually antagonistic positions from Episcopalian Anglicanism through Scottish and Ulster Presbyterianism to civil-war sectarianism, and from High Churchmanship, which regarded Rome as a branch of the universal church, to Low Churchmanship and Nonconformity, which had not all ceased to identify the Pope with Antichrist. Only when a foreign enemy was clearly Catholic, and perceived as posing a threat of the reconversion of the British Isles, did a sense of a common cause emerge. But this was not the case between 1660 and 1688, or after 1763. At times, Britain had Catholic allies, like Austria in the wars of Queen Anne's reign. In the American War, Britain faced a continental coalition including the undeniably Protestant United Provinces. After 1793, Britain was at war with atheist France in alliance with Christian states of many denominations. Protestantism was not enough; indeed nothing was enough to unify the three kingdoms in a shared identity if 'identity' is conceived as an essence or principle. But this is a nineteenth-century assumption. Rather, 'identity' should be understood as a descriptive term, deployed for political purposes, not the reflection of an 'underlying' reality.

It seems rather that 'British' was used during these years as a synonym for Englishness, Welshness, Scottishness and to a lesser extent Irishness without the meanings of those identities in popular discourse being essentially modified. This explains why the identities of the four component parts of the British Isles were not equally robust. Wales's identity was in long-term decline before the nineteenth century. Scotland was the loser from the Revolution of 1688, bound by force to an English Whig myth that condoned the extension of English influence, and deprived of its Parliament by the Union of 1707. Protestant Ireland, which retained the Dublin Parliament until the Union of 1801, was similarly locked into an English Whig historical scenario, but one which was openly rejected by the Catholic majority of its population.

The commonly used name for this composite polity was 'England', a conventional usage, just as the citizens of the United States today refer to themselves as 'Americans' in disregard of the many other states occupying the American continent. Edmund Burke, whom everyone knew to be Irish born, wrote of himself in c.1790 as 'an Englishman'.[59] The Scottish MP David Scott complained in the House of Commons about an Irish MP in 1805: 'we commonly, when speaking of British subjects, call them English, be they English,

Scotch or Irish; he, therefore, I hope, will never be offended with the word English being applied in future to express any of his majesty's subjects, or suppose it can be meant as an allusion to any particular part of the united kingdom'.[60] No other MP contested his claim. What changed this situation fundamentally was not the weakening of the English formula for describing a free, law-bound, patriotic people but the increasing participation of Irish and Scots in military, overseas and imperial enterprise after c.1776: the term 'British' now came into vogue, but mainly as a euphemism for the Irish and Scots when abroad.

With the exception of hated tax officials, England lacked powerful centralising institutions of government apart from the church: law and religion rather than a bureaucracy had long functioned as the symbolic agencies of state-building. Indeed the term 'state' was not often used; the conventional term was 'kingdom'. Because England was usually seen as a personalised kingdom rather than an abstract and secular state, and because the notion of 'the community of the realm' had been strong since the Middle Ages, registering a sense of popular involvement in the conduct of that kingdom, no clear antagonism developed in England between the ideas of 'the nation' and 'the state', as often happened in Europe, at least until the rise of radicalism after 1815. If so, it was not that 'the upper classes' appropriated 'patriotism' in a cynical manoeuvre to defend their ascendancy, but rather that all groups, Whig and Tory, rich and poor, could more easily picture themselves as patriotic participants in a national epic. In 1776–83 and 1793–1815 that epic took on tragic and sanguinary dimensions that only bound its participants closer together. Although a strand of ruthless satire of monarchs continued throughout the century, George III emerged from his early unpopularity to win widespread respect and even affection among his subjects.[61]

The identity that triumphed in the wars of 1793–1815 was largely England's. Wellington was born in Ireland, but pointed out that a man's being born in a stable did not make him a horse. Nelson was a loyal Norfolk man; Collingwood bore a famous Northumbrian name. England was repeatedly in the front line. It was English fleets that ruled the waves, whatever the Scot James Thompson had written in 1740 in 'Rule Britannia'. For this combination of xenophobia and armed assertion the term used when overseas was 'British', but the English at home normally called themselves English, and local identities took priority in Wales, Ireland and Scotland also.[62] It might be argued that the assembly of these societies into the Union of 1801 was political more than cultural, but the opposite view has also been expressed.

War meant that English national identity was strengthened around the core of providential mission, a self-image Protestant and constitutionalist. So successful was this idea (attracting a wealth of images and celebration that reached a crescendo in 1814–15) that the later doctrine of 'nationalism' never fully replaced it. By 'nationalism' we mean the racial-linguistic premises of national identity that took shape on the continent in response to the advance of Jacobinism and the dictatorship of Napoleon. These new ideas had some points of similarity with the older premises of 'providential' identity, and later seemed to be synonymous with them; at the time there were fundamental differences.

Older ideas survived in England into the twentieth century, producing a society markedly less open to racialism than many societies in Europe. This was less true of Scotland and Ireland, which in the nineteenth century were to develop forms of 'nationalism' (forms that never, however, persuaded all of the Scots or Irish). Scottish and Irish identities in the eighteenth century were less triumphalist than England's, lacking the English sense of providential destiny, and their societies were less robustly successful; the scene was set for the rise of different ways of picturing collective identity in Scotland and Ireland in the idiom of Romantic nationalism. Yet by 1832, this could hardly be foreseen.

Oligarchy: the Hanoverian succession, 1714–1760

Northern Europe was not the libertarian Utopia that later Whig myth depicted. In 1694 a Whig, Robert Molesworth, had warned of the authoritarian tendencies of Lutheranism (a warning that, arguably, was vindicated in the twentieth century). Germany indeed was 'freer then any other part of *Europe*, till at length 'twas lorded by *Captains*, (which in process of time grew *Princes* and *Electors*)'. Lutheranism, Molesworth argued, 'has succeeded as effectually in this Design' of establishing slavery 'as ever Popery did'.[63] The republican John Toland echoed the same concerns in 1701, on the eve of the Commons vote on the bill that would fix the succession in Sophia, Electress of Hanover, and her heirs. Toland was torn between the need to guard against a Stuart restoration, and the threat to English liberties that a Hanoverian monarch might pose. A 'politick and ambitious *Lutheran* prince' might use his German standing army and co-operate with Anglican clergy to 'make himself as Arbitrary in *England*, as most of the princes are in *Germany*'.[64] Toland suggested the division of the British and Hanoverian successions; this idea was not adopted, but the anti-Hanover rhetoric created by such authors became common property, and was taken up and developed especially by Tories.

In 1714 the installation of the German-speaking Elector of Hanover proved widely unpopular: there were riots throughout England that autumn. The king shared these misgivings. According to Lady Mary Wortley Montagu, whose husband, as a Commissioner of the Treasury, knew the incoming king well, George I had been 'free from ambition' but was propelled to the throne of England by 'the ambition of those about him' in Hanover; 'the natural honesty of his temper, joined with the narrow notions of a low education, made him look upon his acceptance of the crown as an act of usurpation, which was always uneasy to him'.[65] As late as 1828, George III's daughter Princess Augusta reportedly 'said lately to a private friend, "I was ashamed to hear myself called Princess Augusta, and never could persuade myself that I was so, as long as any of the Stuart family were alive; but after the death of Cardinal York [James III's son, in 1807], I felt myself to be really Princess Augusta."'[66]

George I's English Whig minders correctly understood that many of their Tory opponents were implicated in the Stuart cause; this was confirmed by the flight, to escape impeachment, of Henry St John, Viscount Bolingbroke. Once in France he was the focus of an international diplomatic effort aimed at securing financial and military support for a restoration. Louis XIV's death in September 1715 removed France from the equation, since the regent was determined to abide by the terms of the Treaty of Utrecht in order to allow France to recover from a disastrous war, but over time many powers emerged as potential Stuart backers including Spain, Sweden, Russia and finally Prussia. The Fifteen went ahead without a French army. Even so, it achieved striking successes; George I hung on, perhaps by a small margin.[67]

The Tory party had already been blighted in George's eyes for concluding the Treaty of Utrecht in 1713, ending the war but abandoning Britain's allies (as they saw it), including Hanover. The Fifteen meant that George I and George II were convinced beyond the possibility of argument that Tories were crypto-Jacobites; earlier ideals of supra-party ministries were abandoned, and Britain became a one-party state. This tactic, aimed at stability, itself destabilised the state. Much now depended on internal manoeuvres within the governing Whigs. This monopoly contributed to just what the Whigs feared: Tories, systematically excluded from public life, often did turn to the Jacobite option as the only way of retrieving their position. John Wesley echoed such perceptions:

The king of a faction, is but the sovereign of half his subjects. Of this, however, the new-elected monarch did not seem sensible. It was his misfortune, that he was hemmed round by men who soured him with all their own prejudices. None but the leaders of a party were now admitted into employment. The Whigs, while they pretended to secure the crown for their king, were with all possible arts confirming their own interests, extending their connexions, and giving laws to their sovereign. An instantaneous and total change was made in all the offices of trust, honour, or advantage. The Whigs governed the senate and the court; whom they would, they oppressed; bound the lower orders of people with severe laws, and kept them at a distance by vile distinctions; and then taught them to call this – Liberty.

Wesley, however, placed a Hanoverian Tory interpretation on the situation:

> It was thus that this monarch was tutored by the faction around him, to look with an evil eye on subjects that never opposed the succession; subjects that detested a popish monarch, and whose only fault was the desire of being governed rather by a king, than a junto of their fellow-subjects who assumed his power.[68]

Sometimes this was true; but Jacobitism may have had more of a following than Wesley's protest allowed.

In Scotland the options were starker, for the Highland clans retained an ability to turn out large numbers of men in arms. Not all of the clans were Jacobite, so that the art of Scottish politics for forty years became that of managing, buying off or coercing enough of the chiefs to minimise the Jacobites' military potential. This Whig effort finally succeeded: the Forty-five was not a rebellion by Scotland against England, since as many Scots fought for King George as for King James. Before this system of suborning had gone far, the Fifteen stood a better chance: it failed chiefly because its component parts could not co-ordinate action. In Ireland, remarkably, nothing happened: persecution worked.

This dire strategic situation, and a sense of the insecurity of the succession, led the new Whig ministers to push through the Septennial Act of 1716, extending Parliament's term before the next general election from three years to seven. This profoundly oligarchical move, which according to its critics 'vested the ministry with a dictatorial power over the liberties of the people',[69] was intended to make the Commons more subject to executive control and had just that result. At

Westminster, power was monopolised not just by the Whig party but by the Whig manager most able to hold them together and deliver stable, reliable government to his monarch. That proved to be the achievement above all of Robert Walpole (1676–1745), the king's chief minister from 1721 to 1742. First returned to Parliament in 1701, a leader in that classic show trial, the impeachment of Dr Sacheverell, in 1709–10, Walpole well knew the high stakes for which an ideologically polarised politics was played. Impeached himself in 1712, Walpole turned the tables on his Tory enemies after the accession of George I, arranging the impeachment of Robert Harley and Bolingbroke. A 'country' Whig by instinct, he abandoned his principles to organise the smokescreen behind which court corruption hid after England's first great financial scandal, the bursting of the South Sea Bubble in September 1721. This economic crisis was an index not of a new consumer society, but of governmental corruption.

Previous first ministers like Harley and Henry St John had chosen to move to the Lords (as Earl of Oxford and Viscount Bolingbroke respectively). Although a commoner, deliberately sitting in the lower House of Parliament, Walpole held office because successive monarchs chose him; he was never the people's choice and did not signify the arrival of a society free from the dominance of the nobility. He was, nevertheless, an archetypal House of Commons man. Chesterfield said that he was

> the best parliament-man, and the ablest manager of parliament, that I believe ever lived. An artful rather than an eloquent speaker, he saw, as by intuition, the disposition of the house, and pressed or receded accordingly . . . He was not, it is true, the inventor of

that shameful method of governing which had been
gaining ground insensibly ever since Charles the Second,
but with uncommon skill and unbounded profusion he
brought it to that perfection which at this time dis-
honours and distresses this country.[70]

Walpole knew that his own position depended on the survival
of the Hanoverian dynasty. The British secret service was
highly developed: it uncovered the plot of 1717, involving an
army to be provided by Charles XII of Sweden, and also the
English conspiracy launched in 1722 that carries the name of
its leading figure, Bishop Francis Atterbury. Walpole exploited
the occasion in a show trial in which he may have secured
Atterbury's conviction by forging evidence, and used the
verdict to brand all his Tory opponents as Jacobites.[71] During
the reigns of the first two Georges, recalled John Wesley, 'It
was the artifice . . . to stigmatise all those who testified their
discontent, as Papists and Jacobites. All who ventured to speak
against their [the ministers'] measures, were reproached as
designing to bring in the pretender.' This meant that some
'were now driven by resentment and apprehension into a
system of politics they would not otherwise have dreamt of.
Some of the Tory party, who were men attached to the
protestant religion, and of moderate principles in government,
began to associate with the Jacobites, and to wish in earnest
for a revolution.'[72]

More, indeed, than Wesley knew: of 140 Tory MPs who sat
in Parliament between 1741 and 1745, evidence survives that
at least fifty-six had traceable links to active Jacobite conspiracy
even at that late date; the real figure must have been higher,
had evidence not been destroyed, and the number of passive
sympathisers higher again.[73] This commitment could not be

openly avowed, but an anti-authoritarian rhetoric could: Tory MP Sir John St Aubyn famously said in a Commons debate in 1742 that 'we lived under a Prince who being used to arbitrary power in his dominions abroad, was minded to establish it here'.[74] He had a point: many policy issues could be referred back to the issue of an over-mighty executive. The excise scheme of 1733, which would have converted the customs duties on wine and tobacco into excises, aroused a storm of protest in exactly this idiom; indeed the American controversy over the Stamp Act of 1765 (which extended to the colonies a metropolitan tax on official documents) was a replay of it. In 1733 men feared, or could claim to fear, an army of excise officers, armed with executive power derived from the central government rather than from local JPs, with arbitrary powers of entry and search, the resulting cases subject to the decisions of the Excise Commissioners rather than jury trial. In the face of this storm, Walpole withdrew the scheme. In an era when constitutionalist issues could be a disguise for more serious dynastic politics, Walpole's motto had to be *Quieta non movere*, 'let sleeping dogs lie'.

It was not enough to make George II popular among the political elite. He had, wrote Lady Mary Wortley Montagu, only 'a small understanding' but an authoritarian temperament:

> He looked on all the men and women he saw as creatures he might kick or kiss for his diversion; and, whenever he met with any opposition in those designs, he thought his opposers insolent rebels to the will of God, who created them for his use, and judged of the merit of all people by their ready submission to his orders, or the relation they had to his power.[75]

He was not an obvious improvement on James II.

George II's reign was a public-relations disaster. But this, and the dynastic threat, meant that Walpole became indispensable to the first two Hanoverians in turn. For Walpole, the end justified the means: he raised political corruption to a high art, ironically using James II's techniques of parliamentary management to first pack and then manage the House of Commons. From the 1722 election Walpole had direct control of the 'secret service money', funds voted by Parliament for espionage as part of the 'civil list' or annual royal household expenses and so not subject to direct parliamentary scrutiny. Much of it now found its way to political purposes. According to its opponents, such a system debased public life. John Wesley was moved to fury even thirty years later:

> The vice, luxury, and prostitution of the age, the almost total extinction of sentiment, honour, and public spirit, had prepared the minds of men for slavery and corruption. The means were in the hands of the ministry: the public treasure was at their devotion; they multiplied places and pensions to increase the number of their dependants: they squandered away the money of the nation, without taste, discernment, decency, or remorse: they enlisted an army of the most abandoned emissaries.[76]

It is hard to quantify corruption, but the perception was widespread that it existed.

From this system Walpole profited hugely, building for himself at Houghton in Norfolk a vast mansion that rivalled Marlborough's (but Blenheim Palace was legally funded by a grateful Parliament). The details of Walpole's corrupt financial dealings have been concealed by the weeding of his papers, but the effects of corruption are still to be seen; even so, he was only the most blatant of a political class that profited from the gravy train of early Hanoverian politics. The public saw a different Walpole: the competent financier, the arranger of parliamentary business, a man anxious to keep the land tax low and the landed interest sweet. They read the official press and the subsidised journalists who praised Walpole's regime as delivering civil liberty and religious toleration to a degree hardly known elsewhere in Europe. They did not always hear of the persecution of the opposition press, the stage censorship, the bending of the law to hound political opponents. Were the ministerial Whigs the true friends of liberty, or were they, as Wesley recorded, 'a party, actuated by pride, avarice, and animosity, concealing a love of power under a mask of freedom'?[77]

The accession of George I also meant British entanglement in Hanoverian affairs, for George's first priority was his Electorate. Hanover, unlike England, Scotland and Ireland, boasted little tradition of representative institutions: it had ancient estates, but these had 'slumbered for decades', and the elector ruled consensually through a series of councils whose members were chosen by himself. It could too easily be argued by British critics that Georg Ludwig was an absolute monarch in Hanover.[78] John Wesley, writing of the 'foreign treaties and alliances', recorded: 'It was natural for a king born and bred in Germany, where all sovereignty is possessed upon such precarious tenures, to introduce the same spirit into Britain, however independent on the rest of Europe.'[79] George's position was unchallenged within the Electorate; but Hanover was menaced militarily by the rise of Prussia and, ultimately, Russia. Consequently Britain was drawn into a system of subsidy treaties to defend Hanover's strategic position, notably treaties with neighbouring small states like Hesse-Cassel for the hire of mercenary troops.

From 1721 a parliamentary opposition was created by co-operation between Tories and a group at the opposite end of the spectrum, the Opposition Whigs. A 'country' programme was devised as a lowest common denominator, demanding cheap government, low taxes, an end to corruption and foreign involvements. But these groups worked badly together until in 1730 the Tories suddenly began to give full backing to their Whig allies. This was the result of instructions that the Tory party received from James III in Rome.

Despite his mastery of the black arts, even Walpole's grip on Parliament eventually faltered. The opposition bloc steadily grew in the early 1730s, especially in the 1734 election, and strengthened again from 1737 when Frederick, the Hanoverian Prince of Wales, gave it his backing. Walpole's demand for undeviating loyalty meant that he increasingly alienated, and dismissed, able young men who objected to some aspect of his policy, notably Lord Cobham's friends, William Pitt, the Grenvilles and the Lytteltons. Walpole even lost control of the City of London, where a Jacobite group remained strong, and this group helped push him into war in 1739. Even so, the Tories did not back a key Opposition Whig vote of censure in February 1741, fearing a trick to exclude them, the Tories, from the resulting ministry. Only a direct order from James III reversed this stance. The 1741 election saw yet more ministerial losses, and in January 1742 Walpole lost by one vote a key division in the Commons on an election petition: no longer able to rig the composition of the House, the game was up, and he resigned.

Why, then, had he been so successful for so long? One reason was his willingness to leave religion untouched. Just as Charles II had to lean away from his natural allies, the churchmen, after 1660, so Walpole had to lean away from his natural allies, the Protestant Dissenters, after 1721. He did not purge the universities, the church, or the commissions of the peace of Tories, as the Stanhope–Sunderland ministry of 1717–21 had threatened to do. He resisted parliamentary inquiries into corruption and maladministration, lest they should set precedents. He did not reconstruct Highland society after the Fifteen, as happened after the Forty-five. Lord Hervey, a Walpole loyalist first in the Commons, then the Lords, wrote of him: 'his great maxim in policy was to keep everything else as undisturbed as he could, to bear with some abuses rather than risk reformations and submit to old inconveniences rather than encourage innovations'.[80]

In religious affairs this meant an attempt to placate churchmen. Protestant Dissenters did not find that their hour had come in 1721, although the Whig ministries that followed the accession of George I had seemed to augur a new dawn. Walpole well remembered the cry 'Church in danger' that had made the Whigs' formal victory in the impeachment of Dr Sacheverell recoil on themselves in the general election of 1710. Unexpectedly, Walpole chose to deal with High Churchmen. In Edmund Gibson, Bishop of Lincoln 1716–23 and of London 1723–48, he found a Whig High Churchman able to manage the ecclesiastical interest for him. In 1732 Walpole dissuaded Dissenters from applying for a repeal of the Test and Corporation Acts, and in 1736, when this was proposed in the Commons by an Opposition Whig MP, Walpole spoke and voted against, securing the measure's defeat. Yet Walpole's judgement had its limits. The same year he backed a proposal to relieve his electoral allies the Quakers from the obligation to pay tithes; when this was defeated in the Lords by the bishops, the alliance was broken.

Quieta non movere applied also in foreign affairs, where Walpole's chief goal was to keep the peace; but although this shielded Britain from another Fifteen, it allowed a dynamic France steadily to recover from defeat in Marlborough's wars and to press forward in trade and in colonial expansion, especially in North America and India. A growing mood of xenophobia now cast France as Britain's natural and implacable enemy; if Walpole had an interest in peace, the opposition had an interest in war. It was the opposition that drove Walpole into war with Spain over trade rivalry in 1739, a conflict that escalated to a general European conflict in 1740. Although France was formally not yet at war, the Jacobite option now presented itself once more to French politicians; not necessarily to restore James III to his three kingdoms at once, but perhaps to effect a restoration in Scotland alone, so dividing and weakening British strength.

The result was a major French invasion attempt timed for 1744, aimed against London, aligned with a carefully orchestrated Jacobite conspiracy across England and Scotland, the expedition to be led in person by James III's eldest son, Charles Edward Stuart. It was a real threat, even though, on Walpole's fall, the leading Whigs in opposition had generally accepted ministerial office and abandoned their Tory allies. Again in 1744 the British secret service uncovered the plot, and a violent storm in the Channel smashed the fleet of transports assembled at Dunkirk. France now declared war, but with France unwilling to restart the project, Prince Charles tried an unsupported invasion, carried in only two ships and with only the arms that slender Stuart finances could purchase. Of these two, one ship was intercepted and failed to reach Scotland. Even then, his success was remarkable. Yet France's quickly reactivated plans for an invasion were delayed.

Charles's hastily assembled army achieved successes in Scotland, but, invading England, his council chose not to take the east coast route, which might have captured Newcastle, centre of the coal trade, and produced a financial crisis in London. Instead they advanced south on the western route through Lancashire. Capturing Manchester, they penetrated to Derby. Yet his council was unaware that the government troops standing between them and London were few and disorganised; he was in the hands of advisers, predominantly Scots, swayed by the reluctance of the English to join a rising mostly Scottish in personnel, and who gave priority to Scottish matters rather than to a bid for London. It was his council that compelled Charles to turn back; steadily drained of funds, he was finally brought to a decisive battle at Culloden in April 1746. No overseas aid arrived in time, while the Hanoverians were able to bring back troops from Germany.

What was the significance of the Forty-five? More Englishmen joined the Jacobite invasion than was once thought, but not enough. English Whig opinion often treated the advance of Charles's army as doubly unwelcome because largely Scots. Many denounced a threat to English liberties from a Catholic monarch. On the other hand, few Englishmen were prepared to volunteer to fight for George II, and the social base of the Hanoverian monarchy was shown to be perilously narrow. In 1776 John Wesley wrote that had Charles advanced from Derby, 'he might probably have made himself master of the metropolis, where he would certainly have been joined by a considerable number of his well-wishers, who waited impatiently for his approach'.[81] Many of the most impressive moral figures in public life were in a broad sense against the system, like Alexander Pope, William Law, Samuel Johnson and John Wesley; they came after a generation of Nonjurors who had given up all worldly advantage for principle. It is not clear whether Walpole was more corrupt than other Whig

THE LOYAL ASSOCIATORS

For King & Country

IN
THE YEAR
OF OUR LORD
MDCCXLV.

An Unnatural Rebelion *being rais'd in* Scotland, *in Favour of a* Popeish Pretender, *Several* Worthy Gentlemen, Eminent Merchants, Tradesmen, &c. *Form'd an Association to Defend the Person of* His Most Sacred Majesty *KING GEORGE, together with the* Rights *and* Liberties *of a* Free Born People, *In Commemoration of which* Glorious *and* Loyal Act, *This Plate is Engraved & is most Humbly Inscribed to all true Lovers of* Liberty *&* Property; *by their most Obedient Servt.* Jno. English

8. Whig propaganda, 1745. The engraving depicts solid citizens rallying consensually to defeat the Jacobite menace. In reality, remarkably few Englishmen enlisted to defend the Hanoverian monarch. It purports to be engraved by 'Jno. English'; in fact, the artist was Louis Philippe Boitard, a Huguenot with a desperate pre-commitment against the Catholic Stuarts. Is this image evidence of what occurred?

politicians, like Stanhope and Sunderland, who held power after 1714 and whose influence was limited only by their early deaths; but so it seemed to many.

Even after Culloden, Henry Pelham and the Duke of Newcastle, the main players in the Whig government in London, continued to fear Stuart initiatives, especially if Charles were to leave France not for Rome but Geneva and there abjure Catholicism. In 1750 he clandestinely visited London and was received into the Church of England. But it was too late, and his act did not offset the decision of his younger brother Henry in 1747 to become a cardinal in the Catholic Church. A Jacobite conspiracy followed Charles's visit, known as the Elibank plot, but was again smashed in 1753 by the British secret service. Even so, the 1740s and 50s were years of political instability, not complacent stability.

Meanwhile, Anglo-French rivalry in North America was leading to armed conflict in the Ohio valley, and this triggered the outbreak of war in 1756. Britain's conquest of Canada raised the stakes: in the last Jacobite invasion attempt, in 1759, a French force of no less than 48,000 men was intended to land at Portsmouth, covered by the French fleet. It was this menacing and militarily feasible invasion plan, the like of which was not seen again until 1805, that was destroyed by the Royal Navy's victories at Lagos, off the coast of Portugal, and Quiberon Bay.

Not for nothing was 1759 known as *annus mirabilis*. The whole orientation of British foreign and domestic policy now changed. From an internal focus on threats of dismemberment, or a preoccupation with the intricate politics of minor German territories, British governments now looked outwards to the conquest, extension and exploitation of a world empire. The Duke of Cumberland's savage repression of the Highlands after Culloden was eclipsed: in 1760, on the death of George II, what remained of the Tories returned to court. James III's death in 1766 made no waves in Britain; even the Pope refused to recognise Charles Edward Stuart as his heir. When he in turn died in 1788, his brother Henry's claim to succeed him persuaded no European rulers.

Imperial connections: the significance of empire

Empire has become a fashionable subject, often led by the preoccupations of American academe and fuelled by American postmodernism. The projection of such anti-imperialist sentiments onto Britain has led to claims that eighteenth-century Britain was deeply shaped by its imperial experience; that British culture was profoundly 'imperialist'; that racialism was rampant in Britain, and British public opinion was oriented towards conquest at the expense of liberty. Yet this 'new imperial history' often rests on untested assumptions rather than on adequate research. It is challenged, for example, by Bernard Porter's study of British attitudes to empire in the nineteenth and twentieth centuries that attempts to quantify themes and preoccupations in popular culture. This research reveals a widespread British indifference towards, and ignorance of, all things imperial; it locates eager concern for empire primarily in those small social groups actively involved in its military or civil administration. Such a survey suggests that Britons' sense of superiority was based on cultural, as opposed to racial, assumptions; that strategic calculations revolved around defence against perceived foreign threats rather than 'militaristic' assertion; and that attitudes to the monarchy at home were not projected as imperialism abroad.[82]

If this is true of the nineteenth century, it is probably more true of the eighteenth.

An exception to this general pattern of indifference was in attitudes towards colonies of settlement; but before 1776 these were generally called 'colonies' in the plural rather than 'empire' in the singular, and were unsystematically and miscellaneously understood in terms of discovery, lawful purchase, occupation or beneficial development rather than in terms of the expropriation of and domination over native inhabitants: the first is a view that continues to characterise the United States' attitude to its title to its own vast land empire in North America. In the eighteenth century, apart from the east coast of North America, Britain's overseas possessions were scattered, small, and heterogeneous, acquired for a bewildering variety of reasons. Historical analysis questions the demand to define them as an 'empire' sustained by 'imperialism'.[83] Few Englishmen held such a theoretical vision. After 1707, some Scots sought to persuade London to accept a more coherent and devolved view of the polity as a whole;[84] before the 1780s, this was never achieved.

The English, and to a lesser extent the Scots, sought trade and (though not as fervently as in the seventeenth century) security for their various religious denominations, not a great land empire integrated into the domestic polity. James II had pursued a clearer definition of colonial relations, but had no time to achieve it; the contested and ambiguous outcome of the Revolution of 1688 meant that empire was left similarly undefined. The peripheries (Scotland, Ireland and finally the American colonies) could achieve leverage against England by appealing to 'Revolution principles', the principles allegedly vindicated in 1688. Since people had often understood these differently, it was an argument that the metropolitan government could never decisively win.

Argument was possible partly because possession was not new, and antiquity created complexity. England had had overseas territories before: by the fifteenth century the English came to see large parts of France as 'their' lands more than they saw England as a subordinate kingdom still occupied by Normans as a result of the conquest of 1066. The final loss of these possessions after the battle of Castillon (1453), the last battle of the Hundred Years War, turned England in on itself. Colonial expansion in the New World in the early seventeenth century looked set to reverse this insularity, but in the event was only ever the enthusiasm of small numbers: more English and Scots emigrated to Ulster than to North America, and civil war in the 1640s made inhabitants of the islands look inwards once more. There was even a reverse migration of religious zealots from New England, eager to leap onto the bandwagon of reformation in the homeland.

In 1660 Charles II, and his brother James, returned with wider horizons. Both were fascinated by science, technology, maritime enterprise and trade; both were well aware that the customs revenue rather than the land tax was the backbone of royal finance. New York and Carolina testify by their names to this new enthusiasm for overseas involvement. Although religious geopolitics played a part, and still influenced the decisions of individuals to emigrate, state policy became more and more focused on trade and naval power. Slowly, Britain realigned itself: in 1700–1, about 85 per cent of Britain's trade by value was with continental Europe. By 1750–1, this had fallen slightly to 77 per cent, and thereafter fell dramatically: by 1772–3 it was 49 per cent, and by 1797–8 (although during major continental war) 30 per cent.[85] But after 1814, trade with Europe again grew as a proportion of total British trade: as these fluctuating trends demonstrate, there was no necessarily growing orientation towards 'empire'.

Colonies were one thing; 'empire' was another. Some historians seek to depict 'an empire', and 'imperialism', from an early date. Others doubt that English, or British, policy had such a coherence, and deny that the United Kingdom was established in 1707 for the purposes of overseas expansion. According to this view, the Union was an episode in the European war against France; the Scottish city that traded most with overseas territories, Glasgow, was the most hostile to the Union.[86] England's and Britain's involvements overseas were diverse, and all such engagements depended on the unpredictable outcomes of military conflict. Britain's possessions were too diverse, too far-flung, acquired for too many different reasons, and too often seen as counters to be traded in the great game of European power politics for a clear sense of an empire to emerge. Nor were Britain's overseas possessions united by any coherent, systematic legal or political theory: the legal and constitutional relations between colonies and homeland were defined in imprecise and often contradictory ways, a problem that was demonstrated by the transatlantic controversies that followed 1763 and which paved the way for the breakdown of government in 1776.

The evolution of polities in America was still shaped chiefly by European dynastic contests. This was true of the dispute over the Spanish succession from 1700, for it entailed a decision over the future course of Spain's American possessions and triggered conflicts between English and French settlers there on just that issue. The War of the Spanish Succession was a world war, fought also in North America. It was at this point that French strategy became clear: to pen in the British settlements to the eastern seaboard by promoting a French colony in Louisiana, so ensuring control of the Mississippi, and to secure a fortress at Detroit, commanding the Great Lakes and excluding the British from the north-west. French power would join the two, in alliance with Native American tribes.

British military involvements overseas did not therefore operate in some independent sphere, governed by calculations about 'empire'; they were, from an early date, peripheral extensions of European conflicts. This was true of Franco-British rivalries in North America from 1689 and in India from the 1740s; the Seven Years War began with a failed attempt to prevent the escalation of such conflicts in the Ohio valley. At least until the 1750s, colonial conflicts were of secondary concern to London governments; from the 1760s it was North American colonists who demanded a redefinition of empire more than British imperialists who sought to impose it on them. Britain's concerns focused after 1714 on Hanover, and the continental entanglements that this brought; soon an added threat was identified by France's resurgence. French seaborne trade expanded from some 50 per cent of Britain's in the 1720s to over 80 per cent in the 1780s: British policy failed to check this fundamental and adverse shift in the balance of power.[87]

Although wars after 1689 steadily increased the national debt and gave rise to fears of national bankruptcy, the same wars could act as stimulants to certain sectors of the economy, especially shipbuilding and iron. Technological change sometimes followed this stimulus, like the development of the reverberatory furnace in the 1690s. Successful wars might open export markets and extend colonies (the war of 1776–83 being the chief exception). War in Europe often disrupted continental economies and opened opportunities for British merchants and manufacturers. Debate continues on whether those wars, especially at the end of the eighteenth century, depressed living standards and retarded growth: some argue that industry acquired its capital locally, away from national financial markets; but, if so, the significance of the 'financial revolution' of the 1690s might be revised downwards.

By 1763 the strategy which Britain adopted in 1689, the attempt to reduce the power of France, seemed triumphantly vindicated. France had lost North America; was saddled with debts that it could hardly afford to service; and had suffered humiliating defeats. But defeat only made Europe's superpower more determined to reverse that verdict, and from 1763 French policy was dedicated to doing just that when Britain was reducing its involvement with Europe.[88] That policy succeeded beyond the French minister Choiseul's dreams when, in 1783, the Treaty of Paris recognised the independence of thirteen of Britain's colonies. This had implications for Britain's attitude towards her remaining overseas possessions, finally perceived as an 'empire'. It is debated how far the loss of the Thirteen Colonies redirected British attention to the east. Some have argued for a 'new imperialism' directed towards dark-skinned peoples; yet British commercial and colonial activity in India, China and the East Indies long predated 1783. Where the monopolies enjoyed by the Royal African Company and the Levant Company had been terminated in the 1750s, the East India Company (founded in 1600) retained its unique position, and continued to be the semi-official arm of the state in territorial acquisition as well as trade; its charter was renewed, although reformed, in 1792. In economic terms, the 'first' British empire was still more important than the 'second': after 1783, the area of fastest growth of trade was again North America, as pre-war relations resumed. The east may have captured the imaginations of later anti-imperialists, but eighteenth-century merchants still looked to the bottom line: North America.

The accession of George III (1760) and the controversy it generated

In the reigns of George I and George II the Tory/Jacobite part of the nation adopted and developed a political rhetoric that implicitly challenged the Hanoverian monarchy without specifically addressing it (this would have been treasonable); instead, they denounced ministerial corruption, incompetence, political manipulation, high taxation to fund entanglements abroad, the role of foreigners in British affairs, the growing influence of the army; they summed up these concerns as the insidious advance of 'tyranny' or 'arbitrary power'. It was a rhetoric related to that of the Whigs in the Exclusion Crisis of 1679–81, and all the stronger for this older resonance. This rhetoric proliferated at home, and was absorbed by Britain's colonies in North America. In 1760 the accession of George III at the age of twenty-two, and the eclipse of the Jacobite option, meant that many former Tories and/or Jacobites could move to a position much more sympathetic to the regime, like William Blackstone, England's leading jurist, and Samuel Johnson, England's leading man of letters. Their Whig contemporaries, still fearful, loudly denied that the Tories had undergone any such sea change.

Some historians echoed the concerns of Whigs of Burke's generation, claiming that the accession of George III saw a 'new Toryism'; but this has been cogently refuted.[89] George III was heir to a Whig understanding of the constitution based on the Revolution settlement and on parliamentary consent, a view taught to him by his wholly Whig tutor, John Stuart, Earl of Bute. But this Whig theory was idealistic more than practical. In one crucial respect it looked back before the Walpolian oligarchy to William III's attempt to sustain ministries drawn from men of all parties. This supra-party idealism was put into action when the politicians of the Whig establishment (the Duke of Newcastle, his legal henchman the Earl of Hardwicke, and the man they had recruited to help them win the war, William Pitt) insisted on prolonging a ruinously expensive conflict to secure war aims on the continent that public opinion decreasingly saw as necessary or attainable. This could only end in their departure from the ministry, Pitt in 1761, Newcastle in 1762.

Once in opposition, the Whig 'old corps' spoke a different language, quickly developing a critique of the monarchy while George III sought ministers able to hold together a non-party, coalition government. This attempt produced a decade of political instability in the 1760s. When in 1770 the king finally found a politician able to deliver stability (Frederick, Lord North, the holder of a courtesy title as the son of a peer, and so able to sit in the House of Commons), the opposition groups were even more indignant. The best known of them was led by the Marquess of Rockingham, and it was his secretary, Edmund Burke, who produced the most famous theory of Britain's constitutional ills.[90] The king, it ran, sustained a system of 'double Cabinet' whereby the major decisions were taken behind the scenes by a shadowy group of ministers not subject to parliamentary control; this bid for royal absolutism was concerted by the sinister figure of the Earl of Bute, formally in private life since 1763 but in fact still running the government. So Burke argued, and others found it politically useful to accept this fiction.

9. The Balanced Constitution: Con. In 1770 Lord Bute is upsetting the balanced constitution and its symbols of liberty with the aid of the king's little finger, emerging from a cloud. Was Bute's persisting image wholly mythical?

Burke's theory was a paranoid fantasy that did not describe how the real world worked; as a result, it was worse than useless for the Whigs, and offered them no way of returning to power by deploying a correct analysis of their situation. It led to increasing denunciations within Britain of the policies of George III's ministers on all matters that could seem to have major constitutional implications. In British domestic policy, this began with the controversy got up over the excise on cider proposed by Bute's ministry in 1763; it continued with the outcry manufactured around the figure of John Wilkes, excluded from the Commons in 1764 on charges of blasphemous and seditious libel, but demanding readmission as a right. The outcry over the Stamp Act in 1765 went over the same ground already explored in Walpole's excise scheme in 1733. This rhetoric denouncing 'tyranny' was fully developed on British issues before colonial American problems arose: in Britain, the opposition depicted ministries attempting to rivet the chains of 'slavery' on America as a preliminary to doing the same in Britain also. Colonial political rhetoric, like colonial consumer goods, was mostly imported from the home country: if politicians in London were speaking this language, it could only seem convincing, or at least a golden opportunity, to colonial American politicians also.

Some historians treated Wilkes as expressing, or catalysing, a new middle-class consciousness in British politics; others depicted him as expressing 'radicalism'. Both class and radicalism can now be dated more accurately to the early nineteenth century. Wilkes himself stood in an older tradition, like the journalist and Irish MP Charles Lucas (1713–71) in the Dublin politics of the 1740s, playing on a popular libertarian tradition. Far from embodying a constructive programme to involve the masses or even the middling sort in politics, Wilkes was an

10. The Balanced Constitution: Pro. In *c*.1774, the constitution is depicted as a tripod supporting scales in which 'Religion', 'Law' and 'Authority' balance 'Liberty', 'Right' and 'Obedience'. Who believed this, and why?

opportunist who dropped the mob when he secured a lucrative sinecure from the City of London; just as Wilkes was no radical, his ministerial opponents were no reactionaries.

Wilkes carried forward, but transmuted, the (often covertly Jacobite) early eighteenth-century denunciation of 'arbitrary power' in the hands of Hanoverian monarchs. Nor was he an independent political actor; he was the instrument of Earl Temple, brother-in-law of William Pitt, and as such was in harmony with other developments: the long-standing hostility of early eighteenth-century London to Walpolian government, the hostility of Dissent (now reviving) to the church, the long-standing attachment of a wider public opinion to a constitutionalist libertarianism. The novel ideology of universal manhood suffrage was circulating in small circles in the 1760s, but Wilkes did not adopt it. Radicalism was born in the 1820s, of different parents. Without radicalism, Wilkes in London and Charles Lucas, returned to the Dublin Parliament in 1761, created through the 1760s an idiom of populist, anti-ministerial reform, indebted chiefly to English 'country' Whig ideology.

The American Revolution as an episode in British history

Historians have long debated the question: why did Britain in the late eighteenth century not experience major revolution, as the assumptions of modernism predicted? This problem was created by an arbitrary choice of categories. Britain did experience major, transformative revolution; but it happened among fellow Britons in the North American colonies, and for reasons having nothing to do with class or industrialisation, those twin preoccupations of modernist historians. Within the British Isles, the constitutional transformations of *c.*1828–35 were similarly only distantly related to industrialisation and urbanisation, and their importance was for similar reasons long understated.

Seen in a transatlantic perspective, there was little that was new, and little that was specifically American, about the causes of the American Revolution. It was an episode that looked back more than it looked forward, and one that took place within an English-speaking polity whose political language originated in the British Isles. The paradox of the American Revolution is that it happened in America. Just as Marx and Engels expected revolution to occur in industrial Germany rather than backward Russia, so revolution was, on the surface, far more likely in Britain (and especially England) than in the rural isolation of North America. Yet neither the American nor the French revolutions were the modern episodes that they were later depicted as being, and displayed fewer novel ideas than seems obvious to those unfamiliar with earlier centuries. In the late eighteenth century it was England, not France or North America, that saw the origins of universal manhood suffrage, anti-slavery and women's rights, and the British Isles into the 1840s still seemed to contemporaries to be on the edge of social upheaval: the American and French revolutions, in the shape they took, were largely unexpected, and cannot simply be explained as self-evident conflicts between 'modern' and 'premodern'. Universal suffrage and a dynamic of conflict between rich and poor were themes absent from Thomas Paine's *Common Sense* (1776), the key pamphlet in catalysing the colonial decision to attempt independence, but a tract that came straight out of the mental world of English Deism in the early eighteenth century. Paine was out of date, and could only have an impact in a backward corner of the English-speaking world, where his tract, covertly heterodox, could have a catalytic effect on politicised religious sectarianism that was reminiscent of the 1640s.

One valid explanation of the American Revolution is a transatlantic one. Settlements of constitutional conflicts within the British Isles had often been attempts to cope with religious pluralism and its consequences. At home, solutions were found, although sometimes by narrow margins, but frequently at the price of exporting them to North America. There they eventually recurred in an intractable form. In the British Isles, the Revolution of 1688 produced not settlement but lasting ambiguity and conflict; in 1763–76, again, all appealed to the 'rights of Englishmen'. Colonial Americans had no monopoly on 'liberty'. Nor were they secular, as was the official face of the republic that emerged in 1783; the American Revolution had many of the attributes of seventeenth-century wars of religion in Scotland, Ireland and England.

The American Revolution is difficult to explain chiefly because it has been caught up in the 'myth of origins' of the United States and is normally interpreted there for present-day purposes. Among these presentist adaptations, some common features emerge. The revolution is traced to innovations in British policy alone, and George III or his ministers reproached for the inconsistency of their acts with 'fundamental law'; colonial society is seen as transformingly 'modern' from its outset. These arguments tell us more about the purposes of today than of the 1770s. Innovations in British policy undoubtedly occurred in the 1760s (policy is always changing, like the constitution), but it is debatable whether they were adequate to explain the scale of what followed. They were more than matched by social and intellectual changes within North America that had created a volcano and now triggered its eruption. Moreover, most of the features of colonial American society now hailed as 'modern' were already present to a greater degree in the British Isles, where they did not give rise to any such revolution.

The common myth of 'the American Revolution' as a unified, consensual response to tyranny also ignores the fact that there was no 'America' before 1776 to make a revolution: a united nation was the result of the revolution, not its cause. In 1769 Burke wrote of twenty-six British colonies 'from Nova Scotia to St Nevis': in 1776 half of them rebelled, half did not. Even within the Thirteen Colonies, some people campaigned for independence, some were loyalists, and a body of opinion in the centre was initially undecided. Within the British Isles, too, opinion was similarly divided, some like Josiah Tucker favouring independence for the colonies, others like Samuel Johnson opposing for equally serious reasons: like all great constitutional conflicts, this one took place in a legal grey area and greatly advanced the careers of lawyers.

One such lawyer was that hard realist Jeremy Bentham. He later recalled his views in 1775:

My opinions were at that time opposite to the American side. The turn they took was the result of the bad arguments by which I observed that side supported . . . The Declaration of Rights [Independence] presented itself to my conception from the first, as what it has always continued to be, a hodge-podge of confusion and absurdity, in which the thing to be proved is all along taken for granted . . . Absurdity, if I do not mis-recollect, went so far on that side as to pretend that, in point of fact, they had all along been in a state of

independence of the British Parliament, the contrary of
which was proved so plainly by such a number of acts
of parliament, which were produced.[91]

Colonial lawyers and politicians found reasons to disagree,
and this made the American Revolution an ideological conflict;
less a colonial war of liberation[92] than a civil war among people
who openly subscribed to similar ideals but whose shared
ideology had fallen into schism. Yet if the population of the
Thirteen Colonies was made up of elements comparable to its
British counterpart, the balance of its composition was wholly
different: the Nonconformist denominations, minorities in the
Old World, hugely predominated in the Thirteen Colonies.
Moreover, they had the freedom to become more like themselves, to develop further in an intolerant Congregationalist or
Presbyterian direction, and to revitalise the seventeenth-
century resistance theories that had been held in check at
home by Anglican ascendancy from the 1660s. As well as being
a civil war, the American Revolution contained many of the
elements of a war of religion.

The contrasting 'Whig interpretation' of the revolution is
still heard, and takes a variety of forms. Some authors have
written of a 'radicalism' originating in the 1760s that flowered
in the 1770s as a defence of liberty against heavy-handed
metropolitan exactions, achieving timeless significance as an
assertion of humanity's natural rights. This argument is
vulnerable to the demonstration that 'radicalism' was a later
ideology, born in England in the 1820s, and that its targets
were absent in North America (no heavy tax burden was ever
laid on American shoulders, or even threatened; universal
suffrage was not at issue in 1776; no colonial economist like
Ricardo had pointed a finger at American landowners; atheism

11. The American Revolution. How secular were the causes of this catastrophe? Here four bishops dance around the Quebec Bill, which its opponents denounced as recognising 'popery' in Canada, while the Devil whispers suggestions to Lord North and Lord Bute plays the bagpipes. And how American were the Revolution's causes? This print appeared in the *New American Magazine*, 1 (October 1774), engraved by the American rebel Paul Revere; but he had copied it from an English source, and Dissenting denunciations of 'arbitary power' were already clichés in England.

was almost unknown in the colonies). Colonists, moreover, were proactive from the 1760s, not merely reactive; women, slaves and Native Americans were so obviously excluded from the promise of natural rights language in the 1770s that this language itself becomes the historical phenomenon to be explained rather than the explanatory key that opens all locks.

The famous cry of the revolution was 'no taxation without representation'. This was an ancient English idea, and therefore difficult for the metropolitan government to argue against. But it was only a smokescreen: colonial Britons almost never sought their colonies' representation in the Westminster Parliament, and the idea was hardly ever seriously promoted on either side of the Atlantic. What part of the colonial elite sought, from an early date, was independence. Britain resisted, as England had long resisted the independence of Ireland and Scotland, and as America's northern states in the 1860s resisted the secession of the Confederacy. Grievance is not a puzzle; rebellion is.

Some of the causes of the rebellion were practical and self-interested. Victory over the French brought territorial responsibilities. Partly to minimise expensive conflict with Native Americans, partly to check the rapacity of settlers, the British government in 1763 drew a Proclamation Line around areas of existing white occupation in an attempt to regulate settlement beyond it. From then until 1773 a clear boundary was established stretching from New York to Florida, despite colonial attempts to cheat on land allocations.[93] By the 1770s, this attempt to restrain the depredations of colonists upon the Native Americans was breaking down. Even so, it had involved stationing some 10,000 troops in America, mostly in the newly conquered colonies of Quebec and Florida, or in the backcountry to separate colonists and Indians. The army lived amicably enough with the colonists,[94] but the disaffected intelligentsia of the east coast now got up a heightened denunciation of 'standing' (i.e. regular) armies, held to be proof of a royal conspiracy to rivet the chains of slavery on the people.

What have been called the 'ostensible causes' of the revolution concerned the legitimacy of taxation, an acute problem for the metropolitan government with the massive debt incurred in the Seven Years War. But it was not obvious that taxation would produce such a rhetorically exaggerated reaction. The founding myth of the revolution, as in the Declaration of Independence, was that the colonies merely reacted against 'a design to reduce them under absolute despotism', namely George III's 'direct object' of 'the establishment of an absolute tyranny over these states'. The opposite was nearer the case: George III's ministers had reacted to illegality and conspiracy among the colonists (massive evasion of trade regulations, disregard of property rights, assertions of legislative autonomy) with a policy which combined an abstract theoretical assertion of sovereignty over the colonies with practical appeasement of local elites.

From the Stamp Act in 1765 through the Townshend duties in 1767 (which lightly taxed certain commodities in order to free colonial judges and governors from local political control, and so to enforce trade regulations) to the East India Company tea deal in 1773 (which would have halved its price and undercut the influential colonial merchants who smuggled tea), London attempted to find compromise formulae to raise modest sums in revenue but tended to back down when these provoked loud colonial resistance. Throughout, the issue was expressed as one of constitutional principle, but this failed to disguise colonial self-interest and religious antipathy to English rule, perceived as a militantly Anglican regime: the colonies never groaned under a major tax burden, and were not going to be asked to do so. The army was never used (as it was to be in Ireland before 1798) to round up colonial leaders, break up meetings like the Continental Congress, or shut down printing presses. When troops finally arrived in Boston in 1768 they were at a loss how to act among a population that continued to enjoy the legal rights of Englishmen, since English law put narrow limits on the use of military force. No English bishop would pursue the descendants of those who had fled from Archbishop Laud; but many colonial Nonconformists feared, or claimed they feared, just that.

Meanwhile, the ministry had decided that the loyalty of newly conquered Quebec could only be secured by granting religious toleration and preserving French civil law. In this it was persuaded by Alexander Wedderburn, Solicitor General, who applied to Canada the formula successfully implemented in his native Scotland in 1707 (in 1777 Adam Smith continued to press Wedderburn to use the 1707 model to solve the American problem). The Quebec Act of 1774 was opposed at Westminster and received with outrage in the Thirteen Colonies, whose elites affected to be indignant at the concession to 'popery' and claimed it as proof that the Whig George III and his Whig ministers were in league with the Pope;[95] they were perhaps more alarmed that the Act extended the boundaries of Quebec south and west, blocking the ambitions of many colonial land speculators including Patrick Henry and George Washington. Overnight, their investments in a speculative future settlement, to be called Vandalia, became valueless.[96]

Just as threatening to many colonists was the landmark ruling in *Somerset* v. *Stewart*, a case heard in London by Lord Mansfield in 1772, which made clear (as William Blackstone had argued in his *Commentaries on the Laws of England*, pub-lished in 1765–9) that English common law did not recognise the status of slavery. In a transatlantic polity, it was only a matter of time before the same principle would be applied in North America also. Colonial slave-owners therefore joined colonial merchant smugglers, colonial Dissenters, colonial debtors and colonial land speculators as powerful groups with an interest in emancipation from British policy.

A growing mood of belligerence spread among colonists, who still included people long used to weapons and to murderous conflicts with Native Americans or slaves. Even so, the outbreak of fighting in 1775 was not bound to lead to independence. War in the eighteenth century more often led to stalemate. That this was not the outcome was not primarily due to Congress, or to the patriot militia, but to the courts of Europe. Only the intervention on the rebel side of France and Spain, both of which had engaged in a naval race that tipped the scales against Britain, created a strategic situation in which British victory and a compromised settlement were impossible. Even so, more might have been achieved, but for Lord North's inadequacy as a war minister, for the lacklustre performance of the two senior British commanders, Admiral Richard Howe and his brother General William Howe, and for Britain's failure to co-ordinate strategy with the colonial loyalists, who were in some areas numerous.

In geopolitical terms, the independence of the Thirteen Colonies in 1783 was a long-delayed consequence of the battle of Almanza (1707), a key conflict in the War of the Spanish Succession, fought by Britain and its allies to prevent a French Bourbon from succeeding Carlos II on the Spanish throne and creating the potential for a Franco-Spanish power bloc. The war is famous in British histories for the victories in the Low

Countries and Germany of the 1st Duke of Marlborough, but his remarkable successes conceal the fact that the Whigs failed in their war aim of 'no peace without Spain'. There a different campaign was fought.[97] Its decisive battle, Almanza, was won by another general of genius, James Fitzjames, 1st Duke of Berwick, natural son of James II; so the Franco-Spanish alliance became a looming threat in following decades. If the second and third navies in Europe were combined, they might well prove stronger than the first navy, whose ascendancy was only intermittent. In 1781 the Royal Navy was compelled to withdraw from before Yorktown, the British army there was forced to surrender, and the balance of war tilted decisively.

George Washington's regular troops were significant, but not decisive. A majority of the forces facing the British at Yorktown were French regulars, whether of the army or the navy. Even here, France's intention was not altruistically to bring into being the new social experiment of an independent United States but to weaken both sides so that the French position on the American continent might be retrieved. That this did not happen after 1783 was another improbable outcome of the revolution. It can be attributed not to the strength of the new republic but to the success of the Royal Navy in bottling up the French Revolution and in leading Napoleon to direct an attack ultimately against Russia. In 1783 Britain lost thirteen colonies, but not its navy; and in the next half-century the navy was to matter more.

Why could disaffected colonists not be appeased? Both sides were led to war because of shared but divided world views that would not compromise on the constitutional questions of sovereignty and jurisdiction thought to be at issue. Neither colonies nor metropolis had seriously explored colonial representation at Westminster or a federal solution to the redefinition of the colonies' position: neither side wanted a compromise. The question is why not.

Metropolitan Britons fought the American war out of a commitment to the indivisibility of sovereignty and the sanctity of allegiance; from a calculation that colonial militias might disintegrate in the face of regular troops; and in the belief that, as Wedderburn put it, the colonies were 'to the trade and navigation of the kingdom essential'.[98] The last two were proved wrong: Britons from the Thirteen Colonies proved as militarily unskilled, but as brave and stubborn, as Britons from the homeland; Britain's trade boomed after the colonies secured independence. The first two, however, were preserved in the homeland. The most important outcome of the American war was not initially the independence of the Thirteen Colonies, which only much later became significant in world terms, but Britain's political and ideological cohesion, and naval success, in the face of a major coalition of European powers. Indeed it was Britain that boldly declared war on the United Provinces in December 1780 to deprive the French and Spaniards of the Dutch carrying trade. The American war was in this way a trial run for Britain's survival in the more important conflicts that followed 1789. Out of the American Revolution, the British polity emerged intact; although the kingdom of Ireland threatened to break free, by 1800 this option was blocked. It was not the defeated party, Britain, that collapsed in revolution, but the chief victor, France. Britain by contrast emerged from the war showing every sign of resilience and dynamism. But even the new American republic emerged as something other than a confederal polity: the new constitution of 1787 created a unitary state with a unitary sovereign, defined as 'we the people'.

Colonial Britons fought the American war out of a

conviction that their liberties were in peril from 'popery' and 'arbitrary power'; that the metropolis intended to load a heavy tax burden on them; that they had a religious duty to resist; and that they had a providential destiny to spread (Protestant Nonconformist) civilisation throughout the world (or, at least, North America). Military victory seemed to prove the correctness of this analysis. In reality, since metropolitan 'popery' and 'arbitrary power' were mythical, the problem had been wrongly diagnosed: the new republic therefore inherited the unsolved legal and constitutional problems of its parent, leading to decades of constitutional conflict and a second civil war in the 1860s. Its understandings of 'liberty' had to be adapted to the slave-owning, Indian-expropriating society that was born less of idealism than of lax British rule before 1776. This situation was disguised when the new nation constructed a myth of origins, and when Britain distanced itself from the failures of metropolitan policy by developing a 'Whig interpretation of history' that blamed everything on George III and his ministers. What was vindicated in the new republic were the self-interested motives of the white elite: the release of many planters from debts contracted in Britain; the freedom of merchants to trade outside the Navigation Acts; the freedom massively to extend black slavery; the freedom to disregard treaties with Native Americans, to seize their lands with massive loss of Native American life, and to make fortunes from the development of a conquered continent.

Despite these ultimate sectoral advantages, in the medium term the economic impact of revolution and war on the Thirteen Colonies was severe: the destruction of property and trade, huge states' debts, high taxes needed to service those debts for many years afterwards, and rampant inflation that went with paper currency. Much of the devastation was localised; even averaged across the economy, one recent American estimate suggests that US per capita income fell by a huge 46 per cent between 1774 and 1790, despite some recovery after 1783. Another estimate places American wealth per capita 14 per cent lower even in 1805 than in 1774.[99] In Britain, the opposite was true. Although the national debt rose from £127 million in 1775 to a staggering £232 million by 1783, manufacturing output recovered quickly after the war. Exports were back at their 1772 level by 1783, and 40 per cent higher by 1790. Trade expanded.[100] Perhaps for the first time, Britons began to sense that war was not always an economic disaster.

Surviving revolution: Britain in the wars of 1776–1783 and 1793–1815

Defeat in war often had a major impact on the political cohesion of states, yet Britain not only lost an unwinnable war in 1783 but emerged strengthened in such a way that the outbreak of the French Revolution in 1789 did not see her converted to French principles, nor did the outbreak of war in 1793 see her conquered by the dynamic and protean force of Jacobinism in arms. Why was this?

A partial recasting of the political structure of the British Isles was indeed a result of the American war: Britain's relations with Ireland were transformed. Ireland had previously been brought more securely under London's control after the end of the 'undertaker' system (the reliance on Irish politicians to manage the Dublin Parliament) and the institution of resident Lord Lieutenants from 1767: they were more active political governors, generally in the interest of Britain as a whole. Under Poynings' Law of 1494, the Dublin Parliament was formally subordinated to the English Privy Council. Ireland did not enjoy free trade, either with Britain or the colonies. These restrictions now became targets for resentment, and the chief response of the Ascendancy was to demand equal status. This was achieved in 1779, and the Dublin Parliament, led by Henry Grattan, went on to demand legislative independence for Ireland, which was conceded by the Westminster Parliament's Renunciation Act of 1782.

The Irish Catholic majority was still eyed with distrust by the Ascendancy: some observers predicted that the Catholics would eagerly join any French invasion, and this threat of a general Catholic rising was one inducement to the Ascendancy to create the Volunteer Movement, a private-enterprise Protestant militia (in recent language, a paramilitary organisation), aimed partly to assert Irish independence against London, partly to defend the Ascendancy against the Catholics: the Irish insurrection of 1641 was never forgotten.[101] What would the Catholics do in a crisis? Nobody knew, least of all the Catholics.

Yet after the death of James III in 1766, the papacy recognised George III, not Charles Edward Stuart (1720–88) as the rightful monarch. During the American war, the Irish Catholic leadership was ostentatiously loyal to the Crown since the rebel colonists were the 'Puritan party, Calvinistical and republican', in the words of the Catholic bishop, John Troy, to the papal nuncio in October 1777. Irish Catholic recruitment to the Irish Brigade in the French army collapsed, and the Catholic Irish sought service in the British army instead.[102] Despite its Presbyterianism, Scotland produced a flood of petitions loyal to the Crown: there, the issues of 1776 had been addressed in 1707, and the intelligentsia vigorously supported the Union. Only the evangelical and proletarian

Popular Party within the Kirk openly backed the rebel cause,[103] as did Presbyterian Dissenters from Scotland's national church. Their co-religionists, the Presbyterian Dissenters of Ireland, took the same pro-rebel line, as did many Dissenters, Low Churchmen and men of heterodox theology in England.

These centrifugal forces were not decisive. Wales was largely oblivious to issues of devolution. Scotland did little, despite Scots dissatisfaction at doubts about Scottish loyalty, hangovers from 1745, that frustrated moves to create a Scottish militia during the American war. Whether such a militia would have become politicised, like the Irish Volunteers, is doubtful: Scottish volunteer corps were few, and showed little such drive. If Scotland was generally loyal, Ireland was a society divided between Catholics, Presbyterians and the Church of Ireland: even the latter, the 'Protestant Ascendancy', now began to develop an Irish patriotism defined by a sense of subordination to British interests. Wales as yet had no such marked sectarian divide.

England's tensions were different. There parliamentary reform had until now been a fad pursued by tiny groups, chiefly of heterodox Dissenters. After 1776, war steadily moved the issue centre stage, addressing corruption, waste, taxation and debt, imposed by a House of Commons held to be unrepresentative because insufficiently responsive to the landed interest, not to an urban demos. The 'country party' opposition of Queen Anne's reign was now, belatedly, to score a major success when the Association Movement, beginning in rural Yorkshire, championed a similar programme of cheap and uncorrupt government. It soon became known as 'economical reform'; gradually introduced, it greatly changed the machinery of government even before 1832. Opposition denunciations of 'Old Corruption' in the 1820s were largely out of date: MPs who held government office ('placemen') fell from about 123 in 1790–6 to fifty-seven in 1818.[104]

Yet in its electoral demands (another 100 seats for the counties, and shorter parliaments) the Association Movement of the 1780s failed, not least because it began to attract extremists with their new and revolutionary agenda: universal manhood suffrage, proposed by John Cartwright in *Take Your Choice!* (1776), equal electoral districts, the secret ballot, payment of MPs, annual parliaments and the end of property qualifications for membership of the Commons. As early as the general election of 1780, this revolutionary agenda was openly advocated at the poll for the city of Westminster. Far more extreme than the points ostensibly at issue in America in 1776 or France in 1789, it was Britain's avoidance of this outcome that was basic to its political stability in the next three decades. The same happened in the Dublin Parliament after 1782: following legislative independence, the line was drawn at franchise reform, which would have pointed to the inevitable enfranchisement of the majority Catholic population.

A purely political explanation for Britain's survival in 1783 must include the appointment as first minister of William Pitt the Younger and his ability to create a social constituency out of natural supporters of stable, moderate government; those who distrusted the evident corruption of the Fox–North coalition, which he succeeded; and the friends of reform. Pitt duly proposed a moderate measure of parliamentary reform in 1785, but with few petitions in favour and reformers split between moderates and extremists he was defeated in the Commons. Christopher Wyvill, effective leader of Yorkshire's Association Movement, saw that London's interest in universal suffrage had been 'a disadvantage to the cause'. Pitt's reforming instincts were frustrated by two episodes: the

Regency crisis of 1788, caused by George III's illness, and the French Revolution; but his broadly reformist, meritocratic social constituency had taken shape. Until Burke's intervention in *Reflections on the Revolution in France*, both Pitt's ministry and Fox's opposition contained men for and against different sorts of legislative change. Pitt, in office, took opportunities for financial reform; when George III was ill in 1789–90, it was Pitt who seemed the moderate administrator, resisting an unchecked hereditary authority devolving at once to the Prince of Wales.

Pitt did not immediately introduce 'free trade': Adam Smith's *An Inquiry into the Nature and Causes of the Wealth of Nations* was published in 1776, when public attention was occupied elsewhere, and took long to persuade the elite. Pitt, who read the work, was an early exception. Vested interests were strong, and few European powers were willing to sign the tariff reduction treaties that Pitt sought. The General Chamber of Manufactures, established in 1785, was split on the issue: its very foundation was intended to block Pitt's scheme for a customs union between Britain and Ireland. The following year saw the smaller craft manufacturers opposed to the Eden Treaty with France while manufacturers in newer sectors embraced the measure. Even Pitt's ministry acted on older mercantilist ideas of the supreme importance of the shipping interest in passing the Navigation Act of 1786, a measure aimed to exclude the carriers and shipbuilders of the new United States. Only the Jay treaty of 1794 began the lowering of Anglo-American trade barriers, with the usual result: trade boomed.[105] Some historians have seen a different pattern in the adoption of free trade ideas, slow in respect of foreign trade, fast in respect of domestic trade and social policy, so that free trade became the dominant ideology of

Victorian Britain. This may be debated: perhaps free trade in a diversified, specialised economy was an eighteenth-century assumption to a larger degree than has been appreciated. Yet perhaps the acceptance of Adam Smith's teaching as a ruling ideology only arrived with William Huskisson's economic reforms in the 1820s.

In social policy, free-trade principles were not uniformly adopted. Thomas Malthus's *Essay on the Principle of Population* (1798) warned of the need for strict restraint; he condemned Pitt's Poor Law Bill of 1796 for encouraging the poor to extend their families. The law was not abolished; indeed practice moved in the opposite direction, with the 'Speenhamland system', initiated in 1798, providing for the financial relief of the poor in their own habitations according to the price of bread. Only the new Poor Law of 1834 sought to confine relief to the workhouse. Yet in matters of domestic trade regulation the tide was already running the other way, with Parliament refusing to insist on the enforcement of Elizabethan legislation regulating wages and requiring apprenticeship qualifications. In 1802 a petition from Yorkshire calico printers led to the suspension of these laws, and their abolition in 1809. In 1813 and 1814, the main sections of the Statute of Artificers of 1563 were repealed. Free trade ideals were applied early in the area of labour relations, with results that are still controversial.

With returning political stability came reviving government creditworthiness. Defeat in 1783, a brief decline in government tax revenues in 1783–4, the enormous costs of the war and the prospect of the loss of export markets threatened total financial collapse: it was this that Pitt avoided, and instead it was French finances that collapsed in 1788. By slashing nominal customs rates through the Commutation Act of 1784, Pitt increased tax yields, returned the national budget to surplus, and began to redeem the national debt: whether or not the 'sinking fund' was sound economics, it boosted public confidence.[106]

The events of 1789 threatened to disrupt this programme of recovery. Pitt initially sought to stand aside from the French Revolution, preferring to dwell on its positive aspects, but France seized the strategically crucial Austrian Netherlands, promised support to revolutionary movements everywhere, and in February 1793 declared war on Britain. The British state was involved in the lives of individuals far more by 1815 than it had been in 1660, whether as tax-gatherer, as bureaucratic structure, as contractor, as employer, or as wielder of armed force. The expansion in the numbers of military and naval personnel in the later eighteenth century went with a decline in earlier preoccupations with the threat that they might pose to civil liberties (such rhetoric survived only in backward areas, like the North American colonies) and a decline in the formerly widespread sense that foreign-born monarchs could not be trusted. George III became a patriotic symbol from the 1780s, as George I and George II had never been; the threat of military defeat, especially in 1803–5, gave a series of boosts to national identity.

Yet 'nationalism' was still an unknown phenomenon; anti-Catholicism was at a low ebb until the late 1820s; and what was strengthened was a conception of Englishness, Welshness, Irishness and Scottishness built chiefly around shared histories, shared constitutional liberties, and (where this was the case) shared religion. Challenge from colonial Nonconformity and French Jacobinism made the national identities of the British Isles more like themselves, more dependent on a revitalisation of older institutions and images, rather than creating a new 'Britishness' built on new foundations, however much Scots and Irish elites wished to use 'Britishness' to advance their careers within England's empire.

Britain survived the French Revolution not only by military and naval success, but because the argument at home was largely won by the opponents of 'French principles'. This rallying to the state had begun during the American war; American arguments partly inoculated the British against a French disease. But the implications of this previous outcome were not obvious: both Pitt and Fox sympathised with the French Revolution on its outbreak, seeing in it an auspicious experiment in Whig reform in the manner of 1688. It was Burke's challenge that destroyed this consensus. Fox did not repudiate the revolution, and was compromised by its unfolding horrors. Forced to be either for or against France's new regime, many Whigs crossed the floor in 1794 to support Pitt's ministry. Fox was left with a rump of some fifty MPs who looked increasingly extreme, their occasional support for parliamentary reform a major handicap. Not until the 1820s did they again look like a credible party of government.

In *Reflections on the Revolution in France* Burke cited as a chief cause of France's catastrophe the collapse there of orthodox religion, especially under the impact of an anti-Christian campaign mounted by the unbelieving *philosophes*. In Britain things were different, for its disaffected intelligentsia tended to be Nonconformists; outright atheists (like William Godwin and Jeremy Bentham) were few, and had a substantial influence only later. The idea that it was the strength of religion in Britain that averted revolution was initiated by the French historian Elie Halévy (1870–1937), who argued that 'Methodism was the antidote to Jacobinism'. Since then, historians have recovered the parallel but much larger roles of the established churches of the British Isles and stressed the advance within them of evangelicalism, a movement that looked to individual conversion rather than collective social reform as the engine of change.

However valid these general causes, they operated through contingency, events and personality. Some historians have seen in the coalition of 1794 the origins of a 'new conservatism', but this is as doubtful as a similar argument applied to the 1760s. Both the Pittites and the Whigs who joined them, notably Burke, claimed to stand on the principles of 1688. So did George III throughout his reign: indeed in 1801 he took the view that Pitt's proposal for the removal of civil disabilities from Catholics in Ireland as part of the Union was inconsistent with his coronation oath, and Pitt had to resign. Ireland and Catholic emancipation now, at last, provided the Whig opposition with an ideological framework; it was finally realised in 1828–9, though with unforeseen consequences. The most important reform of the brief Whig ministry of 1806–7, the abolition of the slave trade, was not a ministerial measure, but the achievement of a long-running extra-parliamentary campaign. Whigs were not good at picking winners.

The Jacobin challenge shaped the ideology of the ministerial coalition of 1794, but that ideology was not the same as the 'Conservatism' that emerged after 1832. First, the French threat reinforced the old affirmation of 'church and king', broadening the idea to be symbolic of the social order in general. Second, it provoked a systematic defence of the aristocratic and the hereditary elements in society. Third, it provoked the governing order to a more systematic defence of property: this did have some continuity with what was to follow, but as yet inequalities of property were defended within a providential setting as a divine disposition. Conservatism was a term coined in the 1830s to express Peel's desire to define a new, pragmatic, secular philosophy defending order and property after the world view of 'church and king' had been smashed beyond repair in 1828–32. Conservatism did not exist in the time of Pitt, Burke or Liverpool. During Liverpool's ministry in the 1820s the much older term 'Tory' sometimes crept back to describe the governing party, but their philosophy differed little from that of Pitt and Burke, who remembered the early eighteenth-century meaning of 'Tory' and would have repudiated its application to themselves.

Nor did Fox anticipate the philosophies later termed 'liberalism' and 'radicalism': he was still locked into the dogma that had blighted the Whigs since the early 1760s, attributing all political ills to an attempt by the Crown to establish 'arbitrary power' or to bypass the Commons by a system of 'double Cabinet'. Foxites were therefore ill-prepared for the new forces of Jacobin populism and handled the challenge badly, seeming to give uncritical endorsement to the popular movements of the 1790s that made common cause with the French revolutionaries. By 1794 the ministry had assembled evidence of conspiracy, and a series of treason trials resulted. Yet the government had gone too far in charging the reformers with treason rather than seditious libel, and English juries declined to convict.

The popular movements of the 1790s had their origins in natural-rights theory combined with a long-standing English constitutionalism; not for nothing did Paine title his best-seller *Rights of Man*. But Paine too belonged to an older world, and never quite embraced the doctrine of universal manhood suffrage worked out by the English Unitarian intelligentsia before 1780. Even his attention to natural-rights theory was perfunctory, however prominent it was in revolutionary France. The intellectual heart of his doctrine, as in *Common*

12. The mass meeting, 1795. Orators of the London Corresponding Society address onlookers at Copenhagen Fields, London. But although the crowds were large, how many of them were converted by the message? Is Gillray's satire a reliable guide to what occurred? Whether there was a peaceful English reforming tradition, and, if so, how it related to Jacobinism, are matters of debate.

Sense (1776), was the older English Deist critique of an establishment in which church and state were inseparably linked, and in which the claims of the church to a divine commission rested on a Trinitarian theology that Deists denied. As a challenge to this social nexus, *Rights of Man* (1791) and *Rights of Man. Part the Second* (1792) were catalysts for action, led by Dissenting manufacturers, merchants and professionals, and even freethinking artisan-led societies in England and Scotland. But more effective than this movement was that of the 'church and king' loyalists who intimidated their subversive neighbours. The English trials of twelve alleged Jacobins in 1794 ended in acquittals, but acted to break the confidence of the movement and sap the support of the middling orders. The suspension of habeas corpus (1794) and the Treasonable Practices Act and Seditious Meetings Act (1795) seemed to promise a reign of terror, but none materialised.

The impact of the French Revolution varied: greatest in Ireland, less in Scotland, less again in England, least in Wales. The reform of the Westminster or Dublin Parliaments might have opened the door to revolution, as did reform of the French Estates General, but in Britain and Ireland this demand was resisted. The most electorally quiescent of the kingdoms was Scotland, where electorates, even in county seats, were tiny, and where the 'undertaker' system continued in full force from the 1770s into the 1790s under the control of Henry Dundas: what is now hailed as the 'Scottish Enlightenment' had no discernible impact on the self-interested Scottish elite. Scottish protests were still expressed chiefly as schisms within Presbyterianism over the issue of lay patronage. The French Revolution transformed this picture: Paine became a best-seller in Scotland as well as England, spoke more clearly to a Scottish egalitarian idiom, and appealed to a much larger

social constituency excluded from formal political participation. The year 1792 saw the beginning of significant
reformist protest in Scotland, initially directed against Henry
Dundas but soon aimed more widely: the French offer to aid
revolution everywhere, and military successes of 1792 against
the armies of the absolute princes, polarised Scottish debate
and created harshly antagonistic blocs.

With opinion rallying to Dundas and the established
order, the authorities were able to move against the Scottish
reformers. In a series of trials in the 1790s, often marked by
judicial partiality, several Scottish reformers were convicted.
Transportation often removed them from the scene and
cowed their remaining sympathisers. In the face of persecution, Scots still pursuing their revolutionary objectives were
led into ever more extreme commitments; when the 'British
Convention' was broken up in 1793 its leaders received
sentences of transportation. Dundas profited; opinion rallied
to the old order. Although a society of United Scotsmen was
established to echo the United Irishmen, it did nothing
during the Irish rebellion of 1798. Scotland's landed and
professional elite was at the height of its self-confidence, and
it was resolutely unionist.

Much the same was true in England. Was a revolutionary
movement driven 'underground' there? The latest major study
tips the balance of interpretation towards the existence of a
serious revolutionary threat.[107] Governments at the time took
the danger entirely seriously. The increasing organisation of
Irish unrest, expressed in a body aimed at armed insurrection,
the United Irishmen, also began to spill over in contacts with
English activists. Arrests of a number of Irish leaders compromised the plans for a rising and broke the link with events
in England, although the possibility remained until the

execution of Captain Edward Despard in 1803 destroyed the conspiracy that bears his name. Even without Irish intervention, the English naval mutinies of 1797 balanced the country on the edge of a defeat that might now (unlike in 1783) have been followed by domestic revolution.

Paine's commitments were significantly different from the radicalism of the 1820s. His analysis did not derive from economics. He did not profess to be an atheist. His themes were equality and opportunity rather than suffrage; his enemy was the aristocrat rather than the landowner. Nor did he subscribe to a class-based analysis, and his writings did not produce class politics. His targets were kings, aristocrats, priests, and in general 'the state', depicted as a corrupt and oppressive device to forward the interests of these groups; remove the state, he argued, and 'society' would come into its own, a spontaneously arising creation of innocent individuals. Indeed Paine advocated free trade and free contracts by labour, rejecting state intervention in private affairs. In his vision, all ills were created by the unproductive sector, the aristocrats; he sought only the triumph of the productive sector, the industrious individual. This, it might be argued, was happening anyway; what Paine failed to explain was why the kings, aristocrats and priests managed to retain the power they did.

Historians debate how far Paine's views persuaded a mass audience, and how ready any such audience was to act on his beliefs. O'Connell's Catholic Association in Ireland in the 1820s may better deserve to be called the first mass movement than the quasi-Jacobin societies in English cities in the 1790s. Nevertheless these societies were a new phenomenon, although their leaders were often skilled artisans, seldom labourers: Jacobinism was not the 'working-class movement' it was once hailed as being. It was, however, widespread; it was not confined to London, where the London Corresponding Society drew on extensive craft skills, but included old cities like Norwich, a centre of weaving, and new ones like Sheffield, centre of the metal trades. The term 'corresponding' in their titles indicated their intention to co-ordinate action with like-minded bodies not just in Britain, but more menacingly in France also.

Popular political consciousness was a reality in the 1790s, but what did it mean? It was open to exploitation by the intelligentsia that had developed the doctrine of universal suffrage by 1780, notably the 3rd Duke of Richmond (1735–1806), but also commoners like John Cartwright (1740–1824), John Jebb (1736–86) and John Horne Tooke (1736–1812). Yet it was not clear that popular discontent always deserved the label 'Jacobin'; it often stood in an older English constitutionalist tradition, however much it was reactivated by events in France. English 'Jacobinism' was important, but not important enough to produce revolution.

Paine's influence was also offset by a new development that was deeply to colour society, evangelicalism. As with Methodism, historians debate whether this was a natural extension of eighteenth-century religiosity or a fundamental departure from it. Evangelicalism had its intelligentsia, asso-ciated with a London district: the 'Clapham Sect' congregated around the south London home of William Wilberforce. It included men like John Venn, its vicar, and, at Cambridge, Isaac Milner and Charles Simeon (it was in such a milieu that the historian Thomas Babington Macaulay, self-righteous apologist for the Whig ascendancy after 1830, was brought up). Hannah More had already published *Thoughts on the Importance of the Manners of the Great to General Society* in 1787; now, to Paine's *Rights of Man*, Wilberforce replied with his best-selling *A Practical View of the Prevailing Religious System of Professed Christians in the Higher and Middle Classes of this Country contrasted with Real Christianity* (1797), a work that had a major impact in shaping the restrained manners and moral high-mindedness that came to characterise the elite by the death of George IV in 1830. How far did this higher moral tone among the elite actually inspire the middling and lower orders to refrain from Paineite alternatives? How far did it reinforce the resolution of the elites themselves? Both seem plausible, but more research is needed.

In Ireland the situation was different. There the Protestant landowning elite of the Church of Ireland, seeing themselves as essentially Irish, had pioneered the growth of an Irish patriotism from the 1770s. This patriotism challenged the ancient supremacy of the Westminster over the Dublin Parliament and threatened Irish quasi-independence at the moment of England's greatest weakness during the American war (it did not, however, draw any deeper egalitarian lessons from the American example). Reacting to this pressure, Britain ended many trading restrictions on Ireland and in 1782 repealed the Declaratory Act of 1720 that codified Ireland's subordination. The English Lord Lieutenant and his executive remained in Dublin Castle, and the Irish House of Commons was more vulnerable to the influence of the executive than its English counterpart: Irish activists still had a major target. But the Irish Episcopalian patriots sawed off the branch on which they sat, for their initiatives were paralleled by the rise of autonomous Catholic peasant violence, fuelled by population pressure and the consequent immiseration of the labourer, a cause that waited only for political leadership.

This was suddenly provided in 1789. Ulster Presbyterians and southern Catholics now found in French ideals apparent common ground. Jacobinism created a vision of non-sectarian justice, expressed in 1791 by the creation of the Society of United Irishmen in Dublin and Belfast. Soon, peasant violence on the ground belied this promise of Presbyterian–Catholic co-operation: rural conflict expressed a growing hatred between denominations. But the leadership pressed ahead: in a revolutionary age, this militant but initially non-sectarian platform led in the 1790s to far more serious plans for armed insurrection than was ever the case in England or Scotland. Concessions did not defuse these Jacobin plans: in 1792–3 Catholic Relief bills in the Dublin Parliament, pushed through at the instigation of Pitt's ministry, largely ended restrictions on Catholic education, Catholic entry to the professions, to posts in the administration, or to military office; they allowed Catholics the vote for the first time since 1727, yet left a ban on Catholics sitting in the Dublin Parliament or holding high office. It was a more favourable situation than Catholics enjoyed in England, but without major parliamentary reform, which was not on offer from Pitt, it was not enough to make a significant difference to Irish politics.

Meanwhile, legislation was directed against the conspiracy that Dublin Castle apprehended. Forearmed and forewarned, the castle pre-empted insurrection. United Irish leaders were arrested; the military, using brutal methods, sought out and seized arms in the countryside. Irish activists missed the bus: they failed to liaise with a French expedition in December 1796 or with English naval mutinies in 1797, and when risings broke out in 1798 they turned into a war of religion between Catholic and Protestant rather than into an idealistic Jacobin war of liberation. It was a throwback to the massacre of 1641, and it defined the nature of alignments in Ireland for a century.

Pitt's solution did not flatter the Protestant Ascendancy: he sought to merge the Dublin in the Westminster Parliament, as had been done in 1707 for Scotland, and to couple this with full equality for Catholics. The Dublin Parliament was manipulated, persuaded and bribed into agreement; but George III, ever a Hanoverian appealing to the principles of 1688 and 1714, saw in Catholic emancipation a violation of his coronation oath. Pitt, Cornwallis and Castlereagh, the architects of the Union, resigned. In 1800, Castlereagh predicted: 'Those things which, if now liberally granted, might make the Irish a loyal people, will be of little avail when they are extorted on a future day.'[108] Historians commonly agree with him, and blame George III for blocking a solution to the Irish Problem: it is argued that Catholic emancipation in 1829 and Irish tithe commutation in 1838 were too late. It may equally be debated whether any measure could have solved the problems of Irish society. In face of the demographic reality of a booming Irish population, the Protestant Ascendancy, not the Catholics, now embraced the Union that they had resisted in the 1770s.

In Scotland, revolutionary pressure may have been defused by gradually rising real wages in c.1780–1800 (a pattern opposite to England's). Modest population growth, combined with urbanisation and industrialisation faster than England's, supplemented by large-scale enlistment in the armed forces, kept wages up. By the 1810s this benign pattern was reversed by the flood of rural population into Scottish cities, creating a pool of casual and impoverished labour. A legal decision in 1812, triggered by a weavers' strike, ended the system created by an Act of 1661 which gave Scottish JPs the power to regulate wages and, implicitly, to set them at a level that would allow a worker to maintain himself and a family: henceforward, market forces determined wage rates, and a boost was given to politicised, even revolutionary, trades unionism. English precedents, and contacts with former United Irishmen, now influenced Scotland also: after 1815, organised labour became a phenomenon there, with unforeseeable results. Armed insurrection, on a small scale, was easily suppressed in 1820, but its potential remained and was taken seriously by the government. Yet this was social revolution, focused in areas of rapid industrialisation and forging links with activists in similar industrial districts in England; it was not the war of Scottish liberation that Scottish nationalists later sought. On the contrary, into the late twentieth century Scots played a disproportionately large part in 'the working-class movement' that sought to combine English, Welsh, Irish and Scottish proletarians rather than to divide them on national grounds.

With the American war, 'social control' became a problem in the eyes of the English elite, not because of the impact of the American example (which was hardly felt) but because of the phenomenon of the urban crowd. Even then, the first serious episode of disorder, London's Gordon Riots of 1780, in which some 285 died and much property was destroyed, was triggered by Parliament's attempts to relax ancient anti-Catholic legislation, not by popular support for the ideals of the American revolutionaries. These disturbances were not obviously different from much older manifestations, like the demonstrations that greeted the Tory clergyman Dr Sacheverell in 1710 or the riots at the accession of George I in 1715. In 1791 local elites, in traditional fashion, arranged the mob action that drove the subversive Dissenting minister Dr Joseph Priestley out of Birmingham. But this was the last such example. The growing atrocities of the French Revolution put mob action in a new light: they identified 'the people' as a vast, and unpredictable, threat to 'order' rather than (as hitherto) a social constituency offering a critique of some particular policy only. This fear was never absent until the failure of the Chartist movement in the late 1840s, and was fuelled by a growing evangelicalism among an elite now appalled at the irreligion and immorality of the lower orders.

Britain survived the defeat of the American war because of its economic strength, allowing it to outlast its opponents in a war of attrition; because of its ability to raise loans from the propertied classes (only 20 per cent of the cost of the American war was met from taxation, as against 60 per cent in the French wars of 1793–1815); and because it had a persuasive ideological response to colonial republicanism. It was this power base that the younger Pitt tended and consolidated.[109] What secured financial survival was a fiscal system consolidated in the 1690s and not essentially changed thereafter. The burden of earlier wars was heavy, too: between 1692 and 1801, expenditure on the army, navy and ordnance plus debt charges (which related to former wars) ranged from 84 to 93 per cent of total government expenditure; even in the Napoleonic War, the military burden was still within this range. Given that the church had been endowed in the Middle Ages, the business of the state was, overwhelmingly, war.[110]

If the American war was expensive, the French war was even more so. Pitt met its cost partly by steep increases in the tax rates on luxuries like carriages and servants, partly by an income tax, first levied in 1799, that tapped sources of wealth beyond landed income. The affluence of the middling orders, who substantially footed the bill, was now evident; and after the resumption of war in 1803, the cost steadily escalated again. Britain's economic growth meant that the cost of war could gradually be met more from taxation than from loans; after the mid 1790s it was Britain's ability to pay for ever-higher military expenditure from burgeoning public revenues that gave it the edge over other European states.[111]

Yet the battles still needed to be fought, and here fortune favoured the rich. France's chief invasion attempt in the war of 1793–1801 was directed against Ireland; this miscarried, partly because of the subversion of French naval competence by revolution, partly by the decision of Bonaparte to lead a major expedition to Egypt rather than against England's weakest link. After 1803 French efforts were renewed, this time in alliance with Spain; French policy was to draw away Britain's fleets by a stratagem, allowing Napoleon's army of over 130,000 men, massed at Boulogne, to slip across the Channel. Had this army landed, its victory over Britain's modest land forces would have been assured. It was this outcome that was averted by Nelson's crushing victory at Trafalgar on 21 October 1805, one of the few decisive battles of world history.

Military stalemate between Europe's greatest land and sea powers was the result. Napoleon tried to break it by an economic blockade of Britain, the 'Continental System' of 1807–12, that sought to close all ports under French influence to British ships and so block export markets. Britain responded with Orders in Council blockading all ports from which British ships were barred. Of the two systems, Napoleon's was the more incomplete: British trade often found its way through to countries or ports not securely under French control, and in any case had world markets at its feet, exempt from European competition. Meanwhile the British blockade began to tell against the French economy. In 1808 resistance in Spain to French domination led Britain to send an expeditionary force in support of the Spanish guerrillas; this turned into a full-scale land campaign under Wellington, Britain's most successful general since Marlborough. Well supplied thanks to British naval supremacy, Wellington scored victory after victory against superior French numbers; consequently, France's hold on northern Europe was less than complete. In 1810 Russia reopened its ports to British vessels; in 1812 Napoleon invaded Russia, losing almost all the Grand Army in the Russian winter. In 1813–15 Britain played a leading role in organising and funding the coalition that toppled Napoleon and established a new European order. There was no attempt to destroy France economically, as would happen to Germany after 1918; rather, Castlereagh, the Foreign Secretary, sought to establish a balanced stability while securing Britain's commercial, naval and colonial interests overseas. It was a peace settlement that set the stage for Britain's economic hegemony in the half-century that followed.

Surviving the peace: the challenge of democracy, 1815–1832

What mattered more than conflicts between social groups was their much larger degree of co-operation. Perhaps this grew after 1760 to the point where the British Isles resisted revolution following 1776 and 1789. Even the discontinuity of 1828–32 is hard to explain as a class war. But class conflict was not the only source of major change, and the importance of what happened in 1828–32 has been emphasised. Debate still rages about the causes and consequences of that series of events.

Historians used to depict the old order toppled in 1832 by 'pressure from without', or by long-mounting, 'underlying' causes. Recently the validity of such explanations has been questioned: if a cause is a cause, is the term 'underlying' merely rhetorical? After historians of earlier years explained the outbreak of civil war in the 1640s and the Revolution of 1688 as the result of contingency rather than necessity, a role for contingency becomes more plausible in 1828–32 also. The debate is still between two options: whether reform was compelled by popular demands, or whether one part of the explanation, in addition to long-term change, lies in divisions within the established order, however these are defined.

Some have argued that a politically stable and economically prosperous outcome was assured once Britain pursued 'industrialisation' in response to population growth. Yet other paths were possible, like the Thirteen Colonies' and France's path of revolution or Ireland's of failed revolution and demographic disaster. The possibility of revolution in England, partly resulting from divisions within the elite, cannot be excluded. Such divisions had been seen before 1789: in commercial London's forcing Walpole into war with Spain in 1739, in resisting the Peace of Paris in 1763, and in 1785 when the General Chamber of Manufactures protested at Pitt's policy of moving towards free trade with Ireland. But these instances were limited. Not until after the war could nationwide campaigns be organised without seeming unpatriotic. In 1815 such a campaign was launched to secure repeal of Pitt's income tax of 1798 (a campaign that succeeded in 1816) and against the new Corn Law of 1815, which prohibited imports of corn (i.e. wheat) until the domestic price reached eighty shillings per quarter bushel (a campaign that had to wait for success until 1846).

Except in Ireland, economic debates were becoming more central to political conflict. Economic stress after 1815 added hugely to the pent-up demand for practical remedies for pressing grievances: a poor harvest in 1816, high food prices, a collapse in demand, high unemployment following demobilisation and downward pressure on wages, especially for workers competing with machinery. After 1815 there were increasing demands for the end of restrictive systems in government and economy. The *Manchester Guardian*, founded in 1821, embodied the world view of the northern manufacturing interest. But this interest was not well represented within the parliamentary Whig party, which was overwhelmingly one of blue blood, broad acres, and fashionable London literary salons. They read, and arranged to review each other in, the *Edinburgh Review*.

The politicisation of the artisans had begun in the 1790s, but had been effectively repressed by a government fearful of Jacobin revolution; it resumed after the economic depression in the textile industries caused by war with the United States in 1812–15 and the blockade of American ports. Parliament's response to artisan demands was to repeal ancient legislation, restrictive of trade or protective of labour according to different visions, like the Statute of Artificers (1563) in 1814, and to legislate to protect technological innovation, for example by making frame-breaking a capital offence.

High wartime food prices meant spiralling rents charged by landowners to their tenant farmers. After 1815, reformers contemplated an economy which had over two decades seen a shift away from wages and towards rent. This was indeed a golden age for the landowner, but it generated a reaction: the discontented now drew a connection between landlordism, high taxes, and the immense burden of the national debt. For the first time since c.1640–60, private property in land became a political target. High rents may also have meant a diversion away from capital investment and away from the consumption of manufactures, although this is still disputed. Land had long enjoyed a profitable symbiosis with trade; now, land was increasingly defined as an interest hostile to industry and to labour. With population growth outstripping increases in domestic food supply, the potential for an explosion was present. Yet the regional diversity of a long-established commercial economy helped defuse these pressures: if conditions in one place were bad, things were better elsewhere; if some trades declined, others flourished. Emigration overseas was the tip of the iceberg of geographical mobility within the British Isles. Diversity offset the despair that narrow horizons elsewhere entailed.

By contrast with this hostility to the landed interest, the positive affirmation of democracy was not an ideal that swept the board, even during the French Revolution. The most emphatic advocate for women's rights, Mary Wollstonecraft, ignored women's suffrage in *A Vindication of the Rights of Women* (1792) for the same reason that she there ignored men's suffrage: she conceived of freedom in other ways. What was most at issue, even in 1832, was reform of the institution of Parliament, not the affirmation of the principle of one person, one vote. Parliamentary reform had long been expressed in the 'country' idiom as a demand for cheap, uncorrupt government, and this nexus was still powerful when new elements were finally added to it.

Nevertheless, new ideas were also coined. Widening popular educational movements might now carry with them two new doctrines, radicalism and socialism. Radicalism was a fusion in the early 1820s of three elements: universal suffrage, Ricardian economics, and programmatic atheism. As a practical movement, radicalism seized on a theme that spoke to the daily experience of everyman: the country's ills, it was argued, were the result of high taxation, imposed by Parliament to defend 'Old Corruption'. This vivid image, expressed now in a radical press,[112] captured the popular imagination, and stood behind the successful careers of a host of activists and organisers after 1815: men like Richard Carlile, Major John Cartwright, William Cobbett and Henry Hunt. Sometimes, as with Jeremiah Brandreth in the Pentrich Rising (1817), or Arthur Thistlewood in the Cato Street conspiracy (1820), this indignation spilled over into armed resistance; more often, revolution was a threat rather than a reality.

Socialism was another new development of the 1820s, emerging from the world of early trades unions and their publications.[113] Where radicalism was atheist in its premises, socialism often appealed openly to Christian ideals of fraternity to rescue the working man from the effect of free competition (the reduction of his wage to the subsistence level) by instituting a new system of property ownership. Socialism and radicalism shared many targets, but were not alike; indeed they were ultimately rivals. Of the two, socialism had the greater impact in the long term, radicalism in the short. Radicalism's negative denunciations as yet proved more effective than socialism's positive vision.

The history of movements towards democracy continue to be used in the present as a way of asserting certain political values and claiming that their progressive realisation was embedded in a historical 'process'. Yet recent experience suggests that democracy is seldom if ever primarily a mechanism by which 'the people' express their will in the public arena. It is chiefly a means by which elites govern masses and secure validation for elite decisions. This explains two things: the remarkable slowness of elites to perceive that parliamentary reform could be a vote winner (since those elites preferred the

13. Radical reform, 1819. 'Radical reform', a synonym for universal suffrage, is here associated with French Jacobinism, about to ravish Britannia, who defends 'Religion', armed with 'The Laws' and assisted by 'Loyalty'. How effective was this characterisation in denigrating or resisting a reforming impulse?

familiar and effective means of governing) and the slowness of the masses to seize on universal suffrage as a panacea. Eventually, in the Chartist movements of 1838–48, the masses did just that. Britain's age-old political structures were deeply challenged in the early nineteenth century, and a new set of practices and values did replace them. The historian's task is not to surrender to the assumption that this happened on its merits.

Scotland had for long hardly protested against a franchise even narrower than Ireland's and England's. Scottish society had been concerned with questions of popular sovereignty, popular participation and structures of representation; but these things were debated in their bearing on the Kirk rather than on the Edinburgh Parliament. The extinction of that institution in 1707 made elections to its Westminster successor even more distantly relevant. Meanwhile, Scots became locked in intellectual and practical battles over an issue that later ages were to ignore: the rights of private patrons in the selection of ministers of the Kirk, as opposed to the rights of congregations to choose ministers of their own liking. This conflict led not to political revolution but to religious schism, the 'Great Disruption' that split the Scottish church in 1843.

Even in Scotland, things were changing. The system of managerial control of Scottish politics by the 2nd and 3rd Dukes of Argyll in the early eighteenth century was mirrored by that of another machine politician, Henry Dundas, from 1780 to 1801, and continued by his son Robert, 2nd Viscount Melville, from 1807 to 1829. Yet this stifling system of patronage and conformity eventually generated a reaction. The Edinburgh professor John Robison's book *Proofs of a Conspiracy against all the Religions and Governments of Europe* seemed widely plausible when published in 1798, so justifying principled inaction, but slightly paranoid by 1815. The later stages of what is today called the 'Scottish Enlightenment' lacked the early phases' nervous adherence to the ruling order. The *Edinburgh Review*, refounded in 1802, eventually developed into a house journal for a Scots-inspired reforming interest. In 1826 Sir Walter Scott, of the opposite persuasion, warned: 'Scotland, completely liberalised, as she is in a fair way of being, will be the most dangerous neighbour to England that she has had since 1639.'[114] Historians debate how far he exaggerated; but Scottish ideas were certainly an important component in the intellectual revival of English Whiggism after 1815.

Revolution was seriously feared after 1815, and it fell to Lord Liverpool's ministry (1812–27) to resist the post-war threat. Its policy was one of legal precaution, denounced as repression by reformers: the suspension of habeas corpus in 1817–18; the 'Six Acts' of 1819 aimed against public meetings; the use of spies, and sometimes agents provocateur, against those suspected of revolutionary conspiracy; the prosecution of radical leaders for seditious libel. Liverpool was served by able subordinates, including Huskisson and Peel, who began at an early date a programme of reform that is normally located in later years from Castlereagh's death in 1822. These included, notably, the resumption of the convertibility of sterling into gold in 1821: stable currency was to set the scene for Britain's international position throughout the nineteenth century. Second, customs duties were simplified and reduced; trade expanded, and receipts from customs increased substantially. Returning prosperity in the 1820s permitted the steady reduction in domestic tax rates, following the abolition of income tax in 1816, and this acted to deflect the reformers' claims about taxation as the source of national ills.

Four large questions dominated the agenda in 1800–30: the abolition of slavery; the repeal of the Test and Corporation Acts; Catholic emancipation; and parliamentary reform (here, for short, Abolition, Repeal, Emancipation and Reform). Reform was the most intermittent, and the last to become serious politics. Since the Whig opposition owed its survival to the influence of the great Whig landowners, often through their pocket boroughs, Whigs showed no long-term desire to destroy their electoral power base. Abolition was an extra-parliamentary movement with elite support that eventually wore down the vested interests to which it was opposed. Emancipation was articulately contested, and produced a sophisticated body of theory on each side on the question whether the constitution was to be understood as essentially Protestant. Neither characteristic was true of parliamentary reform: no petitions solely addressed to the issue were presented in 1825–9, and little debate now addressed the issue of 'democracy'.

On the reform of trade, currency, prisons and the law, Liverpool's supporters were united in favour. On one proposed reform they were disastrously divided: the call for Catholic emancipation. Even so, the government's split might not be enough, with the Whig opposition, to produce a majority for such a measure at Westminster. The English political landscape was fundamentally changed by the situation in Ireland, for there the growing popular consciousness of the early nineteenth century followed a different path from England's. There growing mass activism was associated less with radicalism and nascent class politics than with Catholicism. These currents were harnessed best by Daniel O'Connell, a figure who seems to anticipate the romantic nationalism of the European revolutionaries of 1848.

Yet O'Connell's mind was formed not by 1848, but by 1789: the Jacobin ideals of the French Revolution. During the 1790s he converted from Catholicism to Deism in freethinking circles in London and was close to the United Irishmen in Dublin. He resumed Catholic worship only some years after he began to exploit Irish Catholic resentment that Emancipation had not followed the Union of 1801. In 1804 he became a leading light of the elite Catholic Committee, set up to lobby for the Catholic interest. In 1823 he led the founding of the Catholic Association, an unprecedented organisation: structured, subscription-based and populist, it can probably be termed the first mass movement. Its political leverage secured the passage of a Catholic Emancipation Bill through the Commons in 1825; it failed in the Lords. O'Connell broke the impasse by securing his return in a by-election for Co. Clare in 1828, subsequently claiming that existing legislation imposing a declaration against transubstantiation prevented him as a Catholic from taking his seat (his earlier Deism probably meant that this was only a tactic). O'Connell may have had a greater continuity than is now evident with the revolutionary tradition of the United Irishmen in the 1790s. Equally, although the United Scotsmen had numbered only a few hundred in that decade, Scotland after 1815 showed its ability to mobilise large numbers of industrial workers in semi-political strikes and in mass (and menacing) agitation for parliamentary reform. If the Manchester meeting of 1819 which led to the Peterloo Massacre was initially peaceful, the riots in Scotland that followed were not.

Wellington's ministry had already weakened its position in 1828 by conceding to Protestant Dissenters the repeal of the Test and Corporation Acts, long by-passed by annual Indemnity Acts but still, to some, symbolic of the Anglican confessional state in England (or, as Dissenters called it, 'bigotry' and 'prejudice'). The position of Catholics was now anomalous. Against Emancipation was an alliance of 'primarily legalistic constitutional lawyers and fervently evangelical Protestants', but their representation within the political elite was not sufficient to stop concession.[115] After the Co. Clare by-election the Catholic Association threatened disorder, perhaps even armed revolution. Taking this possibility seriously, Wellington and Peel drove Catholic emancipation through Parliament. Their object was to preserve the Union of 1801 by fully incorporating the Irish Catholics within it, since the Catholic Association threatened, at the minimum, the unofficial re-establishment of an Irish Parliament: the 'three kingdoms' dynamic was reasserted. But concession came with an English price, for Peel and Wellington thereby split their own party in England, many Ultras drawing the conclusion that only the unreformed electoral system had allowed the ministry to secure Emancipation in defiance of public opinion. Historians still debate this point; but it was not a Whig but an Ultra Tory, the Marquis of Blandford, who in February 1830 introduced a bill for sweeping parliamentary reform.

As the crisis developed, popular organisations began to make practical politics out of the new principles of radicalism. Thomas Attwood's General Political Union between the Lower and Middle Classes of the People, founded in Birmingham in January 1830, had a primarily economic agenda but swung behind parliamentary reform as a route to reversing the ministry's anti-inflationary policies. Other local political unions followed,[116] yet 'public opinion' was effective only when organised by local activists: this was to remain the case in the new world of politics that followed 1832. William Lovett's and Henry Hetherington's National Union of the Working Classes, founded in London in April 1831, was committed to manhood suffrage. The general election of 1830 gave reformers the occasion for a popular mobilisation that rapidly grew in 1831 and 1832. How many of the working classes were mobilised is unclear; what the political elite saw was the middle classes, seemingly committed in large numbers behind the goal of parliamentary reform.

The Whigs were the part of the elite that regarded the middle classes, once determined on reform, as unstoppable. After the Bristol riots of October 1831, Earl Grey wrote to William IV's private secretary: 'It is . . . undeniable that the middle classes . . . are actuated by an intense and almost unanimous feeling in favour of the measure of Reform': the goal of the ministry was to detach the middle classes from their association with the political unions. Lord Holland observed to Grey: 'If the great mass of the middle class are bent upon that method of enforcing their views, there is not in the nature of society any real force that can prevent them.'[117] Historic Whig willingness to appeal rhetorically to 'the people' over the heads of a parliamentary class implicated in ministerial corruption now had a novel effect: it triggered a new form of mass and quasi-revolutionary politics, unindebted to patrician leadership. Meanwhile, in Ireland, O'Connell was to be overtaken as early as 1833 by other Irish politicians, committed now to a repeal of the Union.

George IV's death meant a general election in July 1830: even now, parliamentary reform was not the dominant issue. The poll produced a Commons split once more between ministry, opposition and the undecided, but in which avowed reformers had made gains, opponents of reform had been diminished, and Liverpool's governing coalition had been further weakened by the alienation of those who had been close to the ministerial reformers Huskisson and Canning. After their stance on Emancipation, Wellington and Peel tried to retrieve the situation by uncompromising hostility to Reform, an unwise position while an economic depression in 1829–30 was reigniting demands for cheap, transparent government. Wellington's announcement in the Lords in November 1830 that he would resist any such measure was meant to halt a steady loss of initiative to the Whigs, but it alienated more than it rallied. Wellington resigned as a tactical ploy, expecting that the Whigs' failure to form a ministry would lead to his restoration in a stronger position. He was wrong.

Grey's Cabinet was overwhelmingly patrician: its thirteen members included nine peers of Great Britain, one Irish peer, one heir to an English earldom, and two commoners who were great landowners.[118] His ministry came to office in 1830 after an acute economic recession: in the face of widespread suffering, they had to produce a measure which explained people's ills and offered hope of general redress, but they lacked economic analysis and competence. The king, too, was afraid of 'revolutionary feelings', worked on by 'the wild and mischievous projects of the Radicals'. Universal suffrage and the secret ballot, he announced, he would never agree to.[119] Nevertheless, there was support from within the cabinet for extensive measures. Grey had to declare in the Lords in November 1831 that his object was not to promote but to rule out 'universal suffrage and annual parliaments'.[120] Although these ideas were not in the bill, it embodied a sweeping cull of the nomination boroughs and a new, uniform, franchise that many regarded as an astonishing and extreme measure.

Historians have debated whether it was nevertheless a moderate step. Certainly, Grey's object was to restore order by repairing aristocratic dominance of the political machine, not

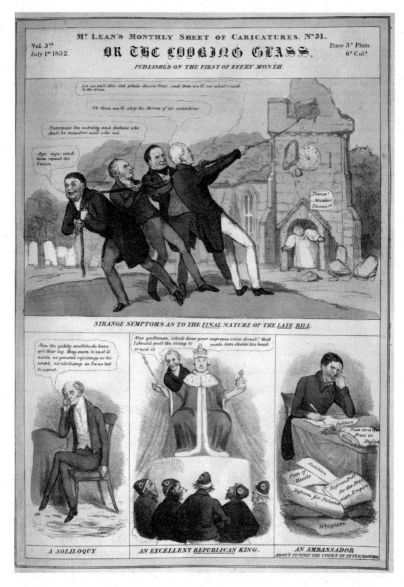

14. The Reform Act, 1832. The Whigs often argued that the 1832 Act was a final measure, but did they believe this? A contemporary satire looks forward to the consequences for the church, the throne, the nobility and the union.

to empower the middle classes or to introduce democracy. As Lord Althorp urged, MPs should, as in former times, represent 'the property, the wealth, the intelligence, and the industry of the country', not population alone, still less population empowered by Jacobin natural rights theory.[121] But contemporaries often saw it differently, and the extensive nature of the bill ensured its defeat. William IV then agreed to a dissolution, and the general election of 1831 tipped the balance decisively in favour of reform. When the Lords blocked a second reform bill in October 1831, a wave of rioting, arson and incitement by the political unions may have seemed the prelude to a revolution like that which had toppled the restored Bourbon monarchy in France in July 1830. This prospect may have influenced William IV to agree to create enough Whig peers to force the measure through the Lords; rather than that, the Lords gave way.

Separate Acts now followed for Scotland and Ireland. As in 1660 and 1688, the consequences there were more dramatic than in England. All Scotland's MPs before 1832 essentially sat for pocket boroughs; now substantial electorates were introduced for the first time, the Scottish electorate growing from 4,239 to some 64,500 in 1832, its antipathy to the former obstructers of reform being especially visceral. Melville's machine politics, in cahoots with the London ministries of the Pitts and the Liverpools, was smashed; the dice were now loaded the other way. Scottish burgh seats became the virtual preserve of Liberals, defined in hostility to English Anglican Toryism.[122] Yet in Scottish county seats, the sloppy drafting of the Act and the persistence of established practices allowed the old, landowning, Tory interest to regain its position by 1840. At Westminster, even less changed: Scottish MPs still largely identified themselves with the ministry (except that this was now Whig) and reaped the usual rewards for doing so.

In Ireland, Catholic emancipation in 1829 had been linked with raising the county franchise from the traditional forty shillings (£2) to £10 in a deliberate attempt to exclude O'Connell's supporters. Ireland was now subject to its own Reform Act that preserved this higher qualification. In an age of reform, the Church of Ireland was in an acutely exposed position, still supported by the tithes of all, Catholics and Presbyterians included, but attended by only some 7 per cent of Ireland's population. Emancipation without franchise extension left Ireland politically even more unstable.

If Britain did not experience revolution in 1832 like that seen in France in 1830, and was also to avoid revolution in the dramatic year of 1848, some have credited the Whigs with this achievement: concession, it is claimed, prevented extreme outcomes, and the terms of the 1832 Act detached the politically active middle classes from the artisan or working-class movements that they might otherwise have led. A related argument suggests that by the 1832 Act Whig landowners gave the landed elite a reprieve. Whether the events of 1828–32 went further than that is a matter of debate; in particular, much depends on whether the world before 1832 is seen as having a degree of coherence, being an order which might be identified as such, like France's social order before 1789.

Was reform the culmination of a reformist tradition, or the product of short-term contingencies? The reforms instituted after 1828 sometimes had remote origins; in the case of Catholic Emancipation and the repeal of disabilities on Protestant Dissenters, those origins lay in the seventeenth century. Overturning these disabilities could be depicted as a victory over 'reaction', or as a redefinition of the entrenched rationale for the state. Other elements of reform prominent after 1828, especially parliamentary reform, had recent roots in the late eighteenth century (the electoral precedents of the Commonwealth having been largely forgotten). There had been some moves to amend Parliament after the 1760s, but basic reform never commanded parliamentary majorities. Some historians have depicted the Reform Act of 1832 as the culmination of a reforming tradition, but this is arguably fanciful. The perception of reformers and their opponents alike was generally that the system was inflexible, resisting structural change, not that it was continually adapting. Parliamentary reform was not just a pragmatic matter: it enlisted ideologies, long bitterly resisted, suddenly and sweepingly victorious. Pragmatic concessions had long been on offer, for instance over religious disabilities; these did not prevent both the friends and foes of the established order from defining it as if those concessions had never occurred. But it was precisely because the state defined by the Revolution settlement proved as successful as it did that practical and pragmatic change could occur; even principles could change, like the abolition of the slave trade in 1807, provided this could be explained in ways that did not call in question the 'Protestant constitution'.

The end of the ancien regime?

Britain survived the French Revolution, only to experience its own years of trauma after 1815 and an episode of upheaval in 1828–35 which saw an end to the legal hegemony of the Church of England, fundamental parliamentary reform, and a complete recasting of local government; arguably, these changes amounted to a social revolution. How this episode is to be explained is a major preoccupation of historians, and constructive debate continues. Much depends on the starting point: what was Britain's state form in the first decades of the nineteenth century? Was it essentially open, democratic, dynamic? Or essentially closed, hierarchical, anachronistic? Are such characterisations admissible historical statements?

The starting point has traditionally been the history of parliamentary reform rather than the history of religious or local government reform. Before 1832 Britain possessed a system of representative government, but how was this to be understood? According to one revealing contemporary defence of that system, democracy in the later sense was understood in a way unfamiliar to later commentators. As Charles Jenkinson, later Lord Liverpool, put it, speaking against Grey's motion for parliamentary reform in 1793, 'We ought not then to begin first, by considering who ought to be the electors, and then who ought to be the elected; but we ought to begin by considering who ought to be the elected, and then constitute such persons electors as would be likely to produce the best elected.' The landed interest 'ought to have the preponderant weight' since it was 'the stamina of the country. In the second place, in a commercial country like this, the manufacturing and commercial interest ought to have a considerable weight, secondary to the landed interest'; plus, thirdly, 'professional people', who were 'absolutely necessary to the composition of the House of Commons'. These professional people 'made that House the representation of the people', exactly because they 'have collectively no *esprit de corps*' – they were not an 'interest' (still less a class). And the professional people could only be returned 'by means of those boroughs which are called rotten boroughs'. Nor was representation intended to give effect to sectional self-interest: 'It was certainly a principle of the British constitution, that monarchy, aristocracy and democracy should serve as a control on each other; but it was likewise a principle, that on ordinary occasions they should and must co-operate.'[123] If so, it is open to debate how far the old order was destroyed by the positive advocacy of democracy, how far by the negative condemnation of the hereditary principle.

In 1827 *Blackwood's Edinburgh Magazine* deplored a reversal in public discourse: John Bull, from boasting that the laws and constitution were 'the perfection of human wisdom', had been persuaded that they were 'so erroneous and defective, that they inflict on him almost every conceivable injury'. One target stood out: 'A war now rages against the Aristocracy, the object of which is to degrade it from its place in society, and to accomplish its virtual annihilation as a separate Estate of the Realm.'[124] Was this an exaggeration? Did the old order indeed have a necessary, interlocking unity? Much depends on definitions. The French term ancien regime was coined in the early 1790s to characterise France's social order before the revolution of 1789: *ancien* chiefly meant old in the sense of previous, but this meaning later changed to add a normative condemnation, society before 1789 being reviled as an anachronistic survival. In the late eighteenth century Britain, like France, often pictured itself as sophisticated and modern; British opinion was therefore often resistant to the revolutionary allegation that Britain, too, represented an instance of the outmoded aristocratic order that the new revolutionary dawn was to dispel. To such Britons it was the French Revolution that represented a step back to an age of barbarism, and many voices echoed Burke in this interpretation. France's declaration of war in 1793 gave a practical but not a historical answer to the point at issue: was British society anachronistic? An answer must address a number of areas.

First, the conceptual. A negative characterisation of British society did arise with the coinage of a key term. 'Old Corruption', an idea that enjoyed currency after 1815, claimed to identify a world of status and hierarchy, and point to its alleged props: privilege, patronage, places, pensions, sinecures. Corruption was old, but 'Old Corruption' was new. It might be asked whether there was anything special in these phenomena: all wars have similar consequences. At the time, however, the label was new, and effective. Against a world so characterised stood, some claimed, a new set of values, some-times expressed in terms of natural rights and equality of opportunity, sometimes in terms of Jeremy Bentham's philosophy of utilitarianism, sometimes in terms of radicalism, with its denigration of the landowner and the established church. Although the nexus of sinecures, pensions and con-tracts used to support government was steadily scaled down from Pitt's ministry of 1784 onwards, enough remained that radicals could ignore this progressive abolition and paint what William Cobbett called 'The Thing' in increasingly threatening hues. This concept, drawing a variety of phenomena together and claiming that they constituted a system, allowed people at the time to hail 1832 as a major watershed, although it equally allowed others to complain that too little had changed.

Second, the perception of general and widespread change in society proceeding independently of the political events of 1828–35. In 1829 a Yorkshire gentleman wrote:

For some time a *Revolution* has been commenced & is regularly *progressing*, in our *feelings*, our *manners*, & our *principles political & religious*. We are no longer the same people that we were seventy years ago: there is no longer the same hospitality amongst acquaintance, nor the same warm attachment amongst connections, even the nearest; there are no *gradations* of rank in society, either in regard to *birth*, to *dress*, to *manners*, nor even to *acquirements*. A general appearance of equality pervades all classes without leaving any line of distinction between them. Even between the *rich* & the *poor* there is little apparent difference; all persons live alike however different may be their income; indeed the fluctuation of property is so rapid, that he who is poor to-day may by some fortunate speculation be rich tomorrow, & the great capitalist may be at once plunged into poverty.[125]

It is a timeless cliché that people are not as they once were, and these remarks need to be interpreted; nevertheless, they were part of a wider body of comment on a shift from an aristocratic to a free-market society. Such transitions happen slowly: if correctly identified here, they must have begun long before 1832 and continued long afterwards. Yet such changes often have symbolic moments and determinative events that end the hegemony of one set of values and promote the extension of others. The year 1832 may have been one such moment.

Third, the impact of the major legislation of 1828–35. Some of the clearest and most testable evidence concerns the nature of the Reform Act of 1832, around which much historical controversy has raged. Yet the 1832 Act's impact cannot be judged by reading its text alone; it must be read against the circumstances that led to it. Here, the evidence does not support the idea that there was a pent-up demand for the franchise over the long eighteenth century that was triumphantly achieved with the passing of the Act: even in the 'first age of party', 1689–1714, this demand was not heard, while after the 1720s the numbers of people voting fell away substantially: many more men had the vote than cast it. This did not imply a political quiescence from which 1832 was an awakening. In some boroughs with householder franchises, participation rates could be substantial, and borough seats were often in commercial and manufacturing centres like Leicester, Norwich and Nottingham, or ports like Bristol, Harwich, Newcastle upon Tyne and Liverpool. Much is often made of the 'unrepresented' state of growing manufacturing towns, yet their inhabitants normally voted in the counties within which those towns were located, and voted on the wide forty-shilling franchise that applied in the counties. One characteristic of the English representative system was that a substantially plebeian electorate (and four-fifths of English MPs sat for boroughs) consistently returned patrician candidates. Of the one-sixth of MPs in 1790–1830 who were merchants or bankers, most sided with the ministry against parliamentary reform. So the absence of any long-term demand for 'democracy' may tell either in favour of, or against, the idea that the 1832 Act represented a fundamental change: 1832 may have initiated a new and democratic era, or this may have been brought about for other reasons entirely. On this reading, the significant increase after 1832 was not in the number entitled to vote, but in the proportion of seats contested; 1832 reinstated two-party politics and the alternation of parties in government (in abeyance since 1714) rather than initiating democracy.

It was conventional to treat parliamentary reform in 1832 as a response to an Industrial Revolution, but the plausibility of this scenario has also weakened as the timing and scale of economic change have been reassessed. Proposals for the reform of Parliament long preceded industrialisation; the novel ideology of universal manhood suffrage was devised in the 1760s for reasons unconnected with economic change, and for half a century achieved no mass audience in growing cities or manufacturing districts. Parliamentary reform was a cry heard in London more than in Leeds, in Westminster more than in Wolverhampton. Not until 1816–17 did agitation for Reform become prominent in industrial areas, and it has not been established that it was the urban or the industrial nature of those areas that caused new political attitudes; rather, Reform was widely seen as a generalised remedy for an economic slump, and recovery in the 1820s stilled those demands until the next recession in 1829–30. It should weigh with those who prefer reductionist explanations that industrialisation had hardly yet developed: in 1832 Britain possessed only 166 miles of railway against the 20,266 miles of the mature system in 1913, and other such indices of output tell the same story. If political change was not compelled by economic change, this may tell in favour of, or against, the idea that 1832 represented a watershed. Political change, if self-caused, might have been sudden rather than incremental; or it might alternatively have been largely irrelevant to the economy's long continuities.

Because of such uncertainties it is still debated how far an erosion in the position of the established order took place over time and was complete before 1832, or how far a hegemonic system retained its grip, despite some degree of numerical erosion, until a late and relatively sudden disintegration. If 'underlying' or 'long term' change did not make a watershed inevitable, we can briefly sum up the other arguments for and against a fundamental transition.

The argument against a watershed points to the areas in which the 1832 Reform Act made little difference. The landed interest still filled the House of Commons, and the number of

MPs who were merchants or manufacturers did not greatly rise. Numbers voting increased from 400,000, but only to about 600,000: there was no intention on the part of the ministry to initiate an age of democracy, and equally little recognition that the middle classes were now to be given political power, let alone the working classes. In the discussions of the Whig government on the contents of the 1832 Bill, the secret ballot was considered, but dropped: the intention was to preserve 'influence'. It was because voting was still open and subject to scrutiny that the qualification was reduced to the level of the £10 householder.[126] Whigs continued to claim that 1832 was final. Even the firebrand Lord John Russell argued thus until 1848; Gladstone voted against Reform in the 1850s, and backed it only from 1865. The really large extensions of the franchise waited for the reform Acts of 1867 and 1884, and it was this later era that saw a marked further rise in the proportion of seats contested at general elections.

The argument in favour of major change invokes other aspects of the question. In one view the end of a social order came when its constitutional-libertarian tradition was brought to merge with resurgent Dissent, joined now by the programmatic atheism that an intelligentsia had propagated. By creating a uniform franchise, the 1832 Act has been argued to have played a large role in the formation of the notion of a singular 'middle class'.[127] Reformers tried to define this middle class as those worthy of the franchise, as distinct from the mob; but class politics was antithetical to the old order.

The Act embodied major advantages for the landed classes in the short term, especially the rise in English county seats from eighty-two to 144, but may have ensured their eventual destruction. It had been passed amidst extra-parliamentary pressure: henceforth Parliament would have to work in the shadow of a militant 'public opinion'. The Act was in some respects intended by its authors to be symbolic: the large number of small borough seats it abolished recognised the validity of the critique of Old Corruption, and it was pushed through despite the shock caused to the political classes.[128] Most of the MPs returned for nomination boroughs were Tories. The Act was not final, as its defenders claimed, but led to further Reform Acts in 1867, 1884 and 1918. Yet the extension of the franchise was not the key theme in 1832, and possibly not even in 1867; what mattered more were the mechanics of representation, not any principled affirmation of the direct representation of the individual.

By 1867, Walter Bagehot was arguing in *The English Constitution* that the state was already a republic in all but name, under a token monarchy. It was also a state significantly more secularised: the Church of England had been the great loser in 1832, vilified by radicals for siding with the old order (the bishops had voted against the first Reform Bill, in October 1831, by twenty-one to two). Old Corruption was an idea that, thanks to radicalism, had centrally included the church. A Unitarian, John Wade, had set out figures for the inequalities of clerical incomes in *The Black Book: or, corruption unmasked* (1820), extended as *The Extraordinary Black Book* (1832). From Jeremy Bentham to James Mill, some intellectuals from the middling orders had been hostile to the church; from the 1800s populist reformers had taken up the cry, as was clear in the Captain Swing riots among landless agricultural labourers in England's south-east and the riots over the Reform Bill in several towns in 1830–2. Until 1914, English politics was heavily shaped by the Protestant Nonconformist assault on the surviving powers of the church, an assault that largely succeeded in marginalising it.

Historians debate whether the changes of these years were part of an integrated programme, changes that share the label 'reform'.[129] Those who deny this tend to conclude that the reforms themselves were not major changes; yet this may be a normative judgement. It seems likely that (except for small groups, such as the followers of Jeremy Bentham) even the Whig parliamentary party did not come to office in 1830 with an organised agenda of legislative change. Most politicians reacted pragmatically to events. What was more in evidence was a law of unintended consequences, as each innovation changed the structure of the system and led on to further innovation.

Fourth, the comparative dimension. The question whether Britain was an ancien regime polity might best be considered in a comparative framework, first between the British Isles and continental Europe, and second between England, Ireland, Scotland and Wales; but little such analysis has yet been undertaken. It seems clear, however, that the internal dynamic within the British Isles did not cease in 1832. Rather, the balance of power tilted markedly, so that Wales, Ireland and Scotland carried far more weight in the century after 1832 than in the century before. If the old order rested on English hegemony, this was profoundly modified.

Such matters are hard to quantify, but one point of access is provided by the controversies of the age about the nature and position of the elite. Some historians have argued that Britain's social order should not be analysed as an ancien regime since, unlike in continental Europe, different social groups did not possess legal immunities. Peers, as well as people, paid taxes and were subject to the criminal law. There is much truth in that argument, seen from a present-day perspective; but it often appeared differently to people at the time. They were aware that differences of status were expressed in terms of 'rank', and that rank was contested. In the countryside, where most people still lived, the idea of a social hierarchy was most palpable (indeed the crisis of 1828–35 was in part a clash between the values of country and town). In England there was one part of the legal code that was intended to, and did, secure special privilege to landed gentlemen: the game laws, codified by the Act of 1671, supplemented and modified by later legislation, but not fundamentally recast until 1831.

In such a mental world a recognition of privilege attached to rank was valued by some, condemned by others. Defenders of the old order used a range of arguments: the positive contribution to society of country gentlemen residing on their estates; the need to keep this practical system in repair by not blurring the distinction between gentlemen and plebeians; the defence of a system associated with the country against the values of townsmen; a siding with the economic plight of the rural labourer, ignored by the London government. The game laws came to symbolise the values of 'land' against the values of 'money'.[130] The redefinition of game as private property rather than as elite privilege, and the collapse of the practice of duelling within a decade of the 1832 Act, is in this view evidence of British society's redefinition away from the assumptions of an old order.

Yet if comparisons with France before 1789 are revealing, comparisons within the British Isles make the pattern far less clear. The term 'Old Corruption' pointed to a particularly English formation, less characteristic of Scotland, Wales and Ireland. Social systems within the British Isles were diverse. In each of its component parts some voices from the 1790s agreed with the Jacobin analysis, developed critiques of

Britain's leading institutions and practices, and found ways of pursuing their interests. Yet these varied considerably between the polities: the intellectual critique of the old order came from a number of sources. One was provided by Scotland, whose intelligentsia abandoned the fervent Unionism of the mid eighteenth century and from the 1790s proved receptive to new ideas, especially political economy and Benthamite utilitarianism. Englishmen educated at Scottish universities imbibed similar doctrines. The *Edinburgh Review* (founded 1802) sold as well in England, and provided a rationale for the revived Whig party that passed the 1832 Reform Act and the reforms that followed.

This was not a common model, however: where Scotland responded to the world after 1815 with the mindset of the *Edinburgh Review*, Ireland's response was the mindset represented in O'Connell's Catholic Association. Catholic emancipation was accompanied by raising the Irish county franchise to exclude those who had supported the Catholic Association. But this formal barrier was to prove ineffective against the populist politics that O'Connell had created. In the nineteenth century, Scotland remained within the Union, arguably at the price of the Union's increasing penetration by Scots values; southern Ireland increasingly resisted both English and Scots world views, threatened to secede, and finally did so to embody a very different outlook that led to its neutrality between Britain and Nazi Germany in the Second World War. This was not the attitude that prevailed in Ireland before 1801.

The hegemony of a new social sector in England was quickly evident with the rejection by Parliament in 1833 of the 'ten hours' movement (an attempt to limit the working day in factories) and the passage of the Poor Law Amendment Act in

1834. This ended the right of the poor to receive parish assistance in their homes and established instead a network of workhouses, far more than had previously existed, designed to be so much more miserable as to promote industriousness as the lesser evil. This was not merely an English Whig innovation; it was inspired by practice elsewhere in the British Isles. Scotland had not developed a compulsory poor-relief system, despite legislative efforts in the late sixteenth and early seventeenth centuries. By the eighteenth, Scotland in principle gave no relief to paupers who were classed as 'able-bodied'; paupers who were aged or infirm depended on meagre charitable collections at church, allocated by the ministers and elders, and administered by the heritors (landowners). Now these quite different Scots assumptions were applied to England and Wales, and widely interpreted as ending an older set of customs and values.

On one side in the emerging debate on the 'condition of England' question were social campaigners, in alliance with Tory paternalists who stressed the moral responsibility of landowners for the well-being of their localities; on the other were Liberal manufacturers, political economists and 'philosophic radicals', the followers of Benthamite utilitarianism, for whom unconstrained choice maximised individual utility. Like most Benthamite schemes, the 1834 Poor Law was implemented only in part, with wide regional variations: workhouses were too expensive, and unemployment was too widespread, to allow such tidy solutions. Yet the point was one of principle. It might be argued that a new view of man as an independent, secular, rational calculator had gained the ascendant; and with the Municipal Corporations Act (1835) this view secured hegemony in local government in England and Wales. National politics continued for many decades to be dominated by the landed elite; but in the towns and cities, in which a growing section of the population spent their lives, a new social constituency was in charge, which came to seem to be self-evidently 'the middle class', defined now as enemies (not, as in the 1820s, as allies) of the working classes.

British society in the late eighteenth and early nineteenth centuries was steadily evolving, innovative, increasingly geographically and socially mobile, technologically minded; but it was all these things within the familiar structures of 'church and state', and these were the primary targets of reformers. Some historians explain this survival in terms of ruthless and successful repression by the ruling orders. Others point to a considerable degree of social solidarity, and doubt the 'contradiction' between 'structure' and 'superstructure' that historians used to depict. Such weighty matters are still at issue when Britain's status as an ancien regime is debated.

Part IV
Some Counterfactuals

Identifying the main lines of historical development of the British Isles has the effect of identifying other, perhaps more plausible, paths that were not taken. It is worth setting these out systematically. Such an exercise warns us against 'naïve counterfactualism', the hopeful and therefore normative belief that but for some single policy mistake, all would have been well. All is never well: history moves through conflict and loss. Yet this does not establish that things could not have been different.

In a wider perspective nothing can be taken for granted, not even the course followed by population totals. It would be easy to envisage a situation in which England and Scotland matched Ireland's runaway population growth, with equally disastrous results. England and Scotland might then have dealt with such a population boom in the Irish manner, by a progressive subdivision of landholdings. This might have kept the custom-bound, corporatist local community in being for some decades more, but with such a response rampant population growth is likely to have immiserated the countryside more than enclosures and internal migration did. Those who idealise the 'moral economy' assume that an old order could have survived, centred on smallholdings and customary use-rights for the poor; but this projection depends on the assumption that the 'customary society' would not have generated a population explosion. Since in Ireland and parts of the Scottish Highlands it did just that, this assumption is implausible. It may be that all the major options pointed forward to widespread distress; in England and Scotland that could have meant revolution, as it did in France after near-famine in 1788–9, rather than Ireland's politically quiescent response to the disaster of the 1840s.

Revolution was avoided chiefly owing to the special case of England. England's pre-industrial and commercial economy was markedly successful even before the growth of manufacturing industry, and this success is generally taken for granted. Yet England could have followed the pattern of that other notable commercial economy, the United Provinces, commercially dynamic in the seventeenth century yet less successful in the eighteenth.[1] Here again, the counterfactual of England's mercantilist failure in the face of French rivalry might have led to revolution at home.

Many of the differences between the United Provinces and England, then Britain, were political; and political counterfactuals are more easily framed than economic ones. The collapse of the English republic in 1660 was by no means inevitable; it might be seen as the result of a military coup by General Monck. Without the army's intervention, England might have continued as a republic on Presbyterian foundations. Yet against this possibility must be set the relative lack, within the British Isles, of regional bases of military power: English, Scottish and Irish monarchical government therefore still tended towards centralised rule. A powerful military regime in England implied England's military dominance of Scotland and Ireland, as Oliver Cromwell had clearly appreciated. Such a republican regime, centralised and militarised, would probably have led, in an age of religious ferment and denominational resistance theory, to far more religiously based armed conflicts than was the case after 1660. Edmund Burke looked back on the restored monarchy, even in the person of Charles II, as a crucial guarantor of political stability and internal peace, and in this he may have been right.

Internal stability was nevertheless not a secure possession, and stability gained in one decade might be lost in the next. So it proved when the fall of the Stuart monarchy in 1688 led to six decades of external war, internal rebellion and religious schism. The deposition of James II was no foregone conclusion. Willem van Oranje's naval expedition might have enjoyed the same logistical ill fortune that later dogged successive Jacobite invasion attempts (and most combined operations in the age of sail). In that event James would have retained authority, beyond challenge from internal enemies. A Catholic monarchy, continued after James's death in 1701 by the son born to him in 1688 and who lived until 1766, might, in a still strongly Protestant polity, have been able to do little more than secure toleration for all religious groups: the Anglican hegemony of the long eighteenth century would have been unseated, and the religious pluralism that followed 1828–9 would have arrived decades earlier.

Whether Parliament would have emerged essentially weakened from this encounter is harder to gauge: the usual celebration of Parliament's powers after 1688 and 1714 rests on a greatly exaggerated estimate of the ability of the Commons to control ministries. In reality, ministries developed powerful means of controlling the Commons rather than vice versa. A continued Stuart monarchy might have made little difference. It would have been denounced by spokesmen for the strident anti-Catholicism still widespread within the British Isles, yet the experience of a tolerant Catholic regime might have meant that this ancient antipathy of Catholic and Protestant weakened two centuries before it did.

Even given Willem van Oranje's landing with a significant army in 1688, the result might have been political compromise rather than James's expulsion. In that case, Parliament's position would have been enhanced at the same time that a larger measure of religious toleration was secured. Even James II's expulsion in 1688 need not have been a final exclusion of the Stuarts: the wide unpopularity of the Williamite and Hanoverian regimes provided serious support for a Stuart restoration in all the component parts of the archipelago. This was practical politics only with military backing from overseas; yet this was often planned, and often possible. The French fleet might have covered a major landing in 1744 with every chance of linking with support in England. The last such invasion attempt was that of 1759, and only the astonishing series of victories of that year removed that possibility.

A Stuart restoration might have reduced or eliminated the bloodshed endemic in England's relations with Scotland and Ireland, but at the price of igniting armed conflict at an earlier date with the New England colonies, animated as they often were with an anti-Catholicism more virulent than anywhere else in the English-speaking world. An American Revolution in 1715 might have stood much less chance of success, with important long-term consequences; in 1715, France would probably not have intervened.

Revolution did occur in 1776, but its inevitability is in doubt. The founding myth of the American republic, drawn from England's Whig political rhetoric of the Exclusion Crisis, presented the alternatives as 'liberty' or 'slavery', independence or permanent imperial subservience. But this was a false antithesis, and the second a misdescription of reality. It is difficult to see Britain's colonies in North America remaining within the empire for more than a few decades: most of the Thirteen Colonies were already developing towards de facto self rule, and would have continued to do so. The real alternatives for the colonies in the 1770s were between, first, a dangerous bid for independence via world war and internal revolution, or, second, a better prospect of independence a few decades later via commonplace political conflict and negotiation. If so, the path actually followed looks less attractive and less inevitable.

It looks less attractive again if the major geopolitical cause of the independence of the Thirteen Colonies had been otherwise. If Britain had been able to fight the war of 1776–83 with one or more significant allies on the European continent, there is every possibility of a different, perhaps a compromised, outcome. Yet successful continental alliances were a major part of British foreign policy throughout this period, and their absence in the 1770s was not inevitable.

Another alternative was a peaceful one. Much would have been different had the Thirteen Colonies followed Canada's peaceful route to negotiated independence. Within North America, the two major acts of genocide that marked the foundation of the United States might have been mitigated. The expropriation and murder of Native Americans by white

settlers might have been under at least some degree of governmental restraint, since relations with the tribes were regulated
in detail by the treaties into which the British government had
entered with Native Americans in order to win their support
against France in the Seven Years War; these obligations the
new American republic disavowed. The practice of negro
slavery, too, would have been checked, since Mansfield's
landmark verdict in *Somerset* v. *Stewart* (1772) clearly established
that English law did not recognise slavery, and the principle
must soon have been applied in the colonies. The anti-slavery
movement developed on any scale first in Britain, not America,
and would have made greater headway at an earlier date
without the American war. Even in an age of revolution,
Britain was compelled by the opinion of its elite to act against
the slave trade, first by the use of the Royal Navy to end the
trade itself, then by buying out the slave-owners. The extent
of slavery in North America was far smaller in 1776 than it
became by the 1860s, and it was still a problem that could have
been contained and solved by the metropolitan government.
The possibility that North America's devastating and essentially
related civil wars of 1776–83 and 1861–5 could both have been
avoided is real.

Internationally, without an American revolutionary war
France would not have collapsed in bankruptcy as it did in
1788, leading to the recall of the Estates General and revolution
in 1789: the absence of revolution would have meant that
France, and Europe generally, could have pursued a path of
meliorist reform. Without the convulsions and losses of war
in 1776–83, 1793–1802 and 1803–1815, Britain's national debt
would have fallen, capital would have been employed instead
in manufacture, trade and agriculture, British (and North
American) society would have been substantially more

prosperous, and the pressures for violent reform at home would have been mitigated.

All these affluent but mundane outcomes were blasted by war and revolution. In that setting, Britain's survival within revolutionary Europe was not a foregone conclusion. Many historians claim that domestic insurrection was a real possibility in the 1790s, even in England. In Ireland, the potential for armed conflict was far greater, and greater again in the event of a French invasion. The failure of the French navy to deliver this outcome in the 1790s is highlighted by the scale of the Irish rebellion which materialised in 1798 even without significant French aid. In combination with mutinies in the fleet in 1797, a successful Irish rising would have destabilised the state and might easily have brought a version of the French Revolution to the British Isles, as happened so often elsewhere in Europe. Even if revolution had been avoided in the 1790s, all was not secure: the significance of the battle of Trafalgar in 1805 was that it smashed a Franco-Spanish naval combination whose aim was to allow the landing in Britain of the vast army that Napoleon had massed at Boulogne. Had this army, the most effective in Europe, set foot on British soil, its success would have been highly likely.

Britain's course of development in the nineteenth century was set within limits established by her survival of war and the threat of revolution. This survival was remarkable. Historians have found a series of ways of describing it as inevitable: the Whig myth of English constitutional liberties; the model of successful capitalist exploitation; the strength of a fiscal-military state. All are open to major objections. At any point between 1660 and 1832, the future was wholly uncertain.

Appendix

Table 1. Population of the British Isles

Totals in millions

	England[1]	Wales[2]	Ireland[3]	Scotland[4]
1541	2.830	0.207		
1641	5.130			
1661	5.280			
1671	5.159			
1681	5.109			
1691	5.094			1.23[5]
1701	5.211			
1706			2.06	
1707				1.048[6]
1711	5.382			
1712			2.32	
1721	5.503			
1731	5.414			
1732			2.53	
1741	5.723			

1744			2.23	
1751	5.922			
1753			2.57	
1755				1.265
1761	6.310			
1767			3.480	
1771	6.623			
1781	7.206	0.545	4.048	1.435
1791	7.846		4.42	
1795				1.526
1801	8.671	0.541	5.216	1.608
1811	9.864	0.611	5.956	1.806
1821	11.456	0.717	6.802	2.092
1831	13.254	0.807	7.767	2.364
1841	14.937	0.911	8.175	2.620

Table 2. Percentage of the population living in towns of 10,000 or more, and total population of those towns in thousands[7]

Year	England and Wales		Scotland		Ireland	
	000s	%	000s	%	000s	%
1650	495	8.8	35	3.5	17	1.1
1700	718	13.3	53	5.3	96	5.3
1750	1021	16.7	119	9.2	161	7.0
1800	1870	20.3	276	17.3	369	7.4

Table 3. Estimates of annual economic growth rates[8]

	National Product	National Product per head
1700–60	0.69	0.31
1760–80	0.70	0.01
1780–1801	1.32	0.35
1801–31	1.97	0.52

Table 4. English land ownership[9]

	1690	1790
Great owners: over 3,000 acres	15–20%	20–25%
Gentry: 300–3,000 acres	45–50	50
Small owners: less than 300 acres	25–35	15

Table 5. Parties in the House of Commons, 1713–1747[10]

The figures are for MPs as returned, before changes on petition that generally favoured the ministry.

Year	Ministerial Whigs	Opposition Whigs	Tories
1713	200	—	358
1715	341	—	217
1722	379	—	178
1727	409	15	130
1734	326	83	149
1741	286	131	136
1747	338	97	117

Table 6. Central Government Income and Expenditure[11]
In £ million.

(1) Year	(2) Total income	(3) Total expenditure	(4) Army, Navy, Ordnance	(5) Debt payments	(6) (4) and (5) as % of (3)	(7) National debt
1661/2	1.45	1.00	0.61	0.04	65%	
1671/2	2.30[12]	2.38	1.17	0.45	68%	
1681/2	1.38	1.06	0.66	0.06	67%	
1692	4.11	4.25	3.39	0.20	84.47%	3.3
1702	4.87	5.01	3.31	1.17	89.42%	14.1
1712	5.75	7.86	4.78	2.36	90.84%	34.9
1722	6.15	6.98	2.78	3.01	82.95%	52.7
1732	5.80	4.97	1.82	2.22	84.34%	50.1
1742	6.41	8.53	5.66	2.04	90.27%	51.3
1752	6.99	7.04	2.98	2.94	84.09%	76.9
1762	9.46	20.04	14.42	4.40	93.91%	126.6
1772	11.03	10.72	4.57	4.69	86.38%	128.7
1782	13.76	29.23	20.12	7.36	94.01%	214.3
1792	18.60	16.95	5.58	9.31	87.85%	241.6
1802	39.1	65.5	37.4	19.9	87.48%	498.6
1812	71.0	87.3	53.4	24.6	89.35%	626.0
1822	61.6	58.4	16.7	31.9	83.22%	831.1
1832	50.6	51.5	14.4	28.3	82.91%	784.2

Table 7. British naval strength[13]

Total displacement in 1,000 tons

	England/ Britain	France	Netherlands	Spain
1660	88	20	62	?
1670	84	114	102	?
1680	132	135	66	(15)
1690	124	141	68	(30)
1700	196	195	113	(20)
1710	201	171	119	(10)
1720	174	48	79	22
1730	189	73	62	73
1740	195	91	65	91
1750	276	115	62	41
1760	375	156	62	137
1770	350	219	79	165
1780	372	271	70	196
1790	473	324	123	253
1800	546	204	40	227
1810	673	246	?	100
1815	616	228	71	60

Table 8. A Divided Society: two national anthems

The origin of this tune and lyrics have consequences for historical interpretation of the early eighteenth century. The Hanoverian version was first published in book form in English in *Thesaurus Musicus* (London: J. Simpson, [1744]), a collection of songs printed and sold separately in previous years (with alterations to the plate of this one), but there with two verses only, and not mentioning King George. The edition of 1745, with George's name, had three verses, as did the version in the *Gentleman's Magazine* (15 October 1745); further verses were therefore devised in the 1740s, probably in response to the Jacobite rising. Yet its origin was much older: the musicologist Charles Burney wrote to Sir Joseph Banks in 1806 that 'Old Mrs Arne, the mother of Dr Arne and Mrs Cibber, a bigoted Roman Catholic, assured me at the time, 1746, that *God save the King* was written and sung for KING JAMES, in 1688, when the Prince of Orange was hovering over the coast: she said she had heard it sung not only at the Playhouse but in the Street'; the composer Dr Arne himself said 'that it was a received opinion that it was written and composed for the *Catholic Chapel* of James II'. Dr Benjamin Cooke, organist of Westminster Abbey, born in 1734, said in 1796 that 'when a boy he remembered to have heard the song sung to the words *God save great James our king*'. French sources credit the music to Jean-Baptiste Lully, who allegedly composed a version with the words *Dieu protège le roi* for Louis XIV in 1686; from there the tune was echoed by Purcell, and the Jacobite version of the words has been traced to *c*.1688–1701; the fifth verse refers to William III. The Hanoverian version was therefore a late attempt to appropriate a Jacobite original. As with all such songs, not yet possessing official status, there were variant texts, and they developed over time; the sixth verses of both versions speak to the Jacobite rebellion of 1745–6. For two Jacobite texts to the tune see James Hogg, *The Jacobite Relics of Scotland* (1819–21), 2nd ser., ed. Murray Pittock (Edinburgh, 2003), pp. 50–3, 493; for a Hanoverian version, Percy A. Scholes, *God Save the Queen! The history and romance of the world's first national anthem* (London, 1954), pp. 3–26, but cf. pp. 49–73. Thurston Dart, 'Maurice Greene and the National Anthem', *Music and Letters*, 37 (1956), pp. 205–10, dates the opening of the Hanoverian version to the late 1730s: 'An eighteenth-century facade, in fact, has been added to a seventeenth-century building', p. 210. Recent historical writing that overlooks the earlier origin of the song and treats it as spontaneously arising evidence for consensual Whig liberty in the 1740s is problematic. There was also a Jacobite version of 'Rule, Britannia!'

A Hanoverian version

1. God save great GEORGE our king,
Long live our noble king,
God save the king.
Send him victorious,
Happy and glorious,
Long to reign over us,
God save the king.

2. O Lord our God arise,
Scatter his enemies
And make them fall;
Confound their politics,
Frustrate their knavish tricks,
On him our hopes we fix,
O save us all.

3. Thy choicest gifts in store
On George be pleas'd to pour,
Long may he reign;
May he defend our laws,
And ever give us cause,
To say with heart and voice
God save the king.

4. Not in this land alone,
But be God's mercies known,
From shore to shore!

A Stuart version

1. Britons who dare to claim
That great and glorious name,
Rouse at the call!
See English honour fled,
Corruption's influence spread,
Slavery raise its head,
And freedom fall!

2. Church, king and liberty,
Honour and property,
All are betray'd:
Foreigners rule the land,
Our blood and wealth command,
Obstruct, with lawless hand,
Justice and trade.

3. Shall an usurper reign,
And Britons hug the chain?
That we'll deny.
Then let us all unite
To retrieve James's right
For church, king, and laws we'll fight,
Conquer or die.

4. Join in the just defence
Of James our lawful prince
And native king:

Lord make the nations see,
That men should brothers be,
And form one family,
The wide world over.

5. From every latent foe,
From the assassins blow,
God save the king!
O'er him thine arm extend,
For Britain's sake defend,
Our father, prince, and friend,
God save the King!

6. Lord grant that Marshal Wade
May by thy mighty aid
Victory bring.
May he sedition hush,
And like a torrent rush,
Rebellious Scots to crush.
God save the king!

Then shall true greatness shine,
Justice and mercy join,
Restor'd by Stuart's line,
Virtue's great spring.

5. Down with Dutch politics,
Whigs, and all fanatics,
The old Rump's cause!
Recall your injur'd prince
Drive Hanoverians hence,
Such as rule here against
All English laws.

6. Borne on the wings of fame,
Charles's heroic name
All his foes dread.
He'll from his father's throne
Pull the usurper down;
Glorious success shall crown
His sacred head.

Bibliography

The purpose of this list is to give general guidance; for more specific references see the notes.

General surveys

Jeremy Black, *Eighteenth-Century Britain 1688–1783* (2nd edn, Basingstoke, 2008)

Ian R. Christie, *Wars and Revolutions: Britain 1760–1815* (London, 1982)

J. C. D. Clark, *English Society 1660–1832: religion, ideology and politics during the ancien regime* (2nd edn, Cambridge, 2000)

Martin Daunton, *Progress and Poverty: an economic and social history of Britain 1700–1850* (Oxford, 1995)

Eric J. Evans, *The Forging of the Modern State: early industrial Britain 1783–1870* (3rd edn, London, 2001)

Douglas Hay and Nicholas Rogers, *Eighteenth-Century English Society: shuttles and swords* (Oxford, 1997)

Boyd Hilton, *A Mad, Bad, and Dangerous People? England 1783–1846* (Oxford, 2006)

Geoffrey Holmes, *The Making of a Great Power: late Stuart and early Georgian Britain 1660–1722* (London, 1993)

Geoffrey Holmes and Daniel Szechi, *The Age of Oligarchy: pre-industrial Britain 1722–1783* (London, 1993)

Julian Hoppit, *A Land of Liberty? England, 1689–1727* (Oxford, 2000)

J. R. Jones, *Country and Court: England 1658–1714* (Arnold, 1978)

Paul Langford, *A Polite and Commercial People: England 1727–1783* (Oxford, 1989)

Frank O'Gorman, *The Long Eighteenth Century: British political and social history 1688–1832* (London, 1997)

Harold Perkin, *The Origins of Modern English Society 1780–1880* (London, 1969)

W. R. Prest, *Albion Ascendant: English history, 1660–1815* (Oxford, 1998)

Richard Price, *British Society 1680–1880* (Cambridge, 1999)

Edward Royle, *Modern Britain: a social history 1750–1997* (2nd edn, London, 1997)

Jonathan Scott, *England's Troubles: seventeenth-century English political instability in European context* (Cambridge, 2000)

J. A. Sharpe, *Early Modern England: a social history 1550–1760* (2nd edn, London, 1997)

W. A. Speck, *Stability and Strife: England 1714–1760* (London, 1977)

F. M. L. Thompson (ed.), *The Cambridge Social History of Britain 1750–1950* (3 vols., Cambridge, 1990)

Foreign policy

Jeremy Black, *Knights Errant and True Englishmen: British foreign policy, 1660–1800* (Edinburgh, 1989)

Jeremy Black, *America or Europe? British foreign policy, 1739–1763* (London, 1998)

Jeremy Black, *A System of Ambition? British foreign policy, 1660–1793* (2nd edn, Stroud, 2000)

Jeremy Black, *The Continental Commitment: Britain, Hanover and interventionism, 1714–1793* (London, 2005)

John Brewer, *The Sinews of Power: war, money and the English state, 1688–1783* (London, 1989)

J. R. Jones, *Britain and the World, 1649–1815* (London, 1980)

Brendan Simms, *Three Victories and a Defeat: the rise and fall of the first British Empire, 1714–1783* (London, 2007)

State formation

Michael Braddick, *The Nerves of State: taxation and the financing of the English state, 1558–1714* (Manchester, 1996)

M. J. Braddick, *State Formation in Early Modern England, c.1550–1700* (Cambridge, 2000)

Brendan Bradshaw and John Morrill (eds.), *The British Problem, c.1534–1707: state formation in the Atlantic archipelago* (London, 1996)

Brendan Bradshaw and Peter Roberts (eds.), *British Consciousness and Identity: the making of Britain, 1533–1707* (Cambridge, 1998)

John Brewer, *The Sinews of Power: war, money and the English state, 1688–1783* (London, 1989)

Tony Claydon, *Europe and the Making of England 1660–1760* (Cambridge, 2007)

Steven G. Ellis and Sarah Barber (eds.), *Conquest and Union: fashioning a British state 1485–1725* (London, 1995)

Alexander Grant and Keith Stringer (eds.), *Uniting the Kingdom? the making of British history* (London, 1995)

Michael Hechter, *Internal Colonialism: the Celtic fringe in British national development, 1536–1966* (London, 1975)

John Kendle, *Federal Britain: a history* (London, 1997)

Jim Smyth, *The Making of the United Kingdom, 1660–1800: state, religion and identity in Britain and Ireland* (Harlow, 2001)

National identity

J. C. D. Clark, 'Protestantism, Nationalism and National Identity, 1660–1832', *Historical Journal*, 43 (2000), pp. 249–76

Tony Claydon and Ian McBride (eds.), *Protestantism and National Identity: Britain and Ireland c.1650–c.1850* (Cambridge, 1998)

Robin Eagles, *Francophilia in English Society, 1748–1815* (London, 2000)

Colin Haydon, *Anti-Catholicism in Eighteenth-Century England, c.1714–1780: a political and social study* (Manchester, 1993)

Paul Langford, *Englishness Identified: manners and character, 1650–1850* (Oxford, 2000)

John Lucas, *England and Englishness: ideas of nationhood in English poetry 1688–1900* (London, 1990)

Peter Mandler, *The English National Character: the history of an idea from Edmund Burke to Tony Blair* (New Haven, 2006)

Alexander Murdoch, *British History 1660–1832: national identity and local culture* (London, 1998)

Gerald Newman, *The Rise of English Nationalism: a cultural history 1740–1830* (2nd edn, London, 1997)

Murray G. H. Pittock, *Inventing and Resisting Britain: cultural identities in Britain and Ireland, 1685–1789* (London, 1997)

Keith Robbins, *Great Britain: identities, institutions and the idea of Britishness* (London, 1998)

Law

J. M. Beattie, *Crime and the Courts in England, 1660–1800* (Oxford, 1986)

John Brewer and John Styles, *An Ungovernable People: the English and their law in the seventeenth and eighteenth centuries* (London, 1980)

Douglas Hay, Peter Linebaugh and E. P. Thompson, *Albion's Fatal Tree: crime and society in eighteenth-century England* (London, 1975)

Peter King, *Crime, Justice and Discretion in England 1740–1820* (Oxford, 2000)

Peter King, *Crime and Law in England 1750–1840: remaking justice from the margins* (Cambridge, 2006)

David Lemmings, *Law and Government in England during the Long Eighteenth Century: from consent to command* (Basingstoke, 2011)

David Lieberman, *The Province of Legislation Determined: legal theory in eighteenth-century Britain* (Cambridge, 1989)

Peter Linebaugh, *The London Hanged: crime and civil society in the eighteenth century* (2nd edn, London, 2003)

Howard Nenner, *By Colour of Law: legal culture and constitutional politics in England, 1660–1689* (Chicago, 1977)

Lisa Steffen, *Defining a British State: treason and national identity, 1608–1820* (Basingstoke, 2001)

E. P. Thompson, *Whigs and Hunters: the origin of the Black Act* (London, 1975)

Scotland

David Allan, *Scotland in the Eighteenth Century: Union and Enlightenment* (Harlow, 2002)

Keith M. Brown, *Kingdom or Province? Scotland and the Regal Union, 1603–1715* (2nd edn, Basingstoke, 1993)

Bruce Lenman, *Enlightenment and Change: Scotland 1746–1832* (2nd edn, Edinburgh, 2009)

John Robertson, *A Union for Empire: political thought and the British Union of 1707* (Cambridge, 1995)

J. S. Shaw, *The Political History of Eighteenth-Century Scotland* (Basingstoke, 1999)

Richard Sher, *Church and University in the Scottish Enlightenment* (Princeton, 1985)

Richard Sher, *Enlightenment and the Book: Scottish authors and their publishers in eighteenth-century Britain, Ireland and America* (Chicago, 2010)

T. C. Smout, *A History of the Scottish People 1560–1830* (London, 1969)

Chris Whatley, *Scottish Society 1707–1830: beyond Jacobitism, towards industrialisation* (Manchester, 2000)

Chris Whatley, *The Scots and the Union* (Edinburgh, 2006)

Ireland

Toby Barnard, *The Kingdom of Ireland, 1641–1760* (London, 2004)

Thomas Bartlett, *The Fall and Rise of the Irish Nation: the Catholic question 1690–1830* (Dublin, 1992)

D. George Boyce, *Nationalism in Ireland* (3rd edn, London, 1995)

S. J. Connolly, *Religion, Law and Power: the making of Protestant Ireland 1660–1760* (Oxford, 1992)

P. J. Corish, *The Catholic Community in the Seventeenth and Eighteenth Centuries* (Dublin, 1981)

L. M. Cullen, *An Economic History of Ireland since 1660* (London, 1972)

David Dickson, *New Foundations: Ireland 1660–1800* (2nd edn, Dublin, 2000)

Marianne Elliott, *Partners in Revolution: the United Irishmen and France* (New Haven, 1982)

F. G. James, *Ireland in the Empire, 1688–1770* (Cambridge, Mass., 1973)

C. D. A. Leighton, *Catholicism in a Protestant Kingdom: a study of the Irish ancien regime* (Basingstoke, 1994)

R. B. McDowell, *Ireland in the Age of Imperialism and Revolution 1760–1801* (Oxford, 1979)

P. McNally, *Parties, Patriots and Undertakers: parliamentary politics in early Hanoverian Ireland* (Dublin, 1997)

T. W. Moody and W. E. Vaughan (eds.), *A New History of Ireland. IV. Eighteenth-Century Ireland 1691–1800* (Oxford, 1986)

C. Ó Gráda, *Ireland: a new economic history, 1780–1939* (Oxford, 1994)

Jim Smyth, *The Men of No Property: Irish radicals and popular politics in the late eighteenth century* (2nd edn, Basingstoke, 1998)

Wales

Sir Reginald Coupland, *Welsh and Scottish Nationalism: a study* (London, 1954)

Geraint H. Jenkins, *Literature, Religion and Society in Wales, 1660–1730* (Cardiff, 1978)

Geraint H. Jenkins, *The Foundations of Modern Wales 1642–1780* (Oxford, 1987)

Philip Jenkins, *The Making of a Ruling Class: the Glamorgan gentry 1640–1790* (Cambridge, 1983)

Prys Morgan, *A New History of Wales: the eighteenth-century Renaissance* (Llandybie, 1981)

Naval and military

Thomas Bartlett and Keith Jeffrey (eds.), *A Military History of Ireland* (Cambridge, 1996)

John Childs, *Armies and Warfare in Europe, 1648–1789* (Manchester, 1982)

J. E. Cookson, *The British Armed Nation, 1793–1815* (Oxford, 1997)

David French, *The British Way in Warfare 1688–2000* (London, 1990)

Jan Glete, *Navies and Nations: warships, navies and state building in Europe and America, 1500–1860* (2 vols., Stockholm, 1993)

Richard Harding, *Sea Power and Naval Warfare, 1650–1830* (London, 1999)

Piers Mackesy, *The War for America, 1775–1783* (London, 1964)

A. T. Mahan, *The Influence of Sea Power upon History, 1660–1783* (Boston, Mass., 1890; London, 1965)

H. W. Richmond, *Statesmen and Sea Power* (Oxford, 1947)

N. A. M. Rodger, *The Command of the Ocean: a naval history of Britain 1649–1815* (London, 2004)

Lawrence Stone, *An Imperial State at War: Britain from 1689 to 1815* (London, 1994)

Intellectual Life and political thought

Alexander Broadie, *The Scottish Enlightenment: the historical age of the historical nation* (2nd edn, Edinburgh, 2001)

Edmund Burke, *Reflections on the Revolution in France*, ed. J. C. D. Clark (Stanford, 2001)

J. H. Burns (ed.), *The Cambridge History of Political Thought 1450–1700* (Cambridge, 1991)

A. C. Chitnis, *The Scottish Enlightenment: a social history* (London, 1976)

J. C. D. Clark, 'Religion and the Origins of Radicalism in Eighteenth-Century Britain', in Glenn Burgess and Matthew Festenstein (eds.), *English Radicalism, 1550–1850* (Cambridge, 2007)

Mark Francis and John Morrow, *A History of English Political Thought in the Nineteenth Century* (London, 1994)

Mark Goldie and Robert Wokler (eds.), *The Cambridge History of Eighteenth-Century Political Thought* (Cambridge, 2006)

T. L. Hankins, *Science in the Enlightenment* (Cambridge, 1985)

Ross Harrison, *Bentham* (London, 1983)

Andrew Hook and Richard B. Sher (eds.), *The Glasgow Enlightenment* (East Linton, 1995)

David Hume, *Essays Moral, Political and Literary*, ed. Eugene F. Miller (2nd edn, Indianapolis, 1987)

David Martin Jones, *Conscience and Allegiance in Seventeenth-Century England* (Rochester, NY, 1999)

J. P. Kenyon, *Revolution Principles: the Politics of Party 1689–1720* (Cambridge, 1977)

John Locke, *Two Treatises of Government*, ed. Peter Laslett (Cambridge, 1988)

Thomas Paine, *Collected Political Writings*, eds. Ian Shapiro and Jane E. Calvert (New Haven, 2013)

Mark Philp, *Godwin's Political Justice* (London, 1986)

Roy Porter, *Enlightenment: Britain and the creation of the modern world* (London, 2000)

Roy Porter (ed.), *The Cambridge History of Science. IV. Eighteenth-Century Science* (Cambridge, 2003)

Jane Rendall, *The Origins of the Scottish Enlightenment 1707–1776* (London, 1978)

John Robertson, *The Case for the Enlightenment: Scotland and Naples 1680–1760* (Cambridge, 2007)

Steven Shapin, *The Scientific Revolution* (Chicago, 1996)

David Spadafora, *The Idea of Progress in Eighteenth-Century Britain* (New Haven, 1990)

William Stafford, *Socialism, Radicalism and Nostalgia: social criticism in Britain, 1775–1830* (Cambridge, 1987)

Larry Stewart, *The Rise of Public Science: rhetoric, technology, and natural philosophy in Newtonian Britain, 1660–1750* (Cambridge, 1992)

Religion

Roger Anstey, *The Atlantic Slave Trade and British Abolition, 1760–1810* (London, 1975)

D. W. Bebbington, *Evangelicalism in Modern Britain: a history from the 1730s to the 1980s* (London, 1989)

John Bossy, *The English Catholic Community 1570–1850* (Oxford, 1976)

Callum G. Brown, *Religion and Society in Scotland since 1707* (2nd edn, Edinburgh, 1997)

Stewart J. Brown and Timothy Tackett (eds.), *The Cambridge History of Christianity. VII. Enlightenment, Reawakening and Revolution 1660–1815* (Cambridge, 2006)

J. A. I. Champion, *The Pillars of Priestcraft Shaken: the Church of England and its enemies, 1660–1730* (Cambridge, 1992)

J. C. D. Clark, 'The Eighteenth-Century Context', in William J. Abraham and James E. Kirby (eds.), *The Oxford Handbook to Methodist Studies* (Oxford, 2009)

Grayson Ditchfield, *The Evangelical Revival* (London, 1998)

William Gibson, *Church, State and Society, 1760–1850* (Basingstoke, 1994)

William Gibson, *The Church of England 1688–1832: unity and accord* (London, 2001)

Gabriel Glickman, *The English Catholic Community 1688–1745: politics, culture and ideology* (Woodbridge, 2009)

Colin Haydon, *Anti-Catholicism in Eighteenth-Century England, c.1714–80: a political and social study* (Manchester, 1993)

David Hempton, *Methodism and Politics in British Society 1750–1850* (London, 1984)

Boyd Hilton, *The Age of Atonement: the influence of evangelicalism on social and economic thought, 1795–1865* (Oxford, 1988)

D. Bruce Hindmarsh, *John Newton and the English Evangelical Tradition between the Conversions of Wesley and Wilberforce* (Oxford, 1996)

Michael A. Mullett, *Catholics in Britain and Ireland, 1558–1829* (London, 1998)

Peter Nockles, *The Oxford Movement in Context: Anglican High Churchmanship, 1760–1857* (Cambridge, 1994)

E. R. Norman, *Church and Society in England 1770–1970* (Oxford, 1976)

Ernest Rupp, *Religion in England 1688–1791* (Oxford, 1986)

John Spurr, *The Restoration Church of England 1646–1689* (New Haven, 1991)

John Walsh, Colin Haydon and Stephen Taylor (eds.), *The Church of England c.1689–c.1833: from toleration to Tractarianism* (Cambridge, 1993)

W. R. Ward, *Christianity under the Ancien Regime 1648–1789* (Cambridge, 1999)

W. R. Ward, *Early Evangelicalism: a global intellectual history, 1670–1789* (Cambridge, 2006)

The economy

J. V. Beckett, *The Agricultural Revolution* (Oxford, 1990)

N. F. R. Crafts, *British Economic Growth during the Industrial Revolution* (Oxford, 1985)

P. G. M. Dickson, *The Financial Revolution in England: a study in the development of public credit, 1688–1756* (London, 1967)

Roderick Floud and Donald McCloskey (eds.), *The Economic History of Britain since 1700. Volume I, 1700–1860* (2nd edn, Cambridge, 1994)

Roderick Floud and Paul Johnson (eds.), *The Cambridge Economic History of Modern Britain. Volume I: Industrialisation, 1700–1860* (Cambridge, 2004)

Pat Hudson, *The Industrial Revolution* (Oxford, 1992)

Ann Kussmaul, *A General View of the Rural Economy of England, 1538–1880* (Cambridge, 1990)

G. E. Mingay (ed.), *The Agrarian History of England and Wales. VI, 1750–1850* (Cambridge, 1989)

Joel Mokyr (ed.), *The British Industrial Revolution: an economic perspective* (2nd edn, Oxford, 1999)

Patrick K. O'Brien, 'The Political Economy of British Taxation, 1660–1815', *Economic History Review*, 41 (1988), pp. 1–32

Patrick K. O'Brien and Philip A. Hunt, 'The Rise of a Fiscal State in England, 1485–1815', *Historical Research*, 66 (1993), pp. 129–76

Patrick K. O'Brien and Roland Quinault (eds.), *The Industrial Revolution and British Society* (Cambridge, 1993)

Mark Overton, *The Agricultural Revolution in England: the transformation of the agrarian economy 1500–1850* (Cambridge, 1996)

John Rule, *The Vital Century: England's developing economy 1714–1815* (London, 1992)

Jan de Vries, 'The Industrial Revolution and the Industrious Revolution', *Journal of Economic History*, 54 (1994), pp. 249–70

A. M. C. Waterman, *Revolution, Economics and Religion: Christian political economy, 1798–1833* (Cambridge, 1991)

Lorna Weatherill, *Consumer Behaviour and Material Culture in Britain, 1660–1760* (London, 1988)

Donald Winch, *Riches and Poverty: an intellectual history of political economy in Britain, 1750–1834* (Cambridge, 1996)

E. A. Wrigley, *People, Cities and Wealth: the transformation of traditional society* (Oxford, 1987)

E. A. Wrigley, *Continuity, Chance and Change: the character of the Industrial Revolution in England* (Cambridge, 1988)

E. A. Wrigley and R. S. Schofield, *The Population History of England, 1541–1871: a reconstruction* (2nd edn, Cambridge, 1981)

Social history

J. V. Beckett, *The Aristocracy in England 1660–1914* (Oxford, 1986)

Asa Briggs, 'The Language of "Class" in Early Nineteenth-Century England', in M. W. Flinn and T. C. Smout (eds.), *Essays in Social History* (Oxford, 1974)

Philip Carter, *Men and the Emergence of Polite Society: Britain 1660–1800* (Harlow, 2001)

Lee Davison et al. (eds.), *Stilling the Grumbling Hive: the response to social and economic problems in England 1689–1750* (Stroud, 1992)

Peter Earle, *The Making of the English Middle Class: business, society and family life in London, 1660–1730* (London, 1989)

Anthony Fletcher, *Gender, Sex and Subordination in England 1500–1800* (New Haven, 1995)

Natasha Glaisyer, *The Culture of Commerce in England, 1660–1720* (Woodbridge, 2006)

M. Golby and A. W. Purdue, *The Civilization of the Crowd: popular culture in England 1750–1900* (London, 1984)

Bridget Hill, *Women, Work and Sexual Politics in Eighteenth-Century England* (London, 1994)

Paul Langford, *Public Life and the Propertied Englishman 1689–1798* (Oxford, 1991)

R. W. Malcolmson, *Life and Labour in England, 1700–1780* (London, 1981)

Marjorie Morgan, *Manners, Morals and Class in England, 1774–1858* (Basingstoke, 1994)

Mark Overton, Jane Whittle, Darron Dean and Andrew Hann (eds.), *Production and Consumption in English Households, 1600–1750* (London, 2004)

John Rule, *The Experience of Labour in Eighteenth-Century Industry* (London, 1981)

John Rule, *Albion's People: English society 1714–1815* (London, 1992)

K. D. M. Snell, *Annals of the Labouring Poor: social change and agrarian England, 1660–1900* (Cambridge, 1985)

Lawrence Stone, *An Open Elite? England 1540–1880* (Oxford, 1984)

E. P. Thompson, *The Making of the English Working Class* (London, 1963)

F. M. L. Thompson (ed.), *The Cambridge Social History of Britain* (3 vols., Cambridge, 1993)

Amanda Vickery, *The Gentleman's Daughter: women's lives in Georgian England* (New Haven, 1998)

Politics

Jeremy Black (ed.), *Britain in the Age of Walpole* (London, 1984)

Jeremy Black (ed.), *British Politics and Society from Walpole to Pitt, 1742–1789* (Basingstoke, 1990)

Jeremy Black, *George III: America's Last King* (New Haven, 2006)

Michael Brock, *The Great Reform Act* (London, 1973)

John Brooke, *George III* (London, 1972)

Reed Browning, *The Duke of Newcastle* (New Haven, 1975)

John Cannon, *Parliamentary Reform, 1640–1832* (Cambridge, 1973)

Ian R. Christie, *Stress and Stability in late Eighteenth-Century Britain: reflections on the British avoidance of revolution* (Oxford, 1984)

Tony Claydon, *William III and the Godly Reformation* (Cambridge, 1996)

Eveline Cruickshanks, *Political Untouchables: the Tories and the '45* (London, 1979)

Eveline Cruickshanks (ed.), *By Force or By Default? the Revolution of 1688–1689* (Edinburgh, 1989)

Eveline Cruickshanks, *The Glorious Revolution* (Basingstoke, 2000)

Grayson Ditchfield, *George III: An Essay in Monarchy* (Basingstoke, 2003)

John Ehrman, *The Younger Pitt* (3 vols., London, 1969–96)

Albert Goodwin, *The Friends of Liberty: the English democratic movement in the age of the French Revolution* (London, 1979)

Jenny Graham, *The Nation, the Law and the King: reform politics in England, 1789–1799* (2 vols., Lanham, 2000)

Edward Gregg, *Queen Anne* (London, 1980)

Philip Harling, *The Waning of 'Old Corruption': the politics of economical reform in Britain, 1779–1846* (Oxford, 1996)

Bob Harris, *Politics and the Nation: Britain in the mid-eighteenth century* (Oxford, 2002)

Tim Harris, *Politics under the Later Stuarts: party conflict in a divided society 1660–1715* (Harlow, 1993)

Tim Harris, *Restoration: Charles II and his kingdoms, 1660–1685* (London, 2005)

Tim Harris, *Revolution: the great crisis of the British monarchy, 1685–1720* (London, 2006)

A. D. Harvey, *Britain in the Early Nineteenth Century* (London, 1978)

Ragnhild Hatton, *George I Elector and King* (London, 1978)

B. W. Hill, *The Growth of Parliamentary Parties, 1689–1742* (London, 1976)

B. W. Hill, *British Parliamentary Parties, 1742–1832* (London, 1987)

Geoffrey Holmes, *British Politics in the Age of Anne* (2nd edn, London, 1987)

J. Ann Hone, *For the Cause of Truth: radicalism in London 1796–1821* (Oxford, 1982)

Henry Horwitz, *Parliament, Policy and Politics in the Reign of William III* (Manchester, 1977)

Ronald Hutton, *The Restoration: a political and religious history of England and Wales 1658–1667* (Oxford, 1986)

J. R. Jones (ed.), *Liberty Secured? Britain before and after 1688* (Stanford, 1992)

Paul Langford, *The Excise Crisis: society and politics in the age of Walpole* (Oxford, 1975)

F. P. Lock, *Edmund Burke* (2 vols., Oxford, 1998–2006)

David Cresap Moore, *The Politics of Deference: a study of the mid-nineteenth century English political system* (Hassocks, 1976)

Jennifer Mori, *Britain in the Age of the French Revolution, 1785–1820* (Harlow, 2000)

Howard Nenner, *The Right to be King: the succession to the crown of England, 1603–1714* (Basingstoke, 1995)

Frank O'Gorman, *Voters, Patrons and Parties: the unreformed electoral system in Hanoverian England, 1734–1832* (Oxford, 1993)

Richard Pares, *King George III and the Politicians* (Oxford, 1953)

W. D. Rubinstein, 'The End of "Old Corruption" in Britain, 1780–1860', *Past & Present*, 101 (1983), pp. 55–86

James J. Sack, *From Jacobite to Conservative: reaction and orthodoxy in Britain, c.1760–1832* (Cambridge, 1993)

W. A. Speck, *Reluctant Revolutionaries: Englishmen and the Revolution of 1688* (Oxford, 1988)

Michael J. Turner, *The Age of Unease: government and reform in Britain, 1782–1832* (Stroud, 2000)

Jacobitism

Eveline Cruickshanks, *Political Untouchables: the Tories and the '45* (London, 1979)

Eveline Cruickshanks and Howard Erskine-Hill, *The Atterbury Plot* (Basingstoke, 2004)

Bruce Lenman, *The Jacobite Risings in Britain, 1689–1746* (London, 1980)

Paul Kléber Monod, *Jacobitism and the English People, 1688–1788* (Cambridge, 1989)

Paul Monod, Murray Pittock and Daniel Szechi (eds.), *Loyalty and Identity: Jacobites at home and abroad* (Basingstoke, 2010)

Éamonn Ó Ciardha, *Ireland and the Jacobite Cause, 1685–1766: a fatal attachment* (Dublin, 2004)

Daniel Szechi, *The Jacobites: Britain and Europe, 1688–1788* (Manchester, 1994)

Daniel Szechi, *1715: the great Jacobite rebellion* (New Haven, 2006)

The American Revolution

James B. Bell, *A War of Religion: dissenters, Anglicans and the American Revolution* (Basingstoke, 2008)

J. C. D. Clark, *The Language of Liberty 1660–1832: political discourse and social dynamics in the Anglo-American world* (Cambridge, 1994)

Stephen Conway, *The War of American Independence, 1776–1783* (London, 1995)

Stephen Conway, *The British Isles and the War of American Independence* (Oxford, 2002)

H. T. Dickinson (ed.), *Britain and the American Revolution* (London, 1998)

Marc Egnal, *A Mighty Empire: the origins of the American Revolution* (Ithaca, 1988)

Richard Middleton, *Colonial America: a history, 1565–1776* (Oxford, 2002)

Hamish M. Scott, *British Foreign Policy in the Age of the American Revolution* (Oxford, 1990)

R. W. Tucker and D. C. Hendrickson, *The Fall of the First British Empire: origins of the war of American independence* (Baltimore, 1983)

Colonies and empire

David Armitage, *The Ideological Origins of the British Empire* (Cambridge, 2000)

C. A. Bayly, *Imperial Meridian: the British Empire and the world 1780–1830* (London, 1989)

C. A. Bayly, *The Birth of the Modern World 1780–1914: global connections and comparisons* (Oxford, 2004)

Istvan Hont, *Jealousy of Trade: international competition and the nation state in historical perspective* (Cambridge, Mass., 2005)

P. J. Marshall, *Problems of Empire: Britain and India, 1757–1813* (London, 1968)

P. J. Marshall (ed.), *The Oxford History of the British Empire: the eighteenth century* (Oxford, 1998)

Peter J. Marshall, *The Making and Unmaking of Empires: Britain, India and America c.1750–1783* (Oxford, 2005)

Brendan Simms, *Three Victories and a Defeat: the rise and fall of the first British Empire* (London, 2007)

Counterfactual analysis

Niall Ferguson (ed.), *Virtual History: alternatives and counter-factuals* (London, 1997)

Geoffrey Hawthorn, *Plausible Worlds: possibility and understanding in history and the social sciences* (Cambridge, 1991)

Philip E. Tetlock and Aaron Belkin (eds.), *Counterfactual Thought Experiments in World Politics* (Princeton, 1996)

Philip E. Tetlock, Richard Ned Lebow and Geoffrey Parker (eds.), *Unmaking the West: 'what if?' scenarios that rewrite world history* (Ann Arbor, 2006)

Endnotes

Introduction

1. Ireland was never included in that construct of 1707, 'Great Britain'. Its inclusion in this book within the term 'the British Isles' implies nothing to the contrary, and merely adopts a familiar shorthand.

2. D. B. Horn and Mary Ransome (eds.), *English Historical Documents 1714–1783* (London, 1969), p. 3. A characteristic of this approach was its refusal to consider seriously the counterfactuals in, for example, the Revolution of 1688 (p. 81), Jacobitism (p. 19) and the American Revolution (pp. 54–6).

3. Richard Price, *British Society 1680–1880: dynamism, containment and change* (Cambridge, 1999).

Part I

1. Patrick O'Brien, 'The Nature and Historical Evolution of an Exceptional Fiscal State and its Possible Significance for the Precocious Commercialisation and Industrialisation of the British Economy from Cromwell to Nelson', *Economic History Review*, 64 (2011), pp. 408–46, at 409.

2. E. A. Wrigley, 'The Growth of Population in Eighteenth-century England: a Conundrum Resolved', *Past & Present*, 98 (1983), pp. 121–50, at 122; E. A. Wrigley, R. S. Davies, J. E. Oeppen and R. S. Schofield, *English Population History from Family Reconstitution* (Cambridge, 1997), p. 548.

3. Wrigley et al., *English Population History from Family Reconstitution*, p. 549.

4. Gregory Clark, *A Farewell to Alms: a brief economic history of the world* (Princeton, 2007), pp. 40–2.

5. E. A. Wrigley and R. S. Schofield, *The Population History of England 1541–1871* (Cambridge, 1981), pp. 228–36, 240, 244, 450–3.

6. Population and food prices in England followed similar paths until *c.*1811, 'when the price index turned down . . . The historic link between population growth and price rise was broken; an economic revolution had taken place. And by an ironic coincidence Malthus had given pungent expression to an issue that haunted most pre-industrial societies at almost the last moment when it could still plausibly be represented as relevant to the country in which he was born': Wrigley and Schofield, *The Population History of England*, pp. 403–4, 412.

7. Clark, *A Farewell to Alms*, Figure 10.2, p. 195.

8. John Walter and Roger Schofield (eds.), *Famine, Disease and the Social Order in Early Modern Society* (Cambridge, 1989), pp. 9–10.

9. Wrigley et al., *English Population History from Family Reconstitution*, p. 348; Wrigley and Schofield, *The Population History of England*, Table A3.3, pp. 532–3.

10. Wrigley and Schofield, *The Population History of England*, p. 228.

11. 'The available evidence suggests that during the seventeenth century changes in proportions never marrying were much more significant than changes in the mean age at marriage in altering overall fertility levels. In the eighteenth century, in contrast, the fall in marriage age dominated nuptiality change and thus fertility. The proportion of women never marrying seems to have risen greatly during late Tudor and early Stuart times, reaching a peak of over 20 per cent among those reaching adult years in the middle decades of the seventeenth century, but to have fallen to less than 10 per cent by the end of the century. Thereafter there was little further change before the middle of the nineteenth century . . . identifying the reason for this change may well be the key to a satisfactory understanding of the links between economic pressures and marriage decisions': Wrigley et al., *English Population History from Family Reconstitution*, pp. 195–7.

12. K. D. M. Snell, *Annals of the Labouring Poor: social change and agrarian England 1660–1900* (Cambridge, 1985), pp. 210–17, 345–52, 376.

13. Martin Daunton, *Progress and Poverty: an economic and social history of Britain 1700–1850* (Oxford, 1995), pp. 136–45.

14. Wrigley et al., *English Population History from Family Reconstitution*, p. 197.

15. Ibid., pp. 219–20, 421, Tables 6.2, 7.27.

16. 'Mortality in the seventeenth century tended to fluctuate violently in the short run, and there is little doubt that it was primarily the changing pattern of mortality fluctuations that determined whether population would grow, stagnate or decline': Michael Flinn et al., *Scottish Population History from the 17th Century to the 1930s* (Cambridge, 1977), p. 4.

17. Stuart Daultrey, David Dickson and Cormac Ó Gráda, 'Eighteenth-Century Irish Population: New Perspectives from Old Sources', *Journal of Economic History*, 41 (1981), pp. 622–7; *idem*, 'Hearth tax, household size, and Irish population growth, 1680–1800', *Proceedings of the Royal Irish Academy*, 82 (1982), pp. 156–75.

18. R. A. Houston, *The Population History of Britain and Ireland, 1500–1750* (Houndmills, 1992), pp. 38–9; D. E. C. Eversley, 'The Demography of the Irish Quakers, 1650–1850', in J. M. Goldstrom and L. A. Clarkson (eds.), *Irish Population, Economy and Society* (Oxford, 1981), pp. 57–88; David Dickson, 'No Scythians Here: women and marriage in seventeenth-century Ireland', in Margaret MacCurtain and Mary O'Dowd (eds.), *Women and Society in Early Modern Ireland* (Edinburgh, 1990), pp. 223–35; William McCafee, 'Pre-Famine Population in Ulster: evidence from the parish register of Killyman', in Patrick O'Flanagan, Paul Ferguson and Kevin Whelan (eds.), *Rural Ireland, 1600–1900: modernisation and change* (Cork, 1987), pp. 142–61, at 151–7.

19. Houston, *Population History*, p. 46.

20. Ibid., p. 30.

21. R. A. Houston, 'The Demographic Regime, 1760–1830', in T. M. Devine and Rosalind Mitchison (eds.), *People and Society in Scotland: a social history of modern Scotland I 1760–1830* (Edinburgh, 1988), pp. 9–26.

22. Houston, *Population History*, pp. 48–9, 69, 71, 89.

23. Ibid., p. 42.

24. Houston, 'The Demographic Regime', p. 13.

25. Ibid., pp. 9–26. 'Late marriage and high celibacy persisted until the second half of the nineteenth century as embedded customs which had outlived the economic circumstances which brought them into being': Houston, *Population History*, p. 86.

26. Flinn et al., *Scottish Population History*, pp. 7–18, 32–5, 249.

27. Daultrey, Dickson and Ó Gráda, 'Eighteenth-Century Irish Population'; L. A. Clarkson, 'Irish Population Revisited, 1687–1821', in Goldstrom and Clarkson (eds.), *Irish Population*, pp. 13–35.

28. K. H. Connell, *The Population of Ireland 1750–1845* (Oxford, 1950), pp. 86–9.

29. 'Given the sources available, it is at this point impossible to determine whether any significant changes occurred in gender roles in heterosexual

relations within marriage in this period': Robert B. Shoemaker, *Gender in English Society, 1650–1850: the emergence of separate spheres?* (London, 1998), p. 71.

30. Rachel Weil, *Political passions: gender, the family and political argument in England, 1680–1714* (Manchester, 1999).

31. Peter Earle, 'The Female Labour Market in London in the Late Seventeenth and Eighteenth Centuries', *Economic History Review*, 2nd ser., 42 (1989), pp. 328–53.

32. Leonore Davidoff and Catherine Hall, *Family Fortunes: men and women of the English middle class, 1780–1850* (London, 1987).

33. Amanda Vickery, 'The Neglected Century: writing the history of eighteenth-century women', *Gender and History*, 3 (1991), pp. 211–19; idem, 'Golden Age to Separate Spheres? a review of the categories and chronology of English women's history', *Historical Journal*, 36 (1993), pp. 383–414.

34. Peter Laslett and Richard Wall (eds.), *Household and Family in Past Time* (Cambridge, 1972), esp. ch. 4, Laslett, 'Mean Household Size in England since the Sixteenth Century', pp. 125–58, at 154. The later decline of living-in service must have altered this pattern.

35. Price, *British Society*, p. 207; G. J. Barker-Benfield, *The Culture of Sensibility: sex and society in eighteenth-century Britain* (Chicago, 1992), pp. 28–32, 126–9, 163–9, 191–8; Ruth Perry, *The Celebrated Mary Astell: an early English feminist* (Chicago, 1986), pp. 99–119.

36. Adam Smith, *An Inquiry into the Nature and Causes of the Wealth of Nations*, eds. R. H. Campbell and A. S. Skinner (2 vols., Oxford, 1979), II, p. 794.

37. *Woman Not Inferior to Man: or, A short and modest Vindication of the natural Right of the Fair-Sex to a perfect Equality of Power, Dignity, and Esteem, with the Men. By Sophia, A Person of Quality* (London, 1739), pp. 1–3, 8, 11, 30, 35–6, 40, 56.

38. *Man Superior to Woman; or, a Vindication of Man's Natural Right of Sovereign Authority over the Woman . . . By a Gentleman* (London, 1739), pp. 1–2, 4, 6, 9–10, 12, 15, 17, 23, 26, 35, 37–8, 66.

39. Naomi Tadmor, 'The concept of the household-family in eighteenth-century England', *Past & Present*, 151 (1996), pp. 111–40; idem, *Family and Friends in Eighteenth-Century England: household, kinship and patronage* (Cambridge, 2001).

40. [Mary Astell], *A Serious Proposal to the Ladies, For the Advancement of their true and greatest Interest* (London, 1694), pp. 2–3, 60–1, 73, 122, 147.

41. [Mary Astell], *Reflections upon Marriage* (3rd edn, London, 1706), Preface,

pp. 31, 56; [Mary Astell], *A Serious Proposal to the Ladies, Part II* (London, 1697), pp. 192, 214.

42. Price, *British Society*, p. 212; Anna Clark, *The Struggle for the Breeches: gender and the making of the British working class* (Berkeley, 1995), pp. 42–62; Davidoff and Hall, *Family Fortunes*, pp. 114–18; Ford K. Brown, *Fathers of the Victorians* (Cambridge, 1961), pp. 81, 104–5, 153–4, 229–33, 238; Catherine Hall, 'The Early Formation of Victorian Domestic Ideology', in Sandra Burman (ed.), *Fit Work for Women* (London, 1979), pp. 15–32, at 21–2.

43. [John Locke], *Two Treatises of Government* (London, 1690), II, s. 2.

44. Clark, *A Farewell to Alms*, pp. 7–8, 113–14, 130–1, 160–2.

45. G. E. Mingay, *English Landed Society in the Eighteenth Century* (London, 1963), pp. 21–6.

46. Daunton, *Progress and Poverty*, pp. 61–87; John Rule, *The Vital Century: England's developing economy, 1714–1815* (London, 1992), pp. 40–7.

47. Geraint H. Jenkins, *The Foundations of Modern Wales 1642–1780* (Oxford, 1987), pp. 96–7, 264–5.

48. J. V. Beckett, 'The Pattern of Land Ownership in England and Wales, 1660–1880', *Economic History Review*, 37 (1984), pp. 1–22; Beckett, *The Aristocracy in England, 1660–1914* (Oxford, 1986), pp. 87–90.

49. Geoffrey Parker, *The Military Revolution: military innovation and the rise of the West, 1500–1800* (Cambridge, 1988), pp. 62–4; John Brewer, *The Sinews of Power: war, money and the English state, 1688–1783* (London, 1989), pp. 29–42, at 40; B. R. Mitchell and Phyllis Deane, *Abstract of British Historical Statistics* (Cambridge, 1962), pp. 389–91.

50. Bryan Keith Lucas, *The Unreformed Local Government System* (London, 1980), pp. 15–37; Asa Briggs, *The Age of Improvement 1783–1867* (London, 1969), pp. 46–7.

51. Daniel Defoe, *A Tour Thro' the Whole Island of Great Britain* (3 vols., London, 1724–6), ed. G. D. H. Cole (2 vols., London, 1968), I, p. 3.

52. Jürgen Habermas, *The Structural Transformation of the Public Sphere* (Cambridge, Mass., 1989); Joad Raymond, 'The Newspaper, Public Opinion and the Public Sphere in the Seventeenth Century', in Raymond (ed.), *News, Newspapers and Society in Early Modern Britain* (London, 1999), pp. 109–40; Harold Mah, 'Phantasies of the Public Sphere: rethinking the Habermas of historians', *Journal of Modern History*, 72 (2000), pp. 153–82; Tony Claydon, 'The Sermon, the "Public Sphere" and the Political Culture of Late Seventeenth-century England', in Lori Anne Ferrell and Peter McCulloch (eds.), *The English Sermon Revised: religion, literature and history 1600–1750* (Manchester, 2001), pp. 208–34.

53. [Daniel Defoe], *A Plan of the English Commerce* (London, 1728), pp. 80–1.

54. Allan I. Macinnes, 'Scottish Gaeldom: the first phase of clearance', in Devine and Mitchison (eds.), *People and Society in Scotland*, I, pp. 70–90.

55. Thomas Bentley, *Journal of a Visit to Paris 1776*, ed. Peter France (Brighton, 1977), p. 27.

56. Lawrence Stone, 'Interpersonal Violence in English Society 1300–1980', *Past & Present*, 101 (1983), pp. 22–33.

57. Daunton, *Progress and Poverty*, pp. 109–10.

58. P. B. Munsche, *Gentlemen and Poachers: the English game laws 1671–1831* (Cambridge, 1981).

59. James Obelkevitch, *Religion and Rural Society: South Lindsey 1825–1875* (Oxford, 1976), pp. 23–102 at 91, argues for the revival of harvest suppers in the mid-Victorian period.

60. Kim Lawes, *Paternalism and Politics: the revival of paternalism in early nineteenth-century Britain* (Basingstoke, 2000); Price, *British Society*, pp. 325–6.

61. Mitchell and Deane, *Abstract of British Historical Statistics*, p. 410.

62. Alan Macfarlane, *The Origins of English Individualism* (Oxford, 1978).

63. [Locke], *Two Treatises*, I, ss. 47, 49.

64. Defoe, *A Tour*, ed. Cole, I, pp. 2, 252.

65. Smith, *Wealth of Nations*, eds. Campbell and Skinner, I, p. 188.

66. Ibid., I, pp. 17–36.

67. For the late displacement of these ideas see Leonard Gomes, *The Economics and Ideology of Free Trade: a historical review* (Cheltenham, 2003); Ronald Findlay and Kevin O'Rourke, *Power and Plenty: trade, war, and the world economy in the second millennium* (Princeton, 2007), ch. 5.

68. Smith, *Wealth of Nations*, eds. Campbell and Skinner, I, p. 409.

69. E. A. Wrigley, *Continuity, Chance and Change: the character of the Industrial Revolution in England* (Cambridge, 1998), pp. 35, 72; N. F. R. Crafts, *British Economic Growth during the Industrial Revolution* (Oxford, 1985), pp. 12–14, 54–5, 66; Peter Mathias, *First Industrial Nation: an economic history of Britain, 1700–1914* (2nd edn, London, 1983), p. 239; for the slowness of labour mobility, Pat Hudson, *The Industrial Revolution* (London, 1992), pp. 80–3.

70. Michael Turner, 'Agricultural Productivity in England in the Eighteenth Century: evidence from crop yields', *Economic History Review*, 35 (1982), pp. 489–510; R. V. Jackson, 'Growth and Deceleration in English Agriculture, 1660–1790', *Economic History Review*, 2nd ser., 38 (1985), pp. 333–51, at 349.

71. Daunton, *Progress and Poverty*, p. 104.

72. Ibid., pp. 92–117.

73. Jackson, 'Growth and Deceleration', p. 339.

74. Calculations from figures in Mitchell and Deane, *Abstract of British Historical Statistics*, pp. 387–8.

75. Gerrrit P. Judd, *Members of Parliament 1734–1832* (New Haven, 1955), pp. 56, 61–2, 69.

76. Swift to Pope, 10 January 1721.

77. Helen E. Witmer, *The Property Qualifications of Members of Parliament* (New York, 1943), pp. 41–3, 85, 140–4, 155.

78. The classic autobiography of Francis Place (1771–1854), a London tailor, first a journeyman and then a successful master, is eloquent testimony to the importance of 'credit' and the difficulty of obtaining it.

79. C. R. Dobson, *Masters and Journeymen: a prehistory of industrial relations 1717– 1800* (London, 1980), ch. 9, 'The Combination Acts'.

80. Mark Overton, Darron Dean and Andrew Hann (eds.), *Production and Consumption in English Households, 1600–1750* (London, 2004), p. 173.

81. John Rule, *The Vital Century: England's developing economy 1714–1815* (London, 1992), pp. 263–74, at 264.

82. Patrick O'Brien, 'Political preconditions for the Industrial Revolution', in Patrick K. O'Brien and Roland Quinault (eds.), *The Industrial Revolution and British Society* (Cambridge, 1993), pp. 124–55, at 135.

83. For a middle position, see F. Crouzet, 'The impact of the French wars on the British economy', in H. T. Dickinson (ed.), *Britain and the French Revolution 1789–1815* (London, 1989), pp. 189–209; for a claim that British growth in 1790–1820 was lower than it would have been, see J. G. Williamson, 'Why Was British Growth So Slow During the Industrial Revolution?', *Journal of Economic History*, 44 (1984), pp. 687–712. For criticisms of this thesis see N. F. R. Crafts, 'British Economic Growth, 1700–1850: some difficulties of interpretation', *Explorations in Economic History*, 24 (1987), pp. 245–68, Joel Mokyr, 'Has the Industrial Revolution Been Crowded Out? some reflections on Crafts and Williamson', *Explorations in Economic History*, 24 (1987), pp. 293–319, and P. K. O'Brien, 'The impact of the Revolutionary and Napoleonic war, 1793–1815, on the Long-run Growth of the British Economy', *Fernand Braudel Center Review*, 12 (1989), pp. 335–95. For an argument that the Napoleonic Wars significantly promoted the Industrial Revolution by making capital available, see Larry Neal, *The Rise of Financial Capitalism: international capital markets in the Age of Reason* (Cambridge, 1990), pp. 216–22.

84. Summed up in O'Brien, 'The nature and historical evolution of an

exceptional fiscal state.' Between 1688 and 1815 British GNP rose by a factor of about three, but tax receipts by a factor of about fifteen; this 'degrades any suggestion that purports to explain Britain's fiscal success as a product of economic growth', p. 420.

85. Arnold Toynbee, *Lectures on the Industrial Revolution in England* (London, 1884).

86. Crafts, *British Economic Growth*, pp. 44–7, 65.

87. Houston, 'The Demographic Regime', p. 22.

88. T. M. Devine, 'Urbanisation', in Devine and Mitchison (eds.), *People and Society in Scotland*, I, pp. 27–52, at 28–9.

89. Donald McCloskey, '1780–1860: A Survey', in Roderick Floud and Donald McCloskey (eds.), *The Economic History of Britain since 1700. Volume I. 1700–1860* (2nd edn, Cambridge, 1994), pp. 242–70.

90. J. G. Williamson, 'Why Was British Economic Growth So Slow During the Industrial Revolution?', *Journal of Economic History*, 44 (1984), pp. 687–712; *idem*, 'Debating the Industrial Revolution', *Explorations in Economic History*, 24 (1987), pp. 269–92; *idem*, 'Did English Factor Markets Fail During the Industrial Revolution?', *Oxford Economic Papers*, 39 (1987), pp. 641–78.

91. John Hatcher, *The History of the British Coal Industry* (Oxford, 1993), I, pp. 68, 547–56; Wrigley, *Continuity, Chance and Change*, p. 54; David Levine and Keith Wrightson, *The Making of an Industrial Society: Whickham 1560–1765* (Oxford, 1991), pp. 2–4 and *passim*.

92. The subject was not placed at the centre of public attention until David Davies' *The Case of Labourers in Husbandry* (Bath, 1795) and F. M. Eden's *The State of the Poor* (4 vols., London, 1797).

93. [Defoe], *A Plan of the English Commerce*, pp. 87–9, 101–2.

94. R. C. Allen, 'Why the Industrial Revolution was British: commerce, induced invention, and the scientific revolution', *Economic History Review*, 64 (2011), pp. 357–84. But if this argument were decisive, an Industrial Revolution would have happened first in Venice or the United Provinces.

95. For an earlier summing-up see R. M. Hartwell et al., *The Long Debate on Poverty: eight essays on industrialization and 'the condition of England'* (2nd edn, London, 1974); more recently, Gareth Stedman Jones, *An End to Poverty? a historical debate* (London, 2004).

96. Harold Perkin, *The Origins of Modern English Society 1780–1880* (London, 1969), p. 136.

97. Wrigley and Schofield, *The Population History of England*, pp. 252, 528.

98. McCloskey, '1780–1860: a survey', in Floud and McCloskey (eds.), *Economic History*, pp. 242–70, at 249–53; Hudson, *Industrial Revolution*, p. 25; C. H. Lee, *The British Economy since 1700* (Cambridge, 1986), pp. 10, 12; Price, *British Society*, p. 27.

99. Patrick K. O'Brien, 'Introduction: Modern Conceptions of the Industrial Revolution', in O'Brien and Quinault (eds.), *The Industrial Revolution and British Society*, pp. 1–30, at 13.

100. A typical example of exaggerated claims for such a discontinuity, Malcolm I. Thomis's *Responses to Industrialisation: the British experience 1780–1850* (Newton Abbot, 1976), was obliged to concede that contemporaries did not appreciate the extent of the changes that historians later celebrated as transformative (pp. 1–2, 19, 23–4, 30, 33, 53). Thomis did not offer a chronological account of how perceptions developed over the seventy years of the study, instead juxtaposing evidence irrespective of its date. Political responses, he noted, were also puzzlingly tardy: 'the reform of the municipal corporations in 1835 was carried out with a strange lack of reference to the social changes involved in industrialisation and the administrative changes that they had necessitated' (pp. 11, 32).

101. E. A. Wrigley, 'The Classical Economists and the Industrial Revolution', in *idem, People, Cities and Wealth: the transformation of traditional society* (Oxford, 1987), pp. 21–45.

102. 'The Industrial Revolution marks the most fundamental transformation of human life in the history of the world recorded in written documents': E. J. Hobsbawm, *The Pelican Economic History of Britain. Volume 3. From 1750 to the Present Day. Industry and Empire* (Harmondsworth, 1969), p. 13; it was 'the most profound and thoroughgoing change yet experienced by mankind in society': Eric J. Evans, *The Forging of the Modern State: early industrial Britain 1783–1870* (3rd edn, London, 2001), p. 129. Such remarks are, implicitly, normative comments on the claims of revealed religion; and this is a judgement that the historian is not competent to pronounce.

103. For an overview see Tony Clarke and Tony Dickson, 'The Birth of Class?', in Devine and Mitchison (eds.), *People and Society in Scotland*, I, pp. 292–309.

104. R. J. Morris, *Class, Sect and Party: the making of the British middle class, Leeds 1820–1850* (Manchester, 1990).

105. E. P. Thompson, *The Making of the English Working Class* (London, 1963); John Rule, *The Labouring Classes in Early Industrial England 1750–1850* (London, 1986).

106. Peter Earle, *The Making of the English Middle Class: business, society and family life in London, 1660–1730* (London, 1989).

107. W. A. Speck, *Stability and Strife: England 1714–1760* (London, 1977), ch. 6, 'The Making of the English Ruling Class'.

108. H. T. Dickinson, *Liberty and Property: political ideology in eighteenth-century Britain* (London, 1977).

109. E. P. Thompson, 'Eighteenth-Century English Society: class struggle without class?', *Social History*, 3 (1978), pp. 133–66, at 155.

110. Macfarlane, *Origins of English Individualism*.

111. For pre-capitalist conflict between employers and employees see Dobson, *Masters and Journeymen*.

112. E. P. Thompson, 'Alexander Pope and the Windsor Blacks', *Times Literary Supplement* (7 September 1973), pp. 1,031–3; Eveline Cruickshanks and Howard Erskine-Hill, 'The Waltham Black Act and Jacobitism', *Journal of British Studies*, 24 (1985).

113. For an argument that class and rights were symbiotic, see Marc W. Steinberg, '"The Great End of All Government . . .": working people's construction of citizenship claims in early nineteenth-century England and the matter of class', *International Review of Social History*, 40, suppl. 3 (1995), pp. 19–50, at 43–6.

114. Geoffrey Holmes, 'The Sacheverell Riots: the crowd and the church in early eighteenth-century London', *Past & Present*, 72 (1976).

115. John Paul De Castro, *The Gordon Riots* (Oxford, 1962); George Rudé, 'The Gordon Riots: a study of the rioters and their victims', in *idem*, *Paris and London in the Eighteenth Century* (New York, 1971).

116. George Rudé, 'English Rural and Urban Disturbances on the Eve of the First Reform Bill, 1830–1831', *Past & Present*, 37 (1967).

117. E.g. Price, *British Society*, p. 33.

118. Ivy Pinchbeck, *Women Workers and the Industrial Revolution 1750–1850* (London, 1930), pp. 125, 283–6, 293; Sonya O. Rose, 'Proto-Industry, Women's Work and the Household Economy in the Transition to Industrial Capitalism', *Journal of Family History*, 13 (1988), pp. 181–93.

119. Davidoff and Hall, *Family Fortunes*, pp. 272, 279, 304–8; Margaret Hunt, *The Middling Sort: commerce, gender and the family in England 1680–1780* (Berkeley, 1996), pp. 124–8.

120. Penelope Corfield, 'Class by Name and Number in Eighteenth-Century Britain', in *idem* (ed.), *Language, History and Class* (Oxford, 1991), pp. 101–30.

121. Henry Mayhew, *London Labour and the London Poor* (4 vols., London, 1851–62).

122. James Hutton, *The Theory of the Earth* (Edinburgh, 1785; 2 vols., Edinburgh, 1795).

123. Maxine Berg, *Luxury and Pleasure in Eighteenth-Century Britain*

(Oxford, 2005). Among the unpopular newly affluent was the Dissenting minister Joseph Priestley, whose Birmingham house was destroyed by rioters in July 1791: he calculated his losses at £4,083 10s. 3d. (pp. 1–2). This was wealth beyond the dreams of Dissenting ministers of the 1660s.

124. 'On the country manners of the present age', *The Annual Register*, 4 (1761), Pt II, pp. 206–8.

125. Gareth Stedman Jones, 'Rethinking Chartism', in *idem, Languages of Class* (Cambridge, 1983), pp. 90–178, denying that 'Chartists must have meant the economic and social, when they spoke about the political'.

Part II

1. Its symbolic last statement was William Ewart Gladstone, *The State in its Relations with the Church* (London, 1838).

2. Thomas Jones, *A Catalogue of the Collection of Tracts for and Against Popery (published in or about the reign of James II.) In the Manchester Library founded by Humphrey Chetham* (2 vols. [Manchester], 1859–65).

3. S. J. Connolly, *Religion, Law and Power: the making of Protestant Ireland, 1660–1760* (Oxford, 1992); Toby Barnard, *A New Anatomy of Ireland: the Irish Protestants, 1649–1770* (New Haven, 2003).

4. One estimate finds 2,029 Puritan ministers leaving the church in 1660–2: Michael Watts, *The Dissenters: from the Reformation to the French Revolution* (Oxford, 1978), p. 219.

5. Anne Whiteman (ed.), *The Compton Census of 1676: a critical edition* (London, 1986).

6. Numbers of Dissenting 'hearers' were a multiple of Dissenting 'members', the ratio differing according to denomination and place: Watts, *Dissenters*, pp. 491–508.

7. Callum G. Brown, 'Religion and Social Change', in Devine and Mitchison (eds.), *People and Society in Scotland*, I, pp. 143–62, at 151.

8. Only from 1756 were these Acts passed annually; until then, they were passed in some years but not in others. Nor did they extend to the Corporation Act of 1661.

9. Jeremy Gregory and Jeffrey S. Chamberlain (eds.), *The National Church in Local Perspective: the Church of England and the regions, 1660–1800* (Woodbridge, 2003).

10. J. C. D. Clark, *The Language of Liberty 1660–1832: political discourse and social dynamics in the Anglo-American world* (Cambridge, 1994).

11. [John Cartwright], *Take Your Choice!* (London, 1776), pp. xii, xxii, 19–22, 37, 40, 70.

12. William Godwin, *An Enquiry Concerning Political Justice* (London, 1793).

13. J. C. D. Clark, *Our Shadowed Present* (London, 2003), ch. 4.

14. J. C. D. Clark, 'Secularisation and Modernisation: the failure of a "Grand Narrative"', *Historical Journal*, 55 (2012), pp. 161–94.

15. For the unexamined assumption that the adjective 'modern' is synonymous with the noun 'modernity', see Alan Houston and Steve Pincus, 'Introduction. Modernity and later seventeenth-century England', in *idem* (eds.), *A Nation Transformed: England after the Restoration* (Cambridge, 2001), pp. 1–19. In the manner of twentieth-century social science, such authors term modernity 'a thing' (p. 10) rather than, as historians record, a doctrine.

16. E.g. Houston and Pincus, 'Introduction', p. 10 for a team of figures, including Pope, Swift and the Jacobites, who 'denounced modernity'.

17. Sir Isaac Newton, *The Chronology of Ancient Kingdoms Amended. To which is Prefix'd, A Short Chronicle from the First Memory of Things in Europe, to the Conquest of Persia by Alexander the Great* (London, 1728).

18. Edmund Burke, *Reflections on the Revolution in France* (London, 1790), pp. 97, 207.

19. James L. Clifford (ed.), *Dr Campbell's Diary of a Visit to England in 1775* (Cambridge, 1947), p. 43.

20. John Gascoigne, *Cambridge in the Age of the Enlightenment: science, religion and politics from the Restoration to the French Revolution* (Cambridge, 1989); L. S. Sutherland and L. G. Mitchell (eds.), *The History of the University of Oxford. V. The Eighteenth Century* (Oxford, 1986), pp. 469–723.

21. William Blackstone, *Commentaries on the Laws of England* (4 vols., Oxford, 1765–9), I, pp. 41–2.

22. Romney Sedgwick (ed.), *The History of Parliament: the House of Commons, 1715–1754* (2 vols., London, 1970), I, pp. 136, 139.

23. Sir Lewis Namier and John Brooke (eds.), *The History of Parliament: the House of Commons 1754–1790* (3 vols., London, 1964), I, pp. 97, 115.

24. Sylvia Walby, *Patriarchy at Work: patriarchal and capitalist relations in employment* (Cambridge, 1986), pp. 94–7, 100–8; Judy Lown, *Women and Industrialisation: gender and work in nineteenth-century England* (Cambridge, 1990), pp. 14–18, 23, 174–9.

25. Emmet Larkin, 'The Devotional Revolution in Ireland, 1850–75', *American Historical Review*, 77 (1972), pp. 625–52.

26. David Hume of Godscroft, *The History of the House and Race of Douglas and Angus* (Edinburgh, 1743).

27. J. E., *Some Considerations on the Naturalisation of the Jews; And how far the*

Publick will Benefit from this Hopeful Race of Israelites (London, 1753), pp. 6, 11.

28. *Limitations For the Next Foreign Successor, or New Saxon Race. Debated in a Conference betwixt Two Gentlemen* (London, 1701); *Four new Songs, and a Prophecy. I. A Song for Joy to our ancient Race of Stewarts* [?Edinburgh, ?1750].

29. John Stevens, *A Brief History of Spain. Containing The Race of its Kings, from the first Peopling of that Country* (London, 1701); *The History of England . . . with The Effigies of all the Kings and Queens of England, from the Norman Race, to the present Time* (2nd edn, London, 1702); Jeoffry Keating, *The General History of Ireland. Containing I. A full and impartial Account of the first Inhabitants of that Kingdom; with the Lives and Reigns of an hundred and seventy-four succeeding Monarchs of the Milesian Race* (London, 1723); Nathaniel Wraxall, *Memoirs of the Kings of France, of the Race of Valois* (London, 1777).

30. George Burges, *A Discourse on the Necessity and Duty of Enlightening the Human Race* (London, 1797).

31. Frederick A. Pottle and Charles H. Bennett (eds.), *Boswell's Journal of a Tour to the Hebrides with Samuel Johnson LLD* (London, 1936), p. 57.

Part III

1. For contrasting recent emphases see especially John Brewer, *The Sinews of Power: war, money and the English state, 1688–1783* (London, 1989); Jeremy Black, *Continental Commitment: Britain, Hanover and interventionism, 1714–1793* (London, 2005); Brendan Simms, *Three Victories and a Defeat: the rise and fall of the first British Empire, 1714–1783* (London, 2007).

2. Jan Glete, *Navies and Nations: warships, navies and state building in Europe and America, 1500–1860* (2 vols., Stockholm, 1993), I, pp. 186, 190, 192, 195.

3. Ibid., I, pp. 217–21; Richard Harding, *Seapower and Naval Warfare, 1650–1830* (London, 1999), pp. 80–2, 118–20, 154–5.

4. Glete, *Navies*, I, p. 265; Harding, *Seapower*, pp. 203–7.

5. Bruce Lenman, *Britain's Colonial Wars, 1688–1783* (Harlow, 2000), p. 170.

6. Glete, *Navies*, I, pp. 271–7; Harding, *Seapower*, pp. 219–21, 227–34.

7. Harding, *Seapower*, pp. 241–8.

8. Glete, *Navies*, I, pp. 275–6, 376–87; Harding, *Seapower*, pp. 258–63.

9. *The Mystery and Method Of His Majesty's Happy Restauration, Laid open to Publick View. By John Price DD one of the late Duke of Albemarl's Chaplains, and Privy to all the Secret Passages, and Particularities of that Glorious Revolution* (London, 1683).

10. Sir John Dalrymple, *Memoirs of Great Britain and Ireland* (3 vols., London, 1790), I, p. 194.

11. William J. Ashworth, *Customs and Excise: trade, production and consumption in England, 1640–1845* (Oxford, 2003), pp. 94–116.

12. Pádraig Lenihan, 'War and Population', *Irish Economic and Social History*, 24 (1997), pp. 18–21.

13. J. G. Simms, 'The Restoration, 1660–85', in T. W. Moody, F. X. Martin and F. J. Byrne (eds.), *A New History of Ireland. III. Early Modern Ireland, 1534–1691* (Oxford, 1991), p. 428.

14. In the 1670s the ministry's schemes to escape from the financial consequences of this step laid technical foundations for the national debt: Henry Roseveare, *The Financial Revolution 1660–1760* (Harlow, 1991), p. 22.

15. [Anthony Ashley Cooper, Earl of Shaftesbury], *A Letter From a Person of Quality, To His Friend in the Country* ([London], 1675), pp. 1–2. Shaftesbury did not yet use the terms 'Whig' and 'Tory', depicting the enemy as an alliance of 'the High Episcopal Man, and the Old Cavalier'.

16. [Andrew Marvell], *An Account of the Growth of Popery and Arbitrary Government in England* ('Amsterdam', 1677).

17. Frederick Holmes, *The Sickly Stuarts: the medical history of a dynasty* (Stroud, 2005).

18. C. D. Chandaman, *The English Public Revenue 1660–1688* (Oxford, 1975), pp. 256–61.

19. J. R. Jones (ed.), *Liberty Secured? Britain before and after 1688* (Stanford, 1992), p. 22.

20. Eveline Cruickshanks, 'Attempts to Restore the Stuarts, 1689–96', in Eveline Cruickshanks and Edward Corp (eds.), *The Stuart Court in Exile and the Jacobites* (London, 1995), pp. 1–13.

21. Eveline Cruickshanks, *The Glorious Revolution* (London, 2000), p. 26.

22. HMC *Manuscripts of the Earl of Egmont* (3 vols., London, 1920–3), III, p. 226; Cruickshanks, *Glorious Revolution*, p. 36; D. W. Hayton (ed.), *The History of Parliament: the House of Commons 1690–1715* (5 vols., London, 2002), I, pp. 553–68, 707–13.

23. Anchitell Grey (ed.), *Debates of the House of Commons, from the Year 1667 to the Year 1694* (10 vols., London, 1763), IX, p. 26.

24. O'Brien, 'The Nature and Historical Evolution of an Exceptional Fiscal State.', *Economic History Review*, 64 (2011), pp. 408–46, at 425–7.

25. Nathalie Genet-Rouffiac, 'Jacobites in Paris and Saint-Germain-en-Laye', in Cruickshanks and Corp (eds.), *The Stuart Court in Exile*, pp. 15–38, at 32.

26. Bruce Lenman, 'The Poverty of Political Theory in the Scottish Revolution

of 1688–1690', in Lois Schwoerer (ed.), *The Revolution of 1688–89: changing perspectives* (Cambridge, 1992), pp. 244–59; Robert Eccleshall, 'The Political Ideas of Anglican Ireland in the 1690s', in D. George Boyce, Robert Eccleshall and Vincent Geoghegan (eds.), *Political Discourse in Seventeenth- and Eighteenth-Century Ireland* (Basingstoke, 2001), pp. 62–80; S. J. Connolly, 'The Glorious Revolution in Irish Protestant Political Thinking', in *idem* (ed.), *Political Ideas in Eighteenth-Century Ireland* (Dublin, 2000); *idem*, 'The Church of Ireland and the Royal Martyr: regicide and the revolution in Anglican political thought, *c.*1660–*c.*1745', *Journal of Ecclesiastical History*, 54 (2003), pp. 484–506.

27. Chesterfield to Philip Stanhope, 7 February 1749, in *Letters written by the late Right Honourable Philip Dormer Stanhope, Earl of Chesterfield, to his Son, Philip Stanhope, Esq.* (2 vols., London, 1774), I, p. 396.

28. Clare Jackson, *Restoration Scotland, 1660–1690: royalist politics, religion and ideas* (Woodbridge, 2003).

29. Ian B. Cowan, 'The Reluctant Revolutionaries: Scotland in 1688', in Eveline Cruickshanks (ed.), *By Force or by Default? the Revolution of 1688* (Edinburgh, 1989); *idem*, 'Church and State Reformed? The Revolution of 1688–89 in Scotland', in Jonathan Israel (ed.), *The Anglo-Dutch Moment* (Cambridge, 1991), pp. 163–84; Bruce P. Lenman, 'The Scottish Nobility in the Revolution of 1688–1690', in Robert Beddard (ed.), *The Revolutions of 1688* (Oxford, 1991); Keith M. Brown, *Kingdom or Province? Scotland and the Regal Union, 1603–1715* (London, 1992).

30. Lenman, 'The Poverty of Political Theory', in Schwoerer (ed.), *The Revolution of 1688–89*, p. 256.

31. H. G. Koenigsberger, *The Habsburgs and Europe, 1516–1660* (London, 1971); J. H. Elliott, *Richelieu and Olivares* (Cambridge, 1984); Richard Bonney, *The European Dynastic States, 1494–1660* (Oxford, 1991); Paul Monod, *The Power of Kings: monarchy and religion* (New Haven, 1999).

32. Edmund S. Morgan, *Inventing the People: the rise of popular sovereignty in England and America* (New York, 1988).

33. Holmes, *The Sickly Stuarts*.

34. Edward Corp (ed.), *The Stuart Court in Rome* (Aldershot, 2003), pp. 4, 10–11.

35. Burke's speech of 5 March 1776, in W. M. Elofson and John A. Woods (eds.), *The Writings and Speeches of Edmund Burke* (9 vols., Oxford, 1981–), III, p. 233; [Samuel Johnson], *The False Alarm* (London, 1770), p. 50.

36. [James III], *Printed, 1742. A Letter, &c.* [?London, 1742] condemned 'the present Arbitrary Government' and renounced 'the Mistakes of former Reigns' (pp. 2, 4).

37. Paul Monod, *Jacobitism and the English People, 1688–1788* (Cambridge, 1989).

38. Lisa Steffen, *Defining a British State: treason and national identity, 1608–1820* (Basingstoke, 2001).

39. John Wesley, *A Concise History of England, from the Earliest Times, to the Death of George II* (4 vols., London, 1776), IV, pp. 31–2.

40. David Hayton, 'Constitutional Experiments and Political Expediency, 1689–1725', in Steven G. Ellis and Sarah Barber (eds.), *Conquest and Union: fashioning a British state, 1485–1725* (London, 1995), pp. 276–305, at 280–4.

41. P. G. M. Dickson, *The Financial Revolution in England: a study in the development of public credit, 1688–1756* (London, 1967).

42. Roseveare, *Financial Revolution*, pp. 6–28. Roseveare questions the claim that the financial developments of the 1690s would have been impossible had James II remained on the throne.

43. D. W. Jones, 'The Economic Consequences of William III', in Jeremy Black (ed.), *Knights Errant and True Englishmen: British foreign policy, 1660–1800* (Edinburgh, 1989), pp. 24–40.

44. Wesley, *Concise History of England*, IV, p. 37.

45. George Hilton Jones, *Charles Middleton* (Chicago, 1967), p. 268; Nathalie Genet-Rouffiac, *Le grand exil: les Jacobites en France 1688–1715* (Paris, 2007), p. 52; *Memoirs of the Marshal Duke of Berwick, written by himself* (2 vols., London, 1779), I, pp. 157–8.

46. Edward Gregg, *Queen Anne* (London, 1980), p. 122.

47. Abel Boyer, *The History of the Life and Reign of Queen Anne* (London, 1722), p. 17.

48. John M. Gray (ed.), *Memoirs of the Life of Sir John Clerk of Penicuik* (Edinburgh, 1892), p. 60.

49. Douglas Duncan (ed.), *History of the Union of Scotland and England by Sir John Clerk of Penicuik* (Edinburgh, 1993), pp. 86–9, 118, 170–1, 199. The crucial division in the Scottish Parliament was carried on 4 November 1706 by 115 to eighty-three.

50. James Otis, *The Rights of the British Colonies Asserted and Proved* (Boston, Mass., 1764), p. 43.

51. James Kelly, 'Public and Political Opinion in Ireland and the Idea of an Anglo-Irish Union', in Boyce, Eccleshall and Geoghegan (eds.), *Political Discourse*, pp. 110–41.

52. Sir John Sinclair (ed.), *The Statistical Account of Scotland* (21 vols., Edinburgh, 1791–9), VI, pp. 586–7.

53. Francis G. James, *Lords of the Ascendancy: the Irish House of Lords and its members, 1600–1800* (Washington, DC, 1995), p. 104.

54. Geraint Jenkins, *Literature, Religion and Society in Wales 1660–1730* (Cardiff, 1978).

55. Éamonn Ó Ciardha, *Ireland and the Jacobite Cause, 1685–1766* (Dublin, 2002), pp. 374–5 and *passim*.

56. Nicholas Canny, 'Identity Formation in Ireland: the emergence of the Anglo-Irish', in Nicholas Canny and Anthony Pagden (eds.), *Colonial Identity in the Atlantic World, 1500–1800* (Princeton, 1987), pp. 159–212, at 205–12.

57. Hayton, 'Constitutional Experiments and Political Expediency', in Ellis and Barber (eds.), *Conquest and Union*, pp. 289–90; *idem*, 'Anglo-Irish Attitudes: changing perceptions of national identity among the Protestant Ascendancy in Ireland, *c.*1690–1750', *Studies in Eighteenth-Century Culture*, 17 (1987), pp. 145–57.

58. S. J. Connolly, 'Varieties of Britishness: Ireland, Scotland and Wales in the Hanoverian state', in Alexander Grant and Keith J. Stringer (eds.), *Uniting the Kingdom? the making of British history* (London, 1995), pp. 193–207, at 207.

59. Burke to Adrien Duport, [post 29 March 1790]: Thomas W. Copeland et al. (eds.), *The Correspondence of Edmund Burke* (10 vols., Cambridge, 1958–78), VI, pp. 104–9, at 106.

60. T. C. Hansard (ed.), *The Parliamentary Debates from the Year 1803 to the Present Time* (20 vols., London, 1812), IV, col. 365.

61. Marilyn Morris, *The British Monarchy and the French Revolution* (New Haven, 1998).

62. Marjorie Morgan, *National Identities and Travel in Victorian Britain* (Basingstoke, 2000).

63. Robert Molesworth, *An Account of Denmark, as it was in the Year 1692* (London, 1694), Preface (n.p.), p. 258.

64. [John Toland], *Limitations For the Next Foreign Successor, or New Saxon Race debated In a Conference betwixt Two Gentlemen* (London, 1701), pp. 4–6. Toland quickly changed his mind when he received official patronage.

65. Lady Mary Wortley Montagu, 'Account of the Court of George I at his Accession', in Lord Wharncliffe (ed.), *The Letters and Works of Lady Mary Wortley Montagu* (3 vols., London, 1837), I, pp. 107–8.

66. L. J. Jennings (ed.), *The Croker Papers: the correspondence and diaries of the late Right Honourable John Wilson Croker* (2nd edn, 3 vols., London, 1885), I, p. 406.

67. Daniel Szechi, *1715: the great Jacobite rebellion* (New Haven, 2006).

68. Wesley, *Concise History of England*, IV, p. 111.

69. Ibid., IV, p. 149.

70. Philip Dormer Stanhope, Earl of Chesterfield, *Characters of Eminent Personages of His Own Time* (London, 1777), pp. 18–19.

71. Eveline Cruickshanks and Howard Erskine-Hill, *The Atterbury Plot* (Basingstoke, 2004).

72. Wesley, *Concise History of England*, IV, pp. 114–5, 123.

73. Ian R. Christie, 'The Tory Party, Jacobitism and the 'Forty-Five: a note', *Historical Journal*, 30 (1987), pp. 921–31.

74. Sedgwick (ed.), *The History of Parliament*, II, p. 402.

75. Wharncliffe (ed.), *Letters and Works of Lady Mary Wortley Montagu*, I, p. 117. Ironically, Sophia, Electress of Hanover, had 'a family feeling for the young man [James Francis Edward Stuart], whom she firmly believed to be as much James the Second's son as George the First was her own': ibid., p. 41.

76. Wesley, *Concise History of England*, IV, p. 161.

77. Ibid., I, p. 134.

78. Nick Harding, *Hanover and the British Empire, 1700–1837* (Woodbridge, 2007), pp. 38–105, at 51; Uriel Dann, *Hanover and Great Britain 1740–1760: diplomacy and survival* (Leicester, 1991), pp. 1–14; Andrew C. Thompson, *Britain, Hanover and the Protestant Interest, 1688–1756* (Woodbridge, 2006); Brendan Simms and Torsten Riotte (eds.), *The Hanoverian Dimension in British History, 1714–1837* (Cambridge, 2007).

79. Wesley, *Concise History of England*, IV, pp. 156–7.

80. John, Lord Hervey, *Some Materials Towards Memoirs of the Reign of King George II*, ed. Romney Sedgwick (3 vols., London, 1931), I, p. 364.

81. Wesley, *Concise History of England*, IV, p. 220.

82. Bernard Porter, *The Absent-Minded Imperialists: what the British really thought about empire* (Oxford, 2004).

83. For the debate on the thesis that empire in the nineteenth century was driven by a complex mix of financial and service-sector activities rather than by a functional 'imperialism' geared to manufacturing see Raymond E. Dumett (ed.), *Gentlemanly Capitalism and British Imperialism* (Harlow, 1999), discussing P. J. Cain and A. G. Hopkins, *British Imperialism* (2 vols., London, 1993).

84. David Armitage, 'Making the Empire British: Scotland in the Atlantic world 1542–1717', *Past & Present*, 155 (1997), pp. 34–63; idem, 'The Scottish Version of Empire: intellectual origins of the Darien venture', in John Robertson (ed.), *A Union for Empire* (Cambridge, 1995), pp. 97–118.

85. Patrick K. O'Brien and S. L. Engerman, 'Exports and the Growth of the

British Economy from the Glorious Revolution to the Peace of Amiens', in Barbara L. Solow (ed.), *Slavery and the Rise of the Atlantic System* (Cambridge, 1991), pp. 177–209, at 182, 186.

86. Lenman, *Britain's Colonial Wars*, pp. 260, 262.

87. Daniel A. Baugh, 'Withdrawing from Europe: Anglo-French maritime geo-politics, 1750–1800', *International History Review*, 20 (1998), pp. 1–32, at 12.

88. Ibid., pp. 1–32; Hamish Scott, 'The Decline of France and the Transformation of the European States System, 1756–1792', in Peter Krüger and Paul W. Schroeder (eds.), *The Transformation of the European States System, 1648–1945* (Münster, 2002), pp. 105–28.

89. Ian R. Christie, 'Was there a "New Toryism" in the Earlier Part of George III's Reign?', *Journal of British Studies*, 5 (1965–6), pp. 60–76; G. M. Ditchfield, 'Ecclesiastical Policy under Lord North', in John Walsh, Colin Haydon and Stephen Taylor (eds.), *The Church of England c.1689–c.1833: from Toleration to Tractarianism* (Cambridge, 1993).

90. Edmund Burke, *Thoughts on the Cause of the Present Discontents* (London, 1770).

91. 'Memoirs of Bentham', in John Bowring (ed.), *The Works of Jeremy Bentham* (11 vols., Edinburgh, 1843), X, p. 63. Bentham later changed his mind when the British government declined to adopt one of his pet ideas, but his position in 1776 is revealing.

92. This theory was revitalised in the 1960s, especially by the work of Bernard Bailyn. But he succeeded in depicting a unified, consensual 'American' ideology only by excluding the writings of the colonial loyalists on the grounds that 'the future lay not with them': *The Ideological Origins of the American Revolution* (Cambridge, Mass., 1967), p. x. The result was to conceal the degree to which similar issues were fought out on both sides of the Atlantic.

93. Wilbur R. Jacobs, *Dispossessing the American Indian* (New York, 1972), pp. 94–103.

94. John Shy, *Toward Lexington: the role of the British Army in the coming of the American Revolution* (Princeton, 1965), pp. 140–8.

95. Philip Lawson, *The Imperial Challenge: Quebec and Britain in the age of the American Revolution* (Montreal, 1989).

96. John C. Miller, *Origins of the American Revolution* (Stanford, 1959), pp. 373–5.

97. Henry Kamen, *The War of Succession in Spain, 1700–15* (London, 1969).

98. Quoted in Lenman, *Britain's Colonial Wars*, p. 222.

99. John J. McCusker and Russell R. Menard, *The Economy of British America,*

1607–1789 (Chapel Hill, 1991), pp. 373–5; Richard Buell, Jr., *In Irons: Britain's naval supremacy and the American revolutionary economy* (New Haven, 1998).

100. Stephen Conway, *The American War of Independence* (London, 1995); idem, *The British Isles and the War of American Independence* (Oxford, 2000), pp. 45–84.

101. Conway, *British Isles and the War of American Independence*, pp. 176–7.

102. Thomas Bartlett, "'A Weapon of War yet Untried": Irish Catholics and the armed forces of the Crown, 1760–1830', in T. G. Fraser and Keith Jeffery (eds.), *Men, Women and War. Historical Studies*, 18 (Dublin, 1993), pp. 65–85, at 71.

103. Robert Kent Donovan, 'The Popular Party of the Church of Scotland and the American Revolution', in Richard B. Sher and Jeffrey R. Smitten (eds.), *Scotland and America in the Age of the Enlightenment* (Edinburgh, 1990), pp. 81–99.

104. R. G. Thorne (ed.), *The History of Parliament: The House of Commons, 1790–1820* (5 vols., London, 1986), I, pp. 297–8.

105. Judith Blow Williams, *British Commercial Policy and Trade Expansion 1750–1850* (Oxford, 1972), pp. 227–8.

106. P. K. O'Brien, 'Public Finance and the Wars with France, 1793–1815' in Dickinson (ed.), *Britain and the French Revolution 1789–1815*, pp. 165–87.

107. Jenny Graham, *The Nation, the Law and the King: reform politics in England, 1789–1799* (2 vols., New York, 2000).

108. J. W. Derry, *Castlereagh* (London, 1976), p. 80.

109. John Ehrman, *The Younger Pitt. III. The Consuming Struggle* (London, 1996); M. Duffy, *The Younger Pitt* (Harlow, 2000); E. J. Evans, *William Pitt the Younger* (London, 1999).

110. See Appendix, Table 6.

111. Mitchell and Deane, *Abstract of British Historical Statistics*, pp. 388, 392.

112. Including *Sherwin's Weekly Political Register* (1817–19), Thomas Wooler's *The Black Dwarf* (1817–24), and Richard Carlile's *The Republican* (1819–25).

113. Even Thomas Hodgskin's *Labour Defended against the Claims of Capital* (London, 1825) proceeded from a Ricardian attack on land (pp. 29–31).

114. Scott to J. W. Croker, 19 March 1826, in H. J. C. Grierson (ed.), *The Letters of Sir Walter Scott* (11 vols., London, 1932–7), IX, p. 471.

115. J. P. Parry, *The Rise and Fall of Liberal Government in Victorian Britain* (New Haven, 1993), pp. 52–5.

116. Nancy D. LoPatin, *Political Unions, Popular Politics and the Great Reform Act of 1832* (Basingstoke, 1999).

117. Henry, Earl Grey (ed.), *The Correspondence of the late Earl Grey with His Majesty King William IV and with Sir Herbert Taylor from Nov. 1830 to June 1832* (2 vols., London, 1867), I, pp. 410–11; Holland to Grey, 5 November 1832, Grey MSS, in John Cannon, *Parliamentary Reform, 1640–1832* (Cambridge, 1973), p. 245.

118. Parry, *Rise and Fall of Liberal Government*, p. 93.

119. Sir Henry Taylor to Earl Grey, 14 January 1831; William IV to Earl Grey, 4 February 1831: *Correspondence of the Late Earl Grey*, I, pp. 54–5, 96–7, 268.

120. *Hansard's Parliamentary Debates*, 3rd ser., I (1831), col. 606.

121. Ibid., col. 424.

122. I. G. C. Hutchinson, *A Political History of Scotland 1832–1924* (Edinburgh, 1986).

123. William Cobbett (ed.), *The Parliamentary History of England from the Earliest Period to the Year 1803* (36 vols., London, 1812–20), XXX, cols. 810–11, 813–14, 818.

124. [David Robinson], 'The Game Laws', *Blackwood's Edinburgh Magazine*, 22 (1827), pp. 643–4.

125. A. H. Eyre to Sir Robert Buxton, 31 May 1829: Buxton MSS, Box 110/139, Cambridge University Library.

126. Parry, *Rise and Fall of Liberal Government*, pp. 44–5; E. A. Smith, *Lord Grey 1764–1845* (Oxford, 1991), pp. 259–65; Peter Mandler, *Aristocratic Government in the Age of Reform: Whigs and Liberals, 1830–1852* (Oxford, 1990), pp. 168–9.

127. Dror Wahrman, *Imagining the Middle Class: the political representation of class in Britain, c.1780–1840* (Cambridge, 1995), pp. 1–18.

128. Philip Harling, *The Waning of Old Corruption: the politics of economical reform, 1779–1846* (Oxford, 1996).

129. Derek Beales, 'The Idea of Reform in British Politics, 1829–1850', in T. C. W. Blanning and P. Wende (eds.), *Reform in Great Britain and Germany 1750–1850* (Oxford, 1999), pp. 159–74.

130. Munsche, *Gentlemen and Poachers*, pp. 159–68.

Part IV

1. J. L. van Zanden, *The Rise and Decline of Holland's Economy: merchant capitalism and the labour market* (Manchester, 1993); Jan de Vries, *The First Modern*

Economy: success, failure and perseverance of the Dutch economy, 1500–1815 (Cambridge, 1997).

Appendix

1. E. A. Wrigley, et al., *English Population History from Family Reconstitution 1580–1837* (Cambridge, 1997), Table A9.1, pp. 614–5.

2. Wrigley and Schofield, *Population History*, p. 566; from 1801, census figures. 1781 figure from Eric J. Evans, *The Forging of the Modern State* (3rd edn, Harlow, 2001), p. 512.

3. K. H. Connell, *The Population of Ireland 1750–1845* (Oxford, 1950), Table 4, p. 25, estimates based on hearth tax returns; W. E. Vaughan and A. J. Fitzpatrick (eds.), *Irish Historical Statistics: Population, 1821–71* (Dublin, 1978), pp. 2–3; from 1821, the census of Ireland; Daultrey, Dickson and Ó Gráda, 'Eighteenth-Century Irish Population: new perspectives from old sources', pp. 601–28 (taking upper-bound estimates).

4. R. H. Campbell and J. B. A. Dow (eds.), *Source Book of Scottish Economic and Social History* (Oxford, 1968), pp. 1–2, 8ff, giving the estimates of Alexander Webster, 1755, and Sir John Sinclair, 1795; Flinn et al. (eds), *Scottish Population History*.

5. Houston, *Population History*, p. 29, an estimate based on hearth tax returns.

6. This was Sir John Sinclair's estimate, made in the 1790s. Flinn et al (eds.), *Scottish Population History*, pp. 4, 241–2, points out that this is only a conventional estimate; 'We must accept, therefore, that we cannot know what the long-term trends of population were in the seventeenth and eighteenth centuries . . . There is no good reason to assume that the growth of population in the eighteenth century in Scotland bore any constant relationship to that in England . . . we do not know what the population was in 1700, and no figures advanced by historians should be taken as correct to within 20 per cent.'

7. I. D. Whyte, 'Urbanisation in Early-Modern Scotland: a Preliminary Analysis', *Scottish Economic and Social History*, 9 (1989), pp. 21–37.

8. N. F. R. Crafts, *British Economic Growth during the Industrial Revolution* (Oxford, 1985), p. 45. The discrepancy between the two columns is the effect of population growth: in 1780–1801, for example, almost the whole of the increase in national product was taken up by a larger population, and in 1801–31 about three-quarters was. Estimates are for England and Wales to 1800, and for England, Wales and Scotland 1801–31.

9. F. M. L. Thompson, 'The Social Distribution of Landed Property in England since the Sixteenth Century', *Economic History Review*, 19 (1966), pp. 510–14.

10. Sedgwick, *House of Commons 1715–1754*, I, pp. 19, 23, 34, 37, 42, 46, 57.

11. Calculated from C. D. Chandaman, *The English Public Revenue 1660–1688* (Oxford, 1975), pp. 332–3, 350, 355, 362; Mitchell and Deane, *Abstract of British Historical Statistics*, pp. 386–8, 389–93, 401–2.

12. Including the French war subsidy of 1672–4.

13. Glete, *Navies*, I, pp. 192, 195, 241, 256, 263, 271, 311; II, p. 376. It should be noted that these figures for total naval tonnage give only an approximate indication of naval strength; in particular, France's periodic concentration on ships of the line (often superior, ship for ship, to their English counterparts) added significantly to France's naval potential. Furthermore, questions of maintenance meant that the proportion of ships in commission or ready for sea could vary considerably, making comparisons doubly difficult: N. A. M. Rodger, *The Command of the Ocean: a naval history of Britain 1649–1815* (London, 2004), pp. 606–17.

Index

www.vintage-books.co.uk